CW00924463

Planning in the Face of Conflict

The Surprising Possibilities of Facilitative Leadership

John Forester

American Planning Association
Planners Press

Making Great Communities Happen

Chicago | Washington, D.C.

Copyright © 2013 by the American Planning Association

205 N. Michigan Ave., Suite 1200, Chicago, IL 60601-5927
1030 15th St., NW, Suite 750 West, Washington, DC 20005-1503

www.planning.org/plannerspress

ISBN: 978-1-61190-118-4 (pbk.)

Library of Congress Control Number: 2013943868

Printed in the United States of America

All rights reserved

Contents

Part 2 Learning and State Policy Making

Part 3 Land Use and Community Planning

Part 4 Community Development and Governance

Part 5 Environmental and Regional Planning

Part 6 Deep Value Differences and Reinventing Community Problem Solving

Conclusion
Planning, Learning, and Governing Through Conflict   297

Acknowledgments

Without the generosity, curiosity, and passion of the insightful practitioners whose words animate these pages, this book would not have been possible. These interviewees more than once said, "I've never done an interview like this," and they trusted me to explore with them what they did even more than what they thought. I ended interviews grateful, and I remain grateful for the windows on the world of practice these practitioners have shared with us. I'm grateful too for years of bright, challenging, creative students at Cornell who've found these "profiles of practitioners" among the most valuable materials they've ever read. Without continuous student enthusiasm and learning from these profiles, I might have kept these interviews tucked away in my own research files.

Thanks go too for early interviewing assistance to Irene Weiser, Kristen Grace, and Erika Lund. For transcription assistance, my thanks go to Logan Axelson, Kathrin Bolton, Carol Cook, Daniel Forester, Alison Goldberg, Tanneasha Gordon, Emmelia Hudson, Emily Hunter, Renee Kincla, Nicole Kindred, Brian Kreiswirth, Rebecca Liu, Andy Love, Ellen Macnow, Anisa Mendizabal, Steve Mikulencak, Ji Eun June Park, Linda Phelps, Leslie Shieh, Caroline Stem, Matt Styer, Christy Tao, Grzegorz Wieclaw and Rachel Weiner. For the title of chapter 3, thanks to Flavien Glidja. When I was marooned between projects, Sara Cobb urged publication and Eric VanderMaas provided crucial editorial help to transform prized teaching materials into a coherent book. Early research support for conducting these interviews came from the University of Victoria's Institute for Dispute Resolution and Cornell's Clarence S. Stein Institute for Urban and Landscape Studies. Thanks for the cover and design advice to Anne Kilgore.

For ongoing conversations about the intersection of research, pedagogy, mediation, and planning, continuing thanks to David Laws. I alone though remain responsible for all errors of editing or interpretation.

An earlier version of Laurence Sherman's profile appeared, with commentary, in *Planning Theory and Practice* in 2011. Along with Gordon Sloan's, Shirley Solomon's, and Susan Podziba's, Frank Blechman's profile dates from 1995. Blechman's was edited for classroom use in 2003 and further edited in 2011. Abridged, Ric Richardson's profile appeared, with commentary, in *Planning Theory and Practice* in 2013. An earlier version of Michael Hughes's profile, with commentary, appeared in *The Consensus Building Handbook* (1999). Lawrence Susskind's profile, a classic in this field, appeared first in *When Talk Works* by Deborah Kolb, et al. (Jossey Bass, 1994); reproduced by permission of John Wiley & Sons, Inc.

Introduction

John Forester

I've been very lucky. I've been able to talk to exceptionally creative, down-to-earth, practical people who walked into messy and contentious public conflicts and emerged with peaceful and productive solutions. It sounds too good to be true, but it isn't.

Public conflicts about place—about land use and the environment, for example—make news all the time. We hear righteous claims on many sides: Protect! Develop! Forever wild! Highest and best use! So we can't help but wonder what resolutions might be possible. Hardly inspiring our confidence, we hear about public failures of environmental governance all too often. Along this contentious way, we don't learn much about the skills of facing passionate conflicts over place and working through them to emerge with real resolutions: outcomes that allow neighbors, developers, environmentalists, community organizers, and government officials to satisfy their interests and to go on with their lives. So this book will show that much more is possible than we ordinarily think, and we have a great deal to learn from an emerging, if not well publicized, group of experienced community problem solvers.

This book presents the stories of these "facilitative leaders," as we can call them, in their own words. The work they present, the moves they've made, the strategies they've used—none of these are rocket science, none is esoteric, and all in fact are simple enough that many of us will read and say: "I can see myself doing that!"; "I could apologize and erase what I'd written so that I could listen again and get it right"; "I could map a group's concerns on the wall, sure!"; and so on. In the face of public disputes, mediators, facilitative leaders, and self-styled community builders turn out to be both ordinary folks and extraordinary practitioners too.

In a uniquely practical way, this book presents inspiring and instructive stories of dealing with our differences in tricky and contentious public cases—

those times when, as citizens or community members, our "sense of place" conflicts with that of others. We examine new possibilities that emerged even after neighbors, residents, or interest groups had been at loggerheads for years, in situations in which few people thought that they could settle their differences, and in cases where neither politics as usual nor the courts nor other means of coercion or persuasion had been successful. In wide-ranging cases concerning land use and the environment, as well as rights and identity, we shall see that community building and peace making in the face of conflict involve surprising and sometimes quite simple practical moves that can help to resolve the divisive issues at hand.

At times, as I have argued in *Dealing with Differences: Dramas of Mediating Public Disputes*, these moves mean refraining from talking about the theological, theoretical, doctrinal, or ideological issues that divide people, but talking instead, in this case, in this locality, about where we should put the stop signs, where we should do very particular, practical, and specific things to address our concerns. Learning what not to talk or argue about and what not to say or do can be every bit as important as learning about techniques or skills that can help us to live together peacefully with those different from us. These cases present practical insights and theory too.

Consider the cases presented here. How did Mike Hughes bring together in the same room—under the auspices of the Colorado State Health Department—sex workers, religious fundamentalists, gay activists, public health workers, community organizers and others in a bottom-up effort to produce HIV/AIDS-focused recommendations to guide public health efforts and programs? How did Lisa Beutler step in after 20 years of political, legal, and media battles dividing environmentalists from off-highway vehicle enthusiasts, hunters, and others to bring the parties together to produce policy-relevant results as well as a standing state-sponsored roundtable to address related issues in the future? How did Shirley Solomon draw upon lessons of South Africa to build bridges and do multistakeholder land-use planning in the Pacific Northwest when trust between Native Americans and county officials was virtually nonexistent?

In these and other cases, when our senses of good places conflict, we shall see that a good deal more can be possible than we often believe. Of course, our initial skepticism can be in itself a substantial problem: if we ordinarily believe and presume far less to be possible than we can actually achieve, we set ourselves up for failure without ever knowing that we're doing so. We believe the door to peaceful, community problem solving stands there locked, and as a result we're all too reasonably ready to believe we cannot walk through it—even if, in actual fact, that door is not locked. We hardly know how often we have been the unwitting prisoners of our own presumptions, however convinced we've been that the others involved were just naysayers, were skeptical of our intentions, were committed to ideals that left us cold, and so on. "They" don't trust us apparently, and so we don't trust them—and we seem to have little together that we could productively discuss. So, for such self-deceptively comforting "good reasons" as these, we may often fail to explore unlocked doors to better futures, and we all pay the price.

This book explores contentious disputes over space and place—how they arise in cities and neighborhoods over environmental and cultural issues, and how we can resolve them practically and creatively. Through a unique collection of insiders' "practice-stories," the accounts of experienced facilitative leaders or intermediaries working on public disputes, we see complexity and conflict, interests and values, technical expertise and personal preferences all woven together. We see how they went about facing anger and distrust, building relationships, enabling learning, fostering creative solutions, transforming problems, and much, much more. The practice stories provide far more than eyewitness accounts but still less than full case studies: in each case, we explore practices of conflict resolution with guides who have been working the territory for decades. We are in the hands, then, of experienced elders, not naïve initiates, and if we read and listen closely, we will find that, indeed, doors will open if we know where to look, and we will find fresh and substantial material for guiding planning practice as will practitioners in diverse fields and students in universities seeking to solve seemingly intractable problems.

So What?: Listening to Learn, Solve Problems, and Plan Together

The methods described here have both moral and ethical implications. They draw upon expertise but go further to invent and to craft possibilities that few parties to disputes might initially have thought possible. For example, these accounts show us "respect" as a practical accomplishment, not simply as a vague value, and we see how deeply committed parties working across boundaries of class, ethnicity, value commitments, and territorial identities can transform thoroughly suspicious and contested relationships into ones enabling mutual learning, growth, and actually useful practical outcomes.

Politically, these striking accounts can make us smarter about power and interdependence, about the distance from abstract claims to concrete gains. We see in case after case how despair and frustration yield to fresh and surprising new perspectives on problems and, crucially, of course, to new options and new opportunities. We see clearly a practical politics of relationship building in the face of difficult and painful histories. We see the creative politics that Hannah Arendt saw — as new moves and actions in settings of conflict enable wholly new relationships to come into being.

Not least of all, to be sure, these profiles provide a scholarly payoff: they give us fresh and rare material with which to examine micropolitics in practice — politically situated performances in passionately contested settings. Critical studies of professional practice have run aground too quickly and for too long on the rocks of overdrawn presumptions of social control (all planning, for example, a priori, must serve those in power; little else is possible) or on the naïve presumptions about dominating good intentions (as if all planning were oriented to the achievement of open communications, power inequalities notwithstanding). As a result of such overly simple, if popular, views of practice, we know far too little about the actual practical challenges that community planners or placemakers really face. These accounts help to provide far more detailed, and far less facile, pictures of practices that can be helpful for communities facing diverse conflicts.

More provocatively, this book upends the traditional rationalist assumption that first we learn, and then we act. These accounts do not suggest that knowledge must precede action nor that research must precede planned change. Rather, they suggest the reverse: what seem to be contrary claims about outcomes — to develop or to maintain open space, to allow off-road vehicles in the parks or not to allow them, and so on — grow out of a pattern of past actions, and so only by dealing with the conflicting agendas of those past actions and demands can we learn actually what we can and ought to do in this or that place.

These practitioners work not just on public conflicts: they work *in* those conflicts. These men and women work in between conflicting and disputing parties. Not only do they listen to these parties' views and perspectives and their anger and demands, but they actually bring multiple and conflicting parties together in the same room to work through their differences — to find real opportunities to serve their various interests.

This means that their practice stories deal with conflicts over land use but much more than that, too. These accounts illuminate the prospects of local democracy every bit as much as they illuminate narrower, conflict-resolution-like work. So these practitioners' accounts teach us about facilitative leaders, for they not only show us ways of settling spatial conflicts, but also providing leadership and facilitating problem solving too. They take traditional community mediation, for example, to a new level of complexity: the numbers of players are bigger, the venues are bigger, the resources at stake are typically bigger, and the level and depth of emotional intensity can be greater as well.

These practitioners are problem solvers, but they are not calculators. They know that when good information is scarce and distrust is abundant, almost everyone can learn. So they know that passionate demands today can, with more information and expertise, become practical proposals tomorrow. In everyday language, these facilitative leaders have to be good listeners. They have to be sensitive to emotion and not run from it. They have to be able to pay attention without being easily distracted, either by appeals to fact or to emotion when either one turns out to be irrelevant in the case at hand. They have to be keenly alert to all the ways that disputing parties can hurt or provoke one another, not working through but escalating tensions by being dismissive or disrespectful or arrogant or overly aggressive or humiliating or racist or sexist.

Especially within liberal democratic politics, where public disputes ought to be decided less through authoritarian decree and more through the will of affected people, through some semblance of participatory and representative processes, we all have a great deal to learn from the real practice of the peacemakers and facilitative leaders among us—in part because so many of us seem either so ready to avoid conflict or so clumsy that we aggravate conflicts despite ourselves. Many of us shun anger or simply respond in kind—as if stupidity evoked by stupidity made us all more intelligent. Many of us feel uncomfortable or impatient with others' emotions, and we risk appearing dismissive, as if others might miraculously welcome our telling them what and how to feel, in a way we would never tolerate ourselves. Many of us think that emotions threaten rational understanding rather than aid it, even as we might be passionately committed ourselves to ideas of objectivity or equity, ideas of justice or freedom from bias. Indeed, many of us embrace a thin view of professionalism that suggests that our cold detachment might often aid our understanding rather than alienating the very people with whom we need or might wish to work.

But even the most basic notions of democracy or citizen involvement, of course, imply not only plurality, the involvement of different people, but people with different views of good spaces and places. So even our ordinary hopes for some nonauthoritarian politics already and inescapably imply that we will always have to address competing and conflicting desires about better and worse land uses, better and worse ways of producing spaces and creating good places.

So, too, do ideas of "participation"—whether direct or representative—imply difference: spatially diffuse parties with differences must learn, in a functioning democratic setting, to work out their differences together, and that means in some ways articulating, perhaps arguing over, those differences of commitments, values, interests, perspectives, backgrounds, or priorities as they promise differing spatial consequences. That's easy to say, but when people's homes and health care and identities are at stake, those differences of perspective and values and interests can matter a great deal: Can I keep this land protected?; Can I fish or hunt where my grandparents did?; Can I get the best health care for my illness here, whether or not you like my sexual preferences?; Can I get better transportation in or through my community?

So the work of those wrestling with public disputes—mediators, facilitators, facilitative leaders, de facto peacemakers, and coalition builders—can teach us very directly about making democracy work, especially when senses of place and space, neighborhood and community, conflict. The work discussed here doesn't itself solve our problems, but these creative and at times surprisingly simple struggles take us to the heart of what we can call "democratic culture"—how we can meet the challenges of dealing with our differences face-to-face, dealing with differences respectfully and very practically, even productively, transforming both our senses of outcomes and our relationships as well. This public work shows us how true democratic politics can be inclusive and can encourage real learning by many parties—instead of encouraging what skeptics always expect from participatory processes: a down-and-dirty, minimalist culture of "let's cut a deal and get out of here."

Method: Exploring Practice Stories

We wanted to learn from practice and perhaps find useful insights, and maybe even better theory, in the fine-grained details these experienced and astute third parties identified as important. So we set out to gather grounded, detailed, and dramatic "practice stories" from practical insiders, but not just from anyone. We searched for practitioners of a certain kind—not people who talk a good game about public disputes and conflicts, but rather those who had walked the walk and had reputations for being thoughtful and experienced and for having been deeply and skillfully involved in working through public disputes structured by passionate differences of race, ethnicity, class, ideology, deep values, cultural background, or deeply vested interests.

We found, curiously enough, that these experienced and thoughtful third parties quickly resisted or even repudiated the label of "mediator" as being far too simple, far too reductive, much too narrow. That made us all the more curious about what these practitioners, working face-to-face in the middle of deeply contested spatial conflicts, really did in the face of passionate urban and environmental claims.

We asked each of our interviewees to walk us through a case or cases that revealed both the messy challenges and the surprising opportunities of their work. We wanted to learn, of course, about the challenges (distrust, anger, lying) that they faced so we could get a feel for the settings and the difficulties, the complexities and the threats, that confronted them. We wanted also to learn about the opportunities they faced—because we wanted to understand much better than we do how in the "real world" these men and women, these practical peacemakers, made sense of what they could actually do about the complex and messy, politicized and often bitterly contested cases that they were working in and on.

The results are striking: Larry Susskind tells us about "light bulbs" that go on in the process. Peter Adler suggests the power, the opportunities and risks, of naming. Lisa Beutler helps us to see anger as fuel for change rather than as an irrational obstacle—and so on. The stories that follow are often moving, memorable, surprising, instructive, even all in all, inspiring.

We have here no simple recipes, but much practical guidance. We have in our repertoires now no technical fixes, but many tricks of the trade. We have uncovered and evoked practical knowledge, and much more, too, for in listening closely to these accounts, we can tap into what we might call "the wisdom" of facilitative leadership, if not also the wisdom of mediation. "Wisdom" here means "good, practical judgment"—situated, not ephemeral, on the ground, not idealistic, alertly engaged, not abstract, not vaguely theoretical, but offering us through the complexity and detail of these practice stories an abundance of practical tips and cues in the face of emotional intensity, political posturing, cultural difference, and real differences of interests or value commitments.

Attentive to process and outcomes both, mediators and facilitative leaders sometimes sense possibilities even when frustrated and distrusting parties in the grip of conflicts might not. These intermediaries don't typically discover solutions themselves (and they don't worry if they don't), but their experience has taught them lessons that too few others of us have learned: if you can create a space in which adversaries can learn together, they can then often invent together and craft solutions together because their learning, about one another and about real options, will have subtly transformed their senses of what's really possible. Despite the adversaries' well-honed distrust and suspicion of one another, they can come to see each others' priorities in new ways, and so they see new opportunities to make moves, in effect to trade, to help others here in return for help there. They come to see, as I discuss in *Dealing with Differences*, that they can maintain, not compromise, their deep value differences with others, and nevertheless they can come to see that even with those differences intact, they can still decide together where the stop signs should go. They come to see more clearly, too, not just what their own independent alternatives really are good for but also what new options they can craft if they work together and negotiate astutely with their neighbors or adversaries. So, we see that informed, expertly advised, accountable parties can make their own agreements, assisted by facilitative leaders or mediators: or to put it more bluntly, mediators don't make agreements any more than midwives make babies.

My *Dealing with Differences* began to explore what facilitative leaders and mediators might really teach community leaders and urban planners—who are all the more expert in the subject matters at hand—about public disputes and conflicts. We need to consider closely, for example, why might planners in many cases scope out a contentious situation and think that little is possible when mediators with exactly the same information might still see many possibilities that promise more for everyone compared to the status quo? When mediators like Adler or Beutler face apparent value conflicts, for example, and still somehow work to bring parties together in situations where planners might otherwise have thrown in the towel, we need carefully and soberly to ask how they were able to see practical opportunities where planners saw only insurmountable obstacles? What can we learn about not quitting too early, about not assuming too quickly that there's nothing we can do?

No other book focuses so clearly on what it is like to work directly on contentious conflicts with government officials and citizens, with community activists and tribal representatives, with environmentalists and developers—to face difficult governance disputes as senses of place and space conflict. The insiders' accounts here are richer than mere war stories, in part because we have been careful to ask a distinctive set of questions so that we could explore lines of practical response. We were careful to ask How did you do that?, not What did you *think* about that?, so that a discussion of attitudes would not preempt our learning more about courses of action and conduct, what happened on the ground. Here we learn about experienced practitioners' moves and practical judgments—how they responded to the surprising details of unique situations—and about these skillful practitioners' own hunches, maxims, and rules of thumb, not least of all their own "practical theorizing."

This book presents in the insiders' own words not just stories of obstacles and opportunities, of do's and don'ts, but perceptions of cues and clues, possible moves, and offers and queries. This book shows us vividly and self-reflectively, even vicariously, what we can do when our senses of good spaces and places conflict.

Part 1
Better Governance When Interests and Values Conflict

Chapter 1

Mediation and Collaboration in Architecture and Community Planning

Laurence Sherman

This profile begins with an early formative experience of designing a new hospital and the practical lessons it taught. Seeing the users talk and negotiate among themselves, architect and planner Laurence Sherman understood that designers and planners might harness the actual stakeholders' energy and differing interests, special knowledge, and practical creativity to reach better outcomes and to produce better projects and products. So he tells us pointedly, not just that "I didn't switch careers and become a mediator," but "I do mediation to do better planning, architecture and public policy."

Sherman worked on issues involving urban transportation, natural resource management, local economic development, and more. Whether in cases of architectural or urban design, larger urban or small community cases, Sherman shows us how our listening and learning can help to evoke smart and responsive proposals for planning projects and then implementation. He shows us no rocket science, no esoteric magic, but instead wise, sensitive, practically pitched, and critically informed planning practices. We see here the seamless integration of process skills, technical expertise, and substantive planning knowledge. —JF

I love doing this work—and there is almost no issue I won't take on. It's never predictable—it's never what should happen—it's never the textbook. I just love the way that it unfolds. It's almost like writing a great novel where the actors take over and tell you what to write.

I was originally trained as an architect and later did graduate work in architecture, urban design, and planning. I started practicing planning and urban design in communities, and it became clear early on that the folks in these communities had a lot of important information that we planners just didn't have. So we had to go to them somehow and find out from them, very often in different cultures.

I worked in Philadelphia in the 1960s during the Model Cities days in the poor ghettoes. The stuff that we knew downtown to put on maps was not the really essential information we needed from the people like residents, youth gangs, and community organizations. I began to realize that if you would listen—and if you would trust what the people were saying to you—you could probably get the goods that you really needed. So we started working on the skills of listening and of getting the people involved in what it was that we were planning.

Later I got more involved in architecture and architectural programming. I found out that the architect typically goes door to door and asks the clients, "What do you need?" And they'll tell you, but when you add it all up, they can't afford it.

An Early Discovery

We devised a way of programming very complicated public buildings—like hospitals—not by going door-to-door and asking people what they wanted in their new hospital—but instead we would build a plastic 3-D model showing the limit of space that the budget would allow you to build. It was the amount of space that the government allocated per dollar or per bed. Then we would color-code chips of the various functions of the hospital, scaled to the model, and we would invite everyone who worked in the hospital to come in and start talking (to us and to one another) about where their colored chips should be located on the model.

They would show us different locations and functions, and we would ask why they did it this way, and they told us. So we would begin to learn what they knew (and we didn't) about how to lay out the hospital—such as the way they worked and the way they would like to have an arrangement of rooms and functions. They would tell us where they'd like to have the entrances and how they'd like to separate the ER from the main entrance—all those kinds of things. They could do it in a three-dimensional way on the plastic model simply by moving their chips into place.

The interesting thing was that they began to have a dialogue of their own; people agreed, people didn't agree. The more they talked about their problems with how they put those chips on the model, the more we realized that they were negotiating among themselves for solutions right then and there. They were the staff of the hospital, and I said to myself, "If they're negotiating, then what the heck am I doing?," and then I realized, "I'm facilitating—I'm not designing the hospital yet—I'm mediating their attempts to resolve their issues."

They were really telling me what the best arrangement of rooms should be within that budget, within that three-dimensional model to meet their functional needs. Very often, they asked for more than there was space for—very often the chips would actually fall off onto the floor when there wasn't enough space left on the model.

So, I would ask them, "What about this chip?"

They would say, "Oh, we have to have this chip."

I'd say, "But there is no room for it."

They'd say, "But we have to have that one."

I'd say, "OK, tell me about this one."

They'd say, "That's the public eye clinic that operates on Tuesdays and Thursdays every week—we have to have it."

And I'd say, "There is another chip on the floor—what's that?"

They'd say, "That's the dental clinic that operates every Monday, Wednesday, and Friday. We have to have that one, too."

So I'd say, "Are you telling me that maybe we should use the same room for two different purposes—and maybe find some space in this model for it?"

Their replies were, "Oh, no, that's absolutely impossible—because of the technical nature and the safety of the equipment."

So as the designers, we had to come up with a way to safely store the equipment so you could use the space for another purpose. They negotiated among themselves to come to the conclusion about how this could work and where it should be in the hospital.

These early experiences never left me. I have a wonderful photograph of these people working on their hospital problem. A surgeon came in wearing his greens, straight from the operating room. He grabs a cup of coffee, and he's participating in this discussion over the model. It occurred to me later that he came in because he didn't want to miss this meeting. He wasn't going to go somewhere else to get what he wanted because his community was discussing the problems and creating the options; I realized how very important it was that all the stakeholders made the meeting, and they did. Then from there with the information we needed from them we'd go on, and we'd design it.

I began to put these experiences together, and I thought that architects, urban designers, and urban planners also need somehow to become facilitators, to help people have constructive dialogue. And sometime after that, in the mid-

1980s, I met Larry Susskind of MIT, who was a prominent planner, educator, and leader in collaborative problem solving and consensus building; I learned from him some of the more scientific aspects of this, and I have been practicing this way ever since.

For me, my earlier work in the '60s and '70s now made more sense—this was a dimension of urban planning and design that I wanted to be a part of. I didn't switch careers and become a mediator. I mediate to do better planning, architecture, and public policy.

I run a lot of these simulated projects for building design in my practice. In planning it's more difficult to sell—even among my own partners. There is a fear that they will lose control of the planning process that they've been hired by the public client to carry out, to have a plan done. It's not as clear to them that if they get into the arena of discussing with stakeholder parties what the issues are, what the program should be for the planning, where the priorities should be, what the terms of reference should be—that they can still manage the process. It's not as clear to the planners that they can still participate—and with the critical information they need.

But the acceptance is coming. Every time, we learn more about our clients and more about the dynamics between the parties, and the parties in a community learn more about how they can legitimately participate in a structured process. It's not willy-nilly—it's not a public meeting that everyone comes to in order to talk and then they go home.

A Big Breakthrough

This brings me to a turning point in my work, the Calgary Transit case. One of my earliest projects involved transportation planning for the City of Calgary. Our firm had planned the fixed rail transit in the northwest sector of the city, and we'd designed all the stations. All the feeder bus lines in this sector of the city were based on the terminus being at a certain place. When the city council got the money to extend the transit line farther out, they needed to then replan all the feeder bus systems to work with the new terminus along the extended line.

The council, in this case, did not trust the transit planners to go to the public and conduct a participation program on a fairly massive scale of rejiggering all the bus lines because they simply didn't think staff had the people skills to do that. So I was hired by the council to facilitate a public process to see if I could get some kind of involvement from the public on what this plan should be.

At our first public meeting we had representatives of 24 neighborhood associations, a major hospital, a major university, the five shopping centers that were served by this system, and the special interest groups, such as seniors and schools, that had big stakes in this system. I insisted that the transit planners and our own technical planners not a make a presentation to begin. Instead, we started out by talking about process. Technical issues can initially intimidate the public. I decided that the transit planners should not be allowed to come on as technical experts until the public understood they needed them; when the public perceived that need, then I had a collaborative relationship develop between the two.

I encouraged that relationship by going to the city council and asking them to give me the parameters within which they would accept a plan generated by the community. They gave me the limits, which were fiscal. They said, "The community can make any plan for the buses that they want to, but they can't spend one dollar more than the present transit subsidy to this sector."

I went back and told them that at the second meeting. They said, "How can we do that?"

I said, "Well, for example, if you double service on one route, then you're going to have to divide it on other routes."

They said, "How are we ever going to keep track of this?"

I said, "Why don't you ask the transportation experts who are here?"

The transit guys stepped up and said, "Well, this is what 'level of service' means, and this is what 'headways' mean, and we can develop a little laptop program that will balance the budget for you as you propose changes."

They then went off, and worked on this together. For me, it was an example of joint fact-finding—where they jointly generated the information that they had to have—because they needed to.

Each constituent group had a representative that came to these meetings. We had about 35 people coming to these meetings to do this planning. Every two weeks we would have a public meeting. We did the whole plan in six weeks. We would take maps, mark them, and do all the kinds of things that people do around land-use and transportation planning. We would divide the groups up into neighborhoods, and there would be a few groups that would be in one district or neighborhood of the area. They would start to lay out where they thought the routes should be. Then they would lean over and start to talk with the next table because the two maps had to mesh, because you had bus lines that had to connect. Sometimes the lines aligned, and sometimes they didn't, and the transportation experts would then have to help them when it didn't work. Then together they would negotiate the best route for a bus that would serve their interests and that also worked for Calgary Transit.

Finally, they had a total plan worked out. Then I reminded them that they needed to go back to their constituent groups—they needed to have their plan ratified. Some representatives volunteered to help one another out because by now they all had a stake in the plan that balanced the budget and gave them the kind of transit service that they wanted throughout their whole sector.

We had another six weeks of ratification meetings with the neighborhoods because it was hard to get them scheduled. I then had to take this plan and present it to the city council, because it would actually make the decision, not these people. They had simply been asked to recommend the plan. Still, in 12 weeks we had the whole thing done, and I was back at the city council—but not only was I back in 12 weeks, but I was back in 12 weeks with a plan that represented the interests and support of all of these stakeholder groups!

They had invented it—they had worked on it and come to consensus.

So I made my presentation to the council, and then council members asked if there were any comments from the public. One lady stood up, and she wore a yellow lapel flower. She said, "Members of the council, I don't want to take a lot of your time, but you'll notice that there are 35 people sitting behind me in the chambers today, and they all have yellow flowers in their lapels. They all represent organizations and institutions that participated in putting together this plan and recommending it to you"— and (I'll quote her here), "We don't want you futzing with our plan!"

I realized, for me, two important lessons: One, the power of the consensus when it was presented back to a political body like the city council; I realized that the council could accept this without having to play referee, without creating winners and losers. And two, at the same time, the council had retained its authority over the product because it had set the parameters at the very beginning. So it wasn't as if they'd waited until the end and then said, "We don't like your plan, and we can't afford it," because the council had said up front what it could support.

This outcome represented a consensus solution struck finally between all the public stakeholders, including the city council: there were no losers. This was a very big breakthrough for me. I went back through other work that I'd done, including the hospital design and city planning, and I realized that when the public, or the stakeholder groups, could agree on something, then this agreement has a huge influence with the people who make the decisions. It's very difficult for people with authority to go against the stakeholders if the stakeholders can agree among themselves what the plan is, as long as the plan is reasonable (i.e., it also meets the interests of the decision makers). If the members of the hospital could agree on the use of space within the allowable budget, it was pretty hard for the architects or the government who was going to fund it to say, "No, that's not a very good plan." These were the people that were going to use the place, and that was very important.

In the hospital case, three years after the programming, when they cut the ribbon to open the new facility, I gave a ride back from the event to a nurse that was there. I recognized her from three years before. As we were driving, I was quite proud of this beautiful building, and I asked, "So what do you think of the hospital?"

She said, "I like it—I got almost everything that I bargained for."

And I realized that she still felt ownership from those first programming sessions. Now she wasn't high in the hierarchy, but she still identified with the design, and her ownership and satisfaction still mattered.

In order to find a consensus, there are three things that any facilitator does. Communication is the first thing that people always have difficulty with, especially with a lot of people around the table because they're not necessarily communicating very well about the problem at hand or about the design or whatever it is that they've collectively agreed upon as an issue that they need to deal with. Very simply, we help people to communicate by asking, by clarifying, by confirming, by probing—by getting people to clarify what matters to them.

The second thing we do is manage the process because people need a structure as an alternative to fighting it out in court or whatever else they do.

The third thing we do is help them to reach closure. People, particularly in large groups, have a hard time coming to a conclusion and sticking with it.

A Traditional Tool for Reaching Consensus: Talking Circles

The "talking circle" is in stark contrast to the typical participatory meeting. The talking circle comes from an aboriginal practice where only the person who is holding the "talking stick" gets to talk. You pass the stick consecutively around the circle—around the entire group that needs to talk to each other. Initially, people need to build confidence in speaking and contributing to the conversation. So the keeper of the circle asks simply that people be brief and that they be respectful and that they make some contribution.

What happens is that people generally come with their complaints or their positions or their postures, but they will begin very modestly. I will often ask them to describe their community, even though they will very often have disagreements about it. It could be a community of a hospital, or a neighborhood, or a workplace. I'll ask them for positive things: what do they like about their place? And as they pass the talking stick around, they begin to have more and more confidence in themselves, and in one another, to begin to cite the problems, and to begin to deal constructively with those problems. If I'm the keeper of the circle, of course, at some point the stick comes back to me, and I can comment on the subject, or redirect it, or ask a question that might help the community that's in the circle to then refocus in some way.

The circle does a lot of moderating itself, because everybody is heard. So you might be sitting across from someone with whom you take issue, but you don't get to answer them until it is your turn. In between, you may have heard a number of other people express themselves, and by the time the stick comes to you, often your initial defensive response is much more positive; I find that people make a contribution to the discussion and go on to something else rather than get hung up with an objection. I find that the more the stick circulates, the more confident people become and the more ownership they take over whatever concern they have collectively—until someone begins to make suggestions about what they might do about it. That begins to circulate around, and they've advised each other about that possible solution to their problem.

It is almost always surprising. I intuit what process to use in each case, and sometimes I say, "Well, let's try a circle." It's just one of the formats for getting people to communicate. For example, I've been invited to come into a community where there has been discord of some kind, with two or three groups who can't agree on something. I might go to a neighborhood meeting early and simply arrange the chairs in a circle. (If it's 30 people or fewer.) When people walk in, I introduce myself and say something about the circle and how it works—the simple rules of respect and responsibility—so that people are familiar with it, and I'll present the reason that I've been asked to come. But first I'll ask people to introduce themselves.

If you can start by being positive, by getting rid of your negativity, it can jump-start a spirit of collaboration in resolving a difficult collective problem. I sometimes mention that, and people get the message. Some people actually talk about it. They'll say, "I came with a very negative attitude, and I'm glad you mentioned it, because here's a positive thing that I'd like to say about my neighborhood first," or something like that. And then everyone then goes around and builds on that suggestion—and the resolution is probably richer than when it was first suggested.

I was invited to a community one night that had a strong community association, but they needed some economic development on their main street. They had decided to form an economic development corporation. The corporation started developing things, and it attracted a lot of economic activity, and the commercial street was thriving. But the corporation was making some decisions that ran against the philosophy of the community and were unpopular.

In the talking circle, I got them to think collectively. Instead of emphasizing the differences between the two sides, I got them to think more collectively by passing the talking stick around and suggesting to them that their central concern had to be what was in the middle of the circle, which was really the community as a whole. Whatever was good for the community was what they had to start with. So it was the mutual gain that they all needed to accept. Then they started around. By the time we had gone around two or three circles, someone suggested, "Well, OK, how about if we take a six-month loan on that piece of vacant property?" and that went around, and people thought about that and commented on it.

Ultimately, there was a resolution about the actions that the corporation was going to take. The corporation generated some of those ideas, so it still felt that it was in control of its own destiny, but now within terms of reference spelled out by the community. But at the same time, it had gained a lot of "buy-in" from the rest of the residents.

I find that, in the circle, people tend to be less confrontational than they might be in other situations. People tend to be less positional, because that appears to be very selfish. I find that people tend to try to express themselves in terms of the interests of the community, or the neighborhood, or whatever they have in common. It's the way they say it that's so important—and how it comes across to other people. You can say practically the same thing and be very confrontational or be very collaborative—and I think the talking circle often helps people to be more collaborative.

You wouldn't want to do this with a group that's too big to handle. My sense is that 10 to 15 people can really talk to each other very well, but I've done it with smaller groups, and I've done it with larger groups. I generally use it with people who have something that is very strong that they have in common, where their community of interests is clear. I'll use it sometimes in a workplace—where everybody is working for the same enterprise, but they have difficulties—or in a geographic neighborhood.

Now, I have experienced situations where we all came from different perspectives, and we didn't know one another, and it took us some time before we actually could create a community of our own interests by being in that circle. We were developing trust. I find that's interesting in that sometimes we tend to be familiar with someone we don't know very well and will never see again. It's like having an intimate conversation with someone on the bus—but with your closest relation, it's very difficult to have the difficult conversation because there is so much more history there and you have so many more agendas that you have to maintain. In the case of the circle, I find the opposite—confidence builds and community builds and intimacy actually builds in the group over time. People become more personal, and they share more of their feelings about even profound, large-scale policies in the neighborhood or the community.

The Framework: Assess, Prepare, Facilitate, and Follow Through

I want to mention something about managing process. All too often, there is the preoccupation with the mediation event, with convening people and getting them together, getting people around the table who are in conflict and then wondering what you're going to do when you get there. I try to use a four-part framework when mediating groups in conflict: assessment, preparation, facilitation, and follow-through; often, the facilitation part is the least important when the other three are done well.

The first one is assessment: learning about the parties, their concerns, and what matters most to them ahead of the mediation. You assess whether these people are emotionally ready and willing to negotiate with one another and to collaboratively solve their problems; sometimes people must question their assumptions, confront their threats and values, and become curious and willing to learn before they are ready to collaboratively negotiate solutions with others. If they are prepared to explore opportunities and options, I then have to think about the kind of process that might be most useful—and then I report to them all about that.

I give them my perspective, characterizing the conflict and what I think they have in common. Very often, I will hear and be able to piece together what they don't because they haven't had good conversations with one another. The commonalities are very often so strong, and they are so surprised by that—because they assume that the other person is taking a position that is offensive and even threatening to them. But it turns out that there is some other force there.

I was once called by the Ontario Solicitor General's office to try to mediate a public conflict over property rights in a cottage community near Toronto where the previous weekend 2,500 angry protestors had marched along a popular beach and were demanding the government protect their access rights to water. The beachfront owners had fenced off their properties to protect their privacy from increasing numbers of unruly vacationers. The question was apparently about access to the beach by the people who live in cottage subdivisions behind the beachfront properties.

The people that owned the beachfront properties said, "This is our private property, and we're going to fence it off and not allow others to mess it up." It wasn't until I interviewed the association leaders of the neighborhoods and reported back that they came to understand that none of the people on the back lots challenged the ownership issue. That wasn't the problem. And when I interviewed the beachfront owners, all of them said, "You know, we never have had a problem with the people on the back lots—they are our neighbors. They're always welcome to come down."

This redefined the issue. It was the increasing numbers of people from Toronto who drove up to the beach for the day that caused problems, an issue all the cottagers shared; further, the issue for the day-trippers was that the province didn't provide enough public park space, and so naturally they found these private beaches. So the locals who thought they were in conflict with one another collectively turned around and said to the province, "This isn't our problem, this is your problem. We demand you build more public park space!" The solicitor general was happy to move the issue to another provincial ministry, and I ultimately had nothing to mediate.

The second part of my framework, if you do proceed with a process, is preparation for that facilitation or mediation, which can also take time and good thought. You need to prepare, in some cases, the parties themselves. You need to train them, or sometimes you need simply to orient them to an unfamiliar process and behavior. You need to get them to agree to an agenda. In fact, preparing the venue, the schedule, and how these people might meet over an informal meal to nurture better relationships, are all-important.

Meals are very important, and they need to be planned very carefully. They shouldn't be sit-down affairs where everyone is assigned a place. They need to be buffet meals where people can mix and choose where they're going to sit and who they're going to talk to—a lot of nice accidents happen over that break. For example, someone's intrigued by something that someone else says, and they will seek them out over a beer or a bowl of soup—they'll ask them about it informally when they would never do it formally. They get into the most wonderful conversations, and when they come back from the meal, or the next morning, a lot of attitudes will be changed and relationships will have been strengthened. That's part of the management of it. You want to provide those opportunities for people. They won't always happen, but they happen a lot.

The third part, the facilitation itself, is about helping people communicate, managing them, and then, finally, getting closure—helping them to come to a consensus conclusion that they will support. Instead of freezing the solution—as with most plans—the agreement is often conditional (i.e., I will do this if you will do that) and contains contingencies (in case things go adrift). This is the built-in flexibility that planning needs.

The fourth part is for the facilitator to help with the follow-through—making sure that what people have agreed upon actually gets done. Before they leave, you not only record what their agreements are, but you also record a to-do list, and you help people agree to take on certain responsibilities. So when people leave, they're satisfied that things will happen. You need to make sure that these things do happen, but invariably things go wrong. So you'll have to reconvene or make some other accommodation, and very often they will agree on dispute resolution mechanisms they can use in the future, because there are going to be unintended consequences.

Exploring Problem-Solving Capacity

I find very often that no matter what group of people—let's call them "the client"—will determine the process to be, they'll call you up later to get help with it. Very seldom do you ever get the chance to actually initiate and to design the process from scratch. The groups in question have determined what it's going to be, and they think they know what their problems are. They think that they need a facilitator or a mediator or someone to "chair the meeting."

You have to live with the constraints—a lot of the times it has to do with the time, or the budget, or the people they've convened. I find it a fascinating challenge to try to mold those preconceptions of the process into something that will work and something that will then produce a usable outcome.

Let me give you an example. I get a phone call from the ministry of natural resources (MNR): would I facilitate a meeting of stakeholders to review six technical options for the extraction of 15 years of timber in an old-growth management area of some 480,000 hectares (about 1.2 million acres) in northern Ontario? MNR has rented a gymnasium in Elk Lake for the weekend and they're going to present their six options (which they've been working on for two years), and then I'm to facilitate the comments from the various stakeholder groups. The purpose of this is to then conclude that one of these options is acceptable and that plan will be recommended to the minister. Under the law, the minister needs to have an indication that the stakeholders buy in to this plan.

I say, "So give me an idea about who you've invited – who you expect to show up."

They say, "Well, it will be the two lumber companies working in the area; it will be someone from the elected council of the local town (Elk Lake), whose industry is dependent on this lumbering; a local business representative; a representative from the Anglers and Hunters Association—because they love to get access to the wilderness country; and the Mining Association, because they'd also like to use the new logging roads for access to the back country; the Tourist Bureau will probably send someone; and there will probably be representatives from eight different environmental groups, all of whom have particular special interests."

I said, "This is not just a public consultation. If you want their acceptance of one of the alternatives, this is going to be a negotiation."

"A what?"

"A negotiation," I explained: "I think there is going to have to be some give-and-take here to reach an agreeable conclusion. We're going to have to find out what peoples' interests are, and we're going to have to find some acceptable criteria for choosing one of these six alternatives—if that's even possible."

I lay out what a facilitator generally does, which is the assessment and the preparation, and the facilitation, and the follow through.

He says, "Oh no, there is no budget for all that—just show up on Friday night in the Elk Lake gymnasium, and we'll pay your expenses to get up there!"

I say, "Well, could I at least have a conference call with everybody? Could we get everybody on one line, and could I introduce myself to them, and could we talk about some kind of an agenda and what people are interested in?"

They thought that would be OK, and they popped for the call. We get everyone on the line, and everyone introduces themselves. I say something about facilitation and what I might be doing. The client indicates that there are these six technical options that they've been working on for two years and that their purpose in having the meeting is to agree on one of the six options.

Finally, I ask the simple question, "Is there anything that's not negotiable?"

At that point the official from the ministry says, "Yes, there is one thing that's not negotiable: the minister has already signed a contract with the two lumber companies for the volume of wood that's going to come out of the forest in the 15-year period."

Well, of course, the environmental people were just apoplectic, "Why on earth would we want to be there?"

I confirmed their frustrations, and I said, "This is a big surprise for all of us—why don't we think about this for a week?"

We get on the phone the next week, and the environmental people have met in the meantime, and they say, "Well, we will come to this meeting on the condition of covering three major issues which form our agenda— (1) access to the area, how they were going to get the lumber out; (2) methods of silviculture, which is how you regenerate the environment after you take the lumber out; and (3) the type of species that would be allowed to be taken out."

I'm beginning to sense that the environmentalists have decided that not negotiating is not as good an option as negotiating. And so they've decided to come to the meeting, and that's key—without the enviros, any agreement is likely to be doubted by the ministry. Their agenda was accepted by the others, and we had our weekend—and they came to a conclusion. In fact, the environmentalists came to a very clever solution with the lumber companies. It all finally hinged on the means of access.

They chose the alternative that used a bridge across the river, the big Montreal River, because you could control access across the bridge. So you could control the truck traffic coming through to exclude the prospectors, the tourists, the anglers, and everyone else. You could keep them out of the entire area because there was only one route into the area.

The lumber companies sensed that they finally had one alternative that the environmentalists could support—which is all they really wanted. They said, "This is a wonderful alternative—we can certainly do that, and in fact we'll build the bridge, and after 15 years, when we leave, we'll take the bridge with us, and we'll sell it for scrap, or whatever."

They agreed on all of it. Now the environmentalists and the lumber companies were really friendly because they both got the best alternative they could live with, and they've got an alternative that will go to the government and presumably be adopted.

I shouldn't have taken that job. I should have said, "No, if I can't do my assessment, I'm not playing"—but something always happens that's interesting.

Why do I think there might be possibilities when others see animosity? I think there are some things that will tell you that nothing is going to happen— but there was nothing in that case that told me that nothing was going to happen. There was some momentum from call to call, from the morning to the afternoon to the evening of the meetings. There was momentum there, so the optimism was not only in me—though I admit to some of that—but it's in the sense you get from everyone else too. You get a sense of people's willingness and capacity to solve the problem—to develop the relationships that are necessary to address the issues.

Now, sometimes that's not so. For example, in the area next to this timber management area, where the people six years before had stopped lumbering, the government decided to try again. I was called and asked to come up there and do the same thing that I had done next door because that had gone well. In this case, the government had established a commission of private citizens and had given it the authority to get agreement to a timber management plan there. So I met with this group, and I said to them, "I will facilitate these stakeholders here, but if they come up with an option that they can all agree upon, will you accept it?" They said no.

I said, "Then I won't do it. Why would I ask these people to work for a whole weekend and come up with an agreement if you can then pull the rug out from under them?" There was no taking these people seriously.

I've come to the conclusion that people need to understand their roles, and they need to be defined—who does what. If you're asked to come to a conclusion, to a consensus, and to make a recommendation, that recommendation should be taken seriously. It doesn't have to be accepted if someone has the authority to say yes or no to it—for example, in Calgary, I had to go to the city council for the final approval. But you have to take people seriously if you're asking them to give you their best advice and their best effort.

I always make a clear distinction between the role and interest of the general public, the stakeholders who are directly affected, and the decision makers, those with the authority and responsibility to finally decide; the general public should always have access to the information and the proceedings, and they may be involved in mapping the issues and the objectives, but they are not expected to negotiate resolutions; the stakeholders who can commit resources and support to a resolution should be included in the group negotiating the proposed outcome, but they may not have the final say—more often they are representatives of bodies that will have that say.

Possibilities for Planners

Why am I optimistic about this process and our professional role as facilitators, and why aren't I put off or discouraged if there's a lot of animosity between parties? I think there must be some reasons for the animosities. So as an impartial facilitator—though I'm actively interested in the quality of the outcomes because I'm also a planner—I sympathize with people who are angry and frustrated and threatened and confused because I understand their need to be heard and respected and their need to understand their roles in the process to get the issue resolved.

So I see contentious meetings as a necessary challenge. If people are locked in, how do you unlock them? That's a whole skill set that a facilitator must have. If people are angry at each other, then I think you have to come to understand the source of that anger. In those cases, I have to take a step back, and that, first of all, means that I'm not trying to do the planning; instead I am trying to understand what the folks are really concerned about. If I expect them to collaborate, to invent solutions and agree, then first I must deal with their emotions. Only then can we move on to collaboration and problem solving.

If the planner thinks of himself strictly as "the planner" and not also as the facilitator—and everyone has to define his or her own role in this—then I think a planner might be right to back off. I don't think they're right not to try and have conflict resolved, but they might not want to try and help get it resolved—they may choose to ask someone else to be the mediator. But if you want to serve as the mediator as well as the planner, and you want to help this community to strengthen itself, then this community will strengthen itself by resolving its own conflicts. A community weakens itself when it must rely on some higher authority to make decisions for it.

Planners taking on mediating roles sometimes can be seen as helping a community to rebuild itself—to rebuild its relationships, however full of conflict. Once a community has begun to feel better about itself and feel better about talking to one another, it will then want to come back to the problem of planning.

In many ways the planner is well prepared to also be the mediator: balancing fact and intuition and knowing to trust intuition; respecting views that differ or even conflict with one another; translating problems and emotions into opportunities and options; knowing how and why to listen and to be curious and ask why a lot; knowing that the outcome must be acceptable to the folks who must own it and live with it. But the planner who wants also to mediate must address new dichotomies: being impartial and still wanting an elegant solution; empowering others to plan; trusting that the essential information will emerge from the dialogue; respecting emotion along with reason.

I need to elaborate on this point about respecting emotion—whether dealing with an individual or the public—because we planners are rarely prepared for this. Indeed, we tend to ask an emotional person or group to settle down, to put aside their emotions for the good of solving the problem, instead of allowing those emotions to lead us to the source of conflicts that often block our chance of planning or designing something important.

I was called one Thursday by the mayor of a rural township near Toronto, asking me to moderate a public meeting that had been widely publicized as a "debate," scheduled for the next Tuesday evening. This meeting was to be held in the local ice arena that seats 700 people, to debate a proposal to build a huge incineration plant that would burn Toronto's garbage and bring much-needed revenue to this municipality. The "debate" would be between the engineering proponents and the opposing environmental experts. The mayor said most residents would be coming to oppose the idea, others from the struggling business community would likely support it, and the council, anticipating violence, had called upon the provincial police to keep order.

I agreed on certain conditions: stop calling the meeting a "debate"—this should be not an exchange between talking heads but rather a public discussion; all of the elected council members must attend, sitting to one side, listening and taking notes, but not to speak; the local media must be invited and have the opportunity to question the panel, as would everyone else attending who wanted to comment. The mayor agreed.

The place was packed. I opened by outlining how the meeting would go and saying that there was one thing that we all in this room had in common: we all needed more information and we all needed to hear more opinions about the proposition. I said the process must occur for a decision to be made, and that was why we were here tonight, for an exchange, not a lecture or a debate.

I could instantly feel the room of 700 people settle down. I had touched upon everyone's assumptions and anxieties, and they saw their roles, and now they understood what was going to take place. The discussion went off very peacefully; everyone who had something to ask or say, pro or con, was recognized, much information and opinion was exchanged, and when people left they all knew they had had the opportunity of being heard, and they had a better idea of what next steps were to be taken and how they might participate. The proposition was ultimately rejected by a special referendum that the council decided to hold, once they had listened very carefully that night.

As I reflect on my experiences as an architect and planner trying to help solve design and planning problems, my biggest lessons are these:

- Teach yourself to reflect on what's going on and learn from it.
- Listen to people, respectfully ask why a lot, and trust them to inform you.
- Think outside the technical/professional box you're in.
- Follow your instincts.

I am continually excited by the designer's capacity to observe, and I am continually surprised by the mediator's power to intervene by getting parties to the table and helping them to resolve their differences. A wise First Nations chief once closed a circle training I attended by saying, "You will never get it right … so just do it." He was advising us to invite those people to our dialogue and to trust them to figure it out.

I have to admit that I worry a lot less than I anticipated. I love doing this work—and there is almost no issue I won't take on. It's never predictable—it's never what should happen—it's never the textbook. I just love the way that it unfolds. It's almost like writing a great novel where the actors take over and tell you what to write.

Afterword

I hope publication of this isn't really so final as the word "afterword" implies, but rather a continuing dialogue about the practical overlay of planning and mediation. These are not strange bedfellows but rather mates at work in the reality of societal diversity and pluralism, competing interests, deep cares and threats, and collective dysfunctions that require collaborative visions and capacities for resolution. Shared unresolved issues—call them conflicts or problems or differences—require processes of conversion from competition to collaboration to consensus. The outcome is not simply an agreement but an agreed-upon plan of action or, as Larry Susskind so usefully recognized, "negotiated investment strategies": negotiated because collaboration is required, investment because commitments are required, strategy because a plan for getting there is needed.

We must continue to strive to clarify what we do and why we do it. I am finding that the description of this essential conversion process seems to expose our inherent mix of planner and mediator "genes" in ways that resonate both for parties in conflict and students.

When we first address our task—either as planners or mediators—we observe interests, data, even natural forces that are in contradiction or conflict; they are competing with one another, and they are certain they must win. Philosopher Bernard Lonergan introduced me to concepts of conversion from knowing to unknowing, from certainty to uncertainty, curiosity, and questioning, from positions to possibilities and visions of what might be. Without our helping parties in conflict to make this conversion away from competing, they cannot be willing to collaborate in inventing the possibilities of mutual gain outcomes. To do this, we must sometimes even help them probe past their positions and interests to what they care and worry about more deeply, often concerns they are unwilling to share until they can sense reduced risk and greater safety among those who they originally perceived as adversaries.

I would argue that while it is the mediator gene that has led us to this point, the planner gene is always present. Now the planner gene kicks in and, with mediator gene support, begins to orchestrate the questioning, the brainstorming, and the search for shared principles of mutual gain that, once identified and adopted, become the bonding element, the reason why people stay at the table. And once mutual gain is within reach, the parties must collaborate to do the hard work of inventing a mutually beneficial outcome. The planner gene guides them through a process of setting goals and priorities, collecting and applying the relevant data, inventing the options, agreeing on the criteria for evaluating the options, and weighing the consequences of alternative futures—all solid planning traditions, typically practiced by mediators as well.

The planner/mediator likewise assists the parties in the final conversion, reaching consensus on the preferred solution and strategies for ensuring its successful implementation.

Nevertheless, while both planners and mediators can identify with this process—even its often common language—they rarely seem to assign themselves to both roles. Part of this problem is in clarifying the process for them, but more serious is the lack of institutional clarity that exists in professional associations and educational programs in which both share a too limited view of what planners and mediators do and think about. Both in practice and in education we need a more integrated practical and theoretical base of understanding of society's need for "interest-based planning" and assisted negotiation affecting public policy, programs, and projects—that is, the stuff of planning.

I observe both professions shying away from the research and education that's needed. Take learned instinct for example. Neither planning nor mediation seems to embrace learned instinct as an essential competency, nor is it part of a pedagogy of communicating, questioning, problem solving, facilitating, and inventing—all essential to developing planner and mediator skills. Instead, the traditional focus is on method—doing it the right way, content over context, when we know in practice there is no universally right way, that what one does or says in practice is a matter of instinct as well as experience, judgment, context, timing and, yes, good fortune. And when the moment goes against us and the luck turns, we must know to respond fairly, honestly, respectfully, and promptly. Ours is an interdisciplinary art and science. Our institutional preparation and support systems must call upon the likes of psychology and communications and philosophy and behavioral science to enrich our instincts, and we must offer learning experiences in our university programs that will give students greater confidence to help society confront its dysfunctions, overcome the obstacles, resolve the differences, and adopt the solutions.

Chapter 2

From Conflict Generation through Consensus Building Using Many of the Same Skills

Frank Blechman

A conflict generator turned conflict resolver, Frank Blechman tells us that many skills he'd used in adversarial settings turned out to be very useful as well when it came time to craft cooperative working agreements. Blechman argues that very often, if we want to get things done on complex public issues, we will need to build supportive coalitions—which will mean practically reconciling, at least temporarily, the differing priorities, interests, and values of coalition members. Because building support from others typically means looking for areas of agreement even when we don't see eye to eye about everything, the distance between the skills of coalition building, dispute resolution, and advocacy can get very small indeed.

But Blechman's story provides us with other surprises, too. We learn how it can be possible at times that even when parties like pro-choice and anti-abortion advocates have fundamental disagreements, they still might make practical agreements. How can it really be, though, in the face of deep value disagreements, that the careful processes of bringing together deeply divided parties might still successfully do practical work—and without asking anyone to make any compromises?

Blechman covers this ground and still more, for his examples show us cases in which county government officials have said, in effect, "You're crazy!" when asked about participating in a collaborative planning process with nearby neighbors; and yet, after skillful process design, they not only participated but began to make practical progress. How's that possible? Read and find out! —JF

⚜

I may, at best, occasionally be impartial, but I'm never neutral. I believe that, in fact, my presence almost always empowers weaker parties by creating explicit ground rules and a forum that allows people who don't have unlimited resources to focus their resources. It creates a framework in which they can play—where the influence of the more powerful parties is somewhat moderated within a set of rules.

I graduated from college in the late 1960s, so I didn't have a choice of graduate school—I had a choice of nationality or uniform color.

Growing up in the South, I'd lived through the experience of the civil rights movement, which had transformed my community and my life. I became very active in antiwar activity but volunteered for the U.S. Navy because I thought that people of conscience needed to be in the system—to serve the country and know how it all works. I emerged a veteran and a conscientious objector. It was fairly unusual to hold such dual status: I did two years in the navy, and then I had two years of alternative service.

The product of all of that was that from 1971 until 1986 I was involved in what I prefer to call "applied political science": issue and political organizing, mostly in the South—working at the community, state, regional, and then ultimately national level.

By 1985 I worked for the lieutenant governor of Missouri, helping her run for the U.S. Senate. When that campaign was over, I was offered a job with something called the "Conflict Clinic," a dispute resolution organization based at the University of Missouri at Saint Louis. I liked Missouri. After 15 years working for nonprofit organizations, political organizations, and other institutions with dubious and transitory funding, the notion of working with something that was actually rooted to a state university, which probably wasn't going to move anywhere, was entirely attractive.

I had just had a baby, and I liked St. Louis. I was hired by the Conflict Clinic as a political analyst—someone who could come in, investigate a complex of public issues, and map out the parties, the issues, the interrelationships, the coalitions, the political histories of the parties, and the prospect of shifts in those alignments over a period of time and under various circumstances. That's something that, as a journalist, which I had been at one point, and as a political activist, too, I had learned how to do quickly.

Five months after I joined the Conflict Clinic in January 1987, its director, Jim Laue, was offered the world's first endowed chair in conflict resolution. So I moved with the clinic to George Mason University in Fairfax, Virginia. Although several associates of the Conflict Clinic did not move to Washington, several of us did. The effect of this was that I was soon transformed from being a political analyst into being a conflict-resolving jack-of-all-trades: facilitator, mediator, dispute resolver, trainer, researcher, salesman, proposal writer, and all the rest.

During the first couple years there, I insisted loudly at every turn that I was not a mediator, that I was not even sure I believed in mediation, and that I wasn't sure I wanted to be seen as such with them. I was largely in charge of developing the training programs. That was a fairly innocuous thing because it was just talking about it—you didn't have to actually do it—and one of the by-products of politics, certainly, is you learn how to talk about things that you don't really do.

We were very successful in developing a series of training programs for citizens and public officials in public interaction, public participation, public negotiation, facilitation of public meetings, public processes, process design, and process management. That ultimately led to some materials we developed on systems design, and gradually I moved more and more into an active interventionist role.

The Conflict Clinic was a private, nonprofit organization. Because of its academic base and foundation funding, it often intervened uninvited in complex public issues. We often engaged—after conflicts had been developing for some time—by offering to bring new ideas and approaches. In some ways, we modeled ourselves on medical clinics in teaching hospitals: places where people could come to get experimental treatments.

On January 1, 1992, the Conflict Clinic merged into George Mason University, and I became a member of the graduate faculty there. I taught several of the skills classes, and I supervised field research, which became an active part of the doctoral program. Every doctoral student was required to join a field research team built around long-term research questions related to five-to-seven-year projects to which doctoral and some masters students committed at least one year. These long-term issues included conflict in divided societies and racial and ethnic conflict in communities. The concept was that these efforts would then spin off various projects and products as they went along. I directed that field research and, meanwhile, practiced on the side.

Skills That Travel: Coalition Building

So my entry into this field was backward. I'd spent most of my career as a conflict generator and still viewed it as my essential skill in conflict analysis and resolution. Conflict generation is the process of simplifying an issue, raising it to visibility and forcing public polarization so that 50 percent plus one landed on my side. It's essentially the opposite of consensus-building processes although it uses all the same skills. The fundamental skill in both is understanding where people are coming from and how far they're willing to move. Getting people to feel comfortable and therefore willing to reveal information that they initially withhold is about trust building, which comes before solution seeking.

I have been influenced by something Sam Rayburn (former Speaker of the U.S. House of Representatives from Texas) is alleged to have said: "Any bill that passes by more than 10 votes wasn't strong enough." I think that's the ultimate statement of the virtue of nonconsensus. If in fact you need only 50 percent plus one to make policy, then getting more than that means you gave up more than you had to. But in many of the public issues that we face today—because over the last generation we have empowered so many people to obstruct so effectively—50 percent plus one often is not enough; 60 percent plus one is not enough; 70 percent plus one is not enough. Sometimes, you need to get closer to 90 percent plus one in order to actually carry out policy. At that point the skills required to get 50 percent plus one have to be retuned toward a different objective: getting enough consent to move forward. Most of the work that I have done as a conflict intervenor falls into the range between 90 percent plus one and 100 percent minus one, rather than the bare majority.

To put what I say into context, let me describe the intellectual framework we developed at George Mason. I think whereas much conflict resolution practiced in this country is built on negotiation theory—or theories of value, communication, or exchange—in contrast, our program did not start from negotiation theory. Indeed, it started from the premises that the conflicts that go on the longest and cause the most damage are rooted in nonnegotiable issues: race, class, gender, religion, nationality, deeply held values—and that those deeply rooted issues, therefore, cannot be resolved by negotiation. The end product of a resolutionary process, therefore, is not an agreement. That created a different framework for what we do.

The end products of the analytical and transformative processes we developed were often understandings rather than agreements. Parties that were deeply divided came together, joined in an analytical process, and went away not having agreed about anything but having come to understand their own and the other's situation better. They acted unilaterally in the future in ways that were less conflictual, more constructive for each, and in fact often they found that while they could not get within a shred of agreement on issue X, that they in fact had dozens of issues, A, B, C, to J, on which they could cooperate, many of which were in fact negotiable.

To Meet or Not to Meet: Pro-Life and Pro-Choice

I'll give you a classic example. In 1987, the pro-choice and pro-life forces in Maryland—which is a historically Catholic state—had really gone to war with each other, and the state police were proposing to go to the legislature seeking new authority to interpose themselves to prevent violence.

There was a meeting arranged between leaders of the pro-choice and the pro-life forces, and they immediately agreed that it would be very undesirable if such legislation was passed. They jointly opposed it on a variety of free speech grounds. As the discussions went forward they discovered, not entirely to their amazement, that they also shared strong common interest in increasing health care for at-risk and pregnant teenagers. And they wound up forming a coalition that voluntarily proposed a set of rules for how they would picket each other — to lower the risk of violence, thereby forestalling the state police proposal.

Simultaneously, they formed a coalition in the legislature to increase state funding and support for prenatal health care. That coalition, despite all the ongoing friction, including actions of outside groups, held up for five years and succeeded in increasing state funding for health care even at times of budget cuts — and that has, at some level, improved the civility of debate.

Now, on the fundamental issue of abortion, needless to say, the two sides did not convince each other and did not agree, and if the purpose of bringing them together was to seek common ground on that issue, they might never have come together, and my guess is that it would have failed. But by bringing them together in a different context, it was possible for them to identify very constructive things that they could do. Adrienne Kauffman (one of our PhD students) did fabulous work on this issue nationwide via Search for Common Ground to create a Network for Life and Choice. This was really remarkable work that's really important for other people to learn.

That's a small example of a nonbargaining process. It was fundamentally an analytical process in which each side went away and took certain actions. Now there were also some agreements, but those came later. Much of the work that we have done in civil wars internationally, outside the U.S., is essentially that kind of work, where we are creating analytical frameworks rather than bargaining frameworks.

Corridor Planning I

In the corridor between Baltimore and Washington, D.C., there are five counties, the two major cities, five other cities, and a great many independent authorities that have special districts of various sorts. Planning in that corridor accordingly has historically been very fragmented.

We were asked by one of the counties to help it consider how to do comprehensive planning, a traditional land-use type of planning, in the part of the county that's in the corridor. Part of the concern was that this is an area which is somewhat more blue collar, a little bit tougher—a little less civil—than other parts of the county: there was a lot of bitterness that the other parts of the county had been getting better services, and there was a feeling that there was no way to open up traditional citizen participation without it getting completely out of hand and becoming explosive.

The county asked us, could we propose a process, could we do process design work, to help them—to give them advice on how they might proceed with comprehensive planning? We pointed out to them that, thanks to the passage at the federal level, of the Intermodal Surface Transportation Efficiency Act (ISTEA), they could not do land-use and transportation planning without also doing environmental planning. And in further discussions with county officials, we pointed out that many other jurisdictions in the corridor were beginning to realize that you couldn't do land-use, environmental, and transportation planning without also doing housing and economic development planning at the same time. But each of these processes had been separate—they were legally required to be separate processes at the local level, managed by different agencies, and, actually, were related to different sets of citizen organizations.

We said to them, "Would you be interested in considering a process that might integrate all of these?"

They said, "Well, we might."

We said, "Would you be interested in considering a process that integrated what you're doing with what's going on with the adjacent jurisdictions in the corridor?"

They said, "You are out of your mind."

We said, "Let's take a look." We then went out and interviewed about 130 people, roughly one-third business, one-third citizen activist and political types, and one-third governmental officials. We then constructed four focus groups representing slightly different geographical areas, but each mixed in terms of the three sectors. And we then constructed, out of those focus groups and out of the interviews, a team of 14 people who represented all of the jurisdictions and all of the sectors to discuss a process for integrated planning. That group, through us, then presented the proposal for a dramatically different kind of process to the planning agencies in two of the counties and to the county council in a third—and it eventually won approval for that new process, which is now beginning.

We played no role in that ongoing planning process. We were not the facilitators or managers. We were agents of process design. It was a consensus-building process in the sense that folks who initially could not sit in the same room with one another ultimately sat down and came to an agreement about how the process ought to work. Obviously, this is not the same as building a consensus on comprehensive planning, land use, transportation, environmental management, growth, economic development, and housing in the corridor, but it's clearly the first step. It's a piece of work that took us nearly eight months.

I think, in a traditional public process, this would indeed be only the first phase. It would be presumed that the facilitators or process designers would then manage the subsequent phases. It was our belief that because people were so intimately involved in the process design, they would act as the guardians of the process. As such, they might not need "professional" mediation or facilitation.

Built into the process was an escape clause, which said that if one of these named things happened, you could call in somebody to help you.

Bridging Gaps

How did we get people who didn't want to sit in the same room to the point of finally agreeing on things? We did just as you would do with an interpersonal mediation.

The first step was sharing information and helping people discover commonalties that they didn't know existed. After the interviews, we issued a series of reports. The first one was a map of issues, showing that there was high consensus, in all areas, about what the most important issues were, and across all sectors. Not in exactly the same proportions, but the number one issue was number one and number 10 was pretty much at the bottom half across the board.

The second report was then a map of process concerns. It led to a wider survey than the people we first interviewed. We asked, "What are your procedural preferences about how certain things ought to happen?" And that information was then fed back to everyone. Then we did the focus groups.

In the focus groups we explicitly asked people to reflect, saying, "Here are the existing processes in each of these jurisdictions; here are the procedural preferences that an unscientific survey has revealed. What do you make of that? What do you think of that?"

We got very constructive suggestions by asking people, "How would you bridge these gaps?" rather than by asking, "Which side do you fall on?" We pushed—we invited—them to serve in the role of consensus builders rather than in the role of advocates.

When people then saw the range of substantive and procedural views, it was clear to many of them (who, as always happens, had been isolated in their own circles) that they could not get their way by saying, "But I want it to be done this way!", no matter how loudly they said it.

That led, in turn, in time, to people listening to one another, considering procedures that would give their point of view the best chance of being heard by people who disagreed, which happened to be the same procedures that give other people the best chance of having their point of view heard.

Had we tried to do it in two months, it would have been impossible. If we had tried to do it in two years, it would also have been much more difficult because people would have had more time to argue for their points of view. We allowed it to move at a reasonable but slightly pressured pace by saying, "We need to move ahead with this because, gosh, there are various federal and state mandates, funding timelines that this needs to move on" (which was true but not entirely persuasive). Everybody knew they were being pushed, and they could stall it if they wanted to, but at that point nobody really wanted to. The more they saw possibilities, the more they wanted to get on with it. And they understood that the way to get on with it was to come to some understanding and to come to an agreement about process, which they did.

That exercise mapped out both various procedural agreements and areas of substantive disagreement. We captured the areas of disagreement as areas of future work. But it also gave people some common floor to stand on as they moved into the substantive work. I think what often happens in public disputes is that people come together to cross a chasm, and they're intensely focused on that chasm. They don't realize they are standing on the same ground. Refocusing, saying "What do we have to build out from?," doesn't happen until several people have already fallen into the chasm. In this case, we explicitly gave everybody a feeling that they were in this together and had already proven that they could work despite their differences.

Building Problem-Solving Capacity

Did we face suspicion or mistrust or feel some resistance from the parties we were working with? Of course. It was enormous. How did we deal with that? I almost always begin a conflict resolution investigation by asking what I consider to be the big question: "Are you having fun yet?" If the parties say, "Yeah, our situation's great, it's wonderful, couldn't be better," I say, "Well, have a wonderful time." It's clear I'm not necessarily going to be very helpful.

But if they say, "Ugh, it's painful, it's stupid, it's miserable, it's wasteful, but I won't give in to that son of a bitch," then I know there's a clear and very constructive role that I can play. Usually when I say, "You know, it appears to me that what you're really asking for here is the other guy's blood, and I'm just curious from an academic point of view, what are you going to do with the blood when you get it?," people will reply, "Oh, no, I don't really want his blood, I really want his concession on this issue or the other."

Once I've turned that corner, and folks have begun to say, "No, I really don't want blood," then I can begin to say, "Oh, well, that's terrible. It really must be awful to be locked into a situation like this." They say, "It is." And I say, "Oh, that's difficult. What are you going to do about it?"

Well, two things have happened here. First of all, I've expressed some empathy. People appreciate that I understand how difficult their situation is and how, of course, they cannot be asked to give in to that son of a bitch. I acknowledge and legitimate their situation. I've always understood that to be the first rule of facilitation, and I think it is certainly also the first rule of complex mediation.

Once we have identified that their situation is complex and difficult, and that they would like to get out of it but they don't know how, then the question is: "How do we introduce new ideas?" Now, because I've grown up in politics and lived in the South and had experience with agriculture extension services, I've been inclined to introduce new ideas not from a base of academic expertise but anecdotally from peer experience. I might say, "Gosh, you are really in a tough situation. You know, I was working with a guy over in Iowa just a couple of weeks ago who had a situation kind of like yours. Would you like to hear about it?"

A story about how somebody took a different approach and how it led to a different result introduces a new idea in a noncritical, nonthreatening way. Maybe I actually bring in a peer of theirs who can say, "Oh, this guy works for a university, but he's OK—yeah, he's a white boy, but he's not a cracker," or, "He is a cracker, but he's still OK."

I can't legitimate myself. I can acknowledge and legitimate parties in conflict, but they have to decide to acknowledge and legitimate me. I know they are not going to choose to acknowledge, legitimate, or accept me because I tell them I'm terrific. In fact, the farther I go promising snake oil, the deeper trouble I'm in. It's pretty important to offer the traditional academic and mediators' disclaimers up front. What we have to offer is not snake oil: it doesn't work all the time. "But gosh," we can say, "we were working with a fella that had a problem kind of like yours. We helped him, might help you."

Once that framework is in place, people make individual decisions. The wonderful thing about a complex public dispute is there are a lot of people involved, people who are interested in public issues—whether it's a matter of vanity, whether it's a matter of power politics, or whether it's just idle curiosity, they want to be where the action is.

You don't have to get everybody to buy in at the same time: that's ideal, but in real life you try to get a few folks first. I mean out of 20 parties in each of seven factions, if you can get two or three of each to say, "I'm willing to give it a try," you begin to build some momentum, and for better or for worse there is crowd psychology that happens here: someone might say, "Well, I don't know that I believe this stuff, but if Joe's willing to try it, I'll give it a try." In fact, they'll say, "Joe and I will make a pact that we'll both walk out if we don't like what we see. But we'll go together just to look see." You build up from what you have, rather than wish for what you don't have. That's a process of identifying possible resources, possible support, and then using those peers to bring additional folks in.

The other piece that's crucial to me is that in a complex public process, not everybody wants to be involved in the same way, and therefore if out of a million people in a corridor I'm going to end up working with maybe 300 or 400, of whom I'm going to work with maybe 30 intensely, that's not a very representative process by any measure. So I have to make the representative quality of it as visible as possible and make it possible for people who feel they are not represented by any of the 30 or any of the 300 to have a voice by other means. In a complex negotiating process you may have a negotiating team of 30 people, and you have public hearings that involve an additional 400, so you also make sure you have survey and comment processes that allow an additional 10,000 to be involved, at which point you've built a whole lot more legitimacy than the 30 will ever have. It also moderates the extreme views within the 30 by providing some calibrating data.

Those 30 who are at the table understand that they are representatives. As the process manager, I'm not just managing the negotiation among them but among them and their constituents, and also among their constituents directly. That's all part of a large public process. If I manage only what's happening at the table, I'm missing 80 percent of the action, and no wonder if I get blindsided over and over again. So I try to pay attention and create explicit vehicles inside the process for that outside stuff to get in and have an impact.

Beyond Gridlock

Maryland and Virginia in the 1980s proposed bypasses that would divert traffic off the Washington Beltway—an eastern bypass and a western bypass, which would have formed an "outer beltway" if both were built. Enough people objected that neither one was going to happen. The transportation agencies faced increased gridlock with no plan for relief.

The Maryland Department of Transportation (MDOT) said, "U.S. Highway 301 goes up eastern Maryland east of Washington, and whether we call it a bypass or not, more and more people are using it. We need to make transportation improvements there. But there's no way we can propose transportation improvements without people saying, 'Agh, a bypass by another name. We recognize what this is. NO WAY!'" MDOT knew it needed to do something other than the usual "decide-announce-defend."

Working with a group of planners and facilitators from Annapolis, Maryland, we designed a process that brought together about a hundred representatives of the four counties and six cities in that corridor along with representatives of environmental groups, business groups, MDOT, and others. We created a framework that used working groups structured by issues. There was an environmental group, an economic development group, and a transportation analysis group.

We created a variety of ways that those groups interacted, but we also forced geographic caucuses. Every three months, whether they liked it or not, all the folks from Anne Arundel County and all the folks from Charles County talked to one another—because ultimately this was going to come down to some regional politics, and I wanted that discussion inside the process, not outside of it.

That's the politics of it as compared to the substance, and that's just another piece of process design. By saying to people, "I acknowledge and legitimize your needs, and I'm making a place for you to get what you want inside this process that looks more attractive than what you can get outside the process," ultimately I can bring most people in—and even if I never completely overcome the suspicions, I balance the suspicion with concrete, attractive opportunities.

Neutrality

Is it difficult to remain neutral during these processes? I guess I'm never neutral. So, yes, it's extremely difficult. I believe that my mere presence in a situation changes the dynamics, changes the way parties behave. I may, at best, occasionally be impartial, but I'm never neutral. I believe that, in fact, my presence almost always empowers weaker parties by creating explicit ground rules and a forum that allows people who don't have unlimited resources to focus their resources. It creates a framework in which they can play—where the influence of the more powerful parties is somewhat moderated within a set of rules.

I'm explicit about my role up front. People ask, "Can you be neutral?," and I say, "Absolutely not, I don't intend to be." Then there's a big sigh of relief—people appreciate that. It's a lot more sensible than saying, "I'm going to put on a black robe and sit behind a bench and keep a poker face." The other side of that is, obviously, that if at some point I become an active advocate for one party, usually that limits my credibility with others and affects my ability to manage the process.

So I try not to become a conspicuous advocate for any party, but I have never been in a complex process where the parties were equally skilled and where I did not wind up having to spend more time with some parties than with others in order to keep the process functioning, and that's not a neutral intervention.

Dealing with imbalances in money, expertise, and time is a problem to be solved just like any other, and once people look at the options, many of them prefer having me act as a balancer as compared to some of the other possibilities. For example, I was involved in a police/community relations situation in Des Moines, Iowa, and the question was, "Would you rather have these turkeys from George Mason University, or would you rather have the U.S. Department of Justice, or would you rather have, you know, the Aryan Brotherhood act as an intervener?" Well, given those choices, we begin to look pretty good.

I may not be an interested party in the sense that I have something to gain from the outcome or that I favor a particular substantive outcome. But I clearly do have very strong opinions about the process. I'm not impartial on that, and I don't pretend to be. Further, when I work on public issues in my own community, I will be impacted by the result. My role requires that I not get too out front about my interests and preferences, but it doesn't mean that I don't have them.

Successes and Challenges

What did I find the most challenging in the corridor process and what was the most satisfying in the end? The satisfying part is that in the end it came together. You never know if it's going to work; it doesn't always work. You give it your best shot, and some days you understand where you screwed up and why it didn't work, and some days you don't even understand what you did wrong. It's always gratifying when it works. The Baltimore-Washington corridor project moved from a point where citizens were saying, "When you present this proposal to the planning board, it's so radical it won't fly," to the point where the planning board was saying, "What's new? What are we paying you this money for? It looks like a few small tweaks on the same old process," and it was approved with boringly little discussion.

The difficult part is that when we went in, what we knew—or what we had been told in advance—was that there were real lunatics out there. We tend to believe that it's not in our interest to start off by treating people like clinical deviants. There are such people. I've worked with them, and you never know, this might be the situation where everybody is clinically loony. It's better to start with the assumption, though, that no matter how much folks have been acting up to get attention, there is a serious person underneath who I can invite to participate constructively.

In order to do this project, we had to do a lot of interviews very fast. So we assembled a team of myself and four other people who had never worked together before. Because we had to get started very fast, we didn't clarify some of internal roles as well as we should have. That made for some real working problems within our team that we then had to go back and patch up later on.

We had to have our own internal conflict analysis. I think we understood that that was going to happen, and we understood that we should take more time up front, but we didn't have it, and we knew we were going to pay for it. When we started paying for it, we recognized it, we stepped back, and we took the time to sort it out, mostly.

I've worked in team negotiations and independently, about half and half. It's a matter of scale. Anytime a situation involves more than 15 or 20 issues and more than a hundred people, I don't like taking those on alone because there's just too much to watch and I don't trust my own judgment, even if I have the time to do it. I want somebody else who has different perspectives and usually that means not just a team but a team that's diverse: that involves someone who is a different age, a different gender, and a different race, who in some way has a dramatically different perspective than I do. It's humbling but helpful.

What would I have done differently in the corridor process design project?

I think I would have done more surveying earlier, before I did interviews. I would have had a stronger base, and it would have made these interviews much more consistent. As it was, I had a general framework for the interviews, but because five different people were doing them, when we went to try to put the pieces together and analyze the results, it was harder than it needed to be: again it's part of our not having gotten our act entirely clear about what information we were trying to gather and how we were planning to analyze it.

Had we done more surveying earlier, it would also have been helpful. But while I love surveying, I know that for purposes of conflict resolution surveying absolutely is no substitute for personal contact. Interviewing is partially information gathering, but it's 60 percent relationship building. You are introducing yourself and inviting people to trust you. It's a negotiation in itself, and if they trust you to share information with you, and you treat that information with the respect that you promise, it's then not a very large leap to say, "Now, will you trust me to put together a meeting where you won't get beaten up?"

So the first step in conflict resolution is that relationship building, and that's why interviewing is an important technique, and that's why it's largely individual. I don't do a lot of group interviewing in the early stages, and that's why I put focus groups behind individual interviews and not in front of them.

Skills for Mediators and Negotiators

So, what skills and knowledge do people need to be effective mediators or negotiators or conflict generators? I think there are only three. The first one far and above the others is honesty. If you lie to yourself you'll get screwed, and you'll screw up everybody else too. And this is true in politics; it's true in life. The people who get in trouble are the people who convince themselves that everything's fine when it's falling apart. So the first skill is honesty, but I know of relatively few schools that teach this, as a skill. But I believe it is a skill that can be taught.

The second skill is patience, understanding that the first answer is not necessarily the right one, and that in public policy issues it's going to be years before you know how good the deal was. You've got to see how it plays out. Patience is absolutely crucial. People who are impatient, again, screw themselves up and everybody else around them. Again, that's a skill that often is not taught but ought to be.

The third skill is the ability to count backward. People who take it one step at a time don't conceptualize the larger process, don't work backward and manage their resources appropriately, go broke halfway through the process. Whether they are spending money or credibility, they run out.

Part of the way I've tried to teach honesty is through practice. In addition to the four introductory theory courses at ICAR, there are three introductory skills courses: Interpersonal and Small Group Conflict, Community and Organizational Conflict, and International Conflict. The difference among them is largely a question of scale and the degree to which culture plays a role in the exercises and simulations that we thrust people into. In all three of those courses we've required people to do some journaling, to take the skills and concepts that we're talking about and reflect on how it applies in their real life, how they have or have not used these skills for better or worse.

It is very easy to tell, reading journals, who is finessing and who is disclosing, and we call students on it. We say to them, "I want to hear more about this. This is a very interesting story, and I'd like you in your entry in next week's journal to tell me more about that. Tell me more about this part or that part, about how you made this judgment. What skill do you already have that anchors your use of this approach?"

Some people have a very hard time doing that because it requires them to admit some things about themselves that they don't like. "I was tired, and so I didn't do what I knew I should have done. I was mad at that person so I didn't do what I knew I should have done."

This is not a confessional process. This is not transactional analysis. We are not asking you to confess your sins and be absolved. But in fact, by acknowledging limits, your own and others, it allows you to work around them much better than by denying them. And those limits are real. Again, that's a problem to be solved just like any other, and maybe that's not honesty, but it's certainly the first step toward it.

Afterword

In 2002, I left teaching at ICAR and the field of conflict analysis and resolution. Since then, I have practiced organizational development and political consulting. As a result, I look back on the things I said in 1993 as quaint and overly optimistic. I now know, for example, that the corridor planning work that I was engaged in then didn't produce all the good things that I anticipated at the time. Many of the agreements and common visions so carefully developed are still not implemented, almost 20 years later. Some of the people and groups that slowly moved from hostility to cooperation have returned to hostility.

I sense that my own maturation has been paralleled by maturation in the field. We have learned that we sometimes have one approach, and not always the best one. We have learned that we can facilitate, mediate, design, and manage without calling ourselves facilitators, mediators, designers, or managers. We have accepted that some of the best conflict resolvers have never taken a course or read our books. We have come to more fully appreciate the role of kindness, gentleness, and generosity in public life.

Yet no matter how partisan, I find myself still looking at situations, and saying to myself, "OK, slow down, let's look for a way out of this morass." In 1993, I thought I had fallen into the strange world of conflict resolution entirely by accident. I now know that it was not an accident. My interest in public action to make lives better has led me to acquire both skills of conflict generation and conflict resolution. I now know that they are two sides of the same coin, and most of the time I need both.

Part 2
Learning and State Policy Making

Chapter 3
Dispute Resolution Meets Policy Analysis: Native Gathering Rights on Private Lands

Peter Adler

Let's say your state legislature faces a property rights conflict so contentious that community and ethnic groups, bank and real estate interests, and others are furious about the legislative proposals at hand. So you get the call from a state agency head to convene an inclusive, well-informed process to recommend to the legislature what it should really do next. You agree. But what now?

Peter Adler's story shows us one way of responding to this challenge, along with a dozen or more practical suggestions that might come in handy in a variety of contentious public policy cases. We can draw lessons here about the design and structuring of community problem-solving processes—from initially doing interviews, to identify stakeholders, to assess the problem at hand, through convening representatives of those stakeholders and managing their expectations and actual conversations, through identifying uncertainties and questions they might wish to explore, through testing their initial findings with constituencies, through framing their decisions about what to do.

Adler's story is distinctive, too, because it stands as a counterpoint to anyone thinking that facilitated or mediated multistakeholder processes have a built-in bias toward the "Build it" versus the "Don't build it" option. His account shows too how tightly interwoven are the practices of assessing a conflict early on, convening the stakeholders not just to argue with one another but to listen and learn, exploring and inventing their practical options from there, and more. We see, not least of all, Adler's way of posing questions, which makes clear he's encouraging a process in which all stakeholders can do better than they could on their own. —JF

⁓✌⁓

> I'd talked with everyone about what a process would need to look like to be safe and comfortable. What I suggested was that we not call it anything like "mediation." We do not call it anything like "facilitation"; we do not call it a "round table," which are words that I've used in many other settings. So, we called it a "study group." I said, "Let's have a study group." That became the strategy—to lower the expectations of it. . . . If I called it "mediation," it would sound like there were deals to be made, and my sense after these interviews was that we didn't want to talk about deals.

How did I come to do mediation and facilitation in planning settings? Actually, a bit like everybody else—it was a tortured trail. Originally, when I was an undergraduate, I thought I was going to be a biologist. I grew up in Chicago and was quite interested in limnology and freshwater streams and the biota of the Great Lakes and that kind of thing. But I got completely detoured into History and English and a lot of other things as an undergraduate. After graduating and spending two years in the Peace Corps in India, I came back and studied sociology.

I did my master's at the University of Missouri, and then a PhD through Antioch's "university without walls" system. Again, I focused on sociology, but I have retained a lot of interest in science and life sciences. I thought I was going to be an academic, but, candidly, by the time I finished my PhD, I thought, "I don't want to do this."

I really wanted to be more in the world of action. Although I valued the connection I had with the university, and I was able to straddle both worlds, I saw myself as a practitioner first and as a researcher second.

So, I spent a couple years working primarily on the Big Island with a rather unusual Outward Bound program that took executives' kids and people of all different walks of life through pretty rigorous wilderness expeditions. The program was a kind of leadership training. It had a lot of different facets to it. One of them was a very strong cultural component.

One of the things that I was learning from teachers and my training was Ho'oponopono, the old Hawaiian dispute resolution method. That's a conflict resolution system that has some similarities to mediation. It's grounded in the Hawaiian family system and is used in extended families to try to correct problems.

Ho'oponopono derives from two words. "Pono" means righteousness, and "Ho'o" is the verb "to make." So it's about making things right, making things righteous again that are out of balance, out of harmony. It's a process that has similarities to mediation, in that there's someone who presides over a process. They have to be a trusted person to preside over it. They're not necessarily neutral, but they do play a leadership role in taking a group through a process of restoring trust or untangling a problem. It's normally done by one of the senior family members. This person is called a "Haku," one who braids things back together again. So to make a long story short, I was taught a version of that.

After I left the Outward Bound School, I stumbled into a job as a director of one of the first community mediation centers here, the Neighborhood Justice Center on Oahu. I helped develop that for five years. I then went to work for the judiciary and the courts to help develop Alternative Dispute Resolution (ADR) programs there. Then, for almost the next nine years, I was working for the Hawaii Justice Foundation, which allowed me to do some private practice work, so it was part-time. So, I continued to do my own ADR, primarily on environmental, public policy, and organizational issues, and some business cases.

I did both mediation and facilitation. And I've worked at both ends of the spectrum—both the prevention planning end of this work as well as the untangling, breaking of impasses, end of things. I think of this as a line—from things that you do at the front end before conflicts have become intractable or highly pitched or highly escalated, to the breaking of impasses.

For example, I spent most of this morning with a group of federal and state agencies and some NGOs that are jointly designing something called the Pacific Basin Information Node. It's really a strategic planning effort in which all agencies are going to put data and analytical tools on a commonly accessible site so as to create new forms of Geographic Information Systems mapping, mechanisms for looking at species—all kinds of different issues. Here with the agencies this morning, part of my job was to lead them through to a conclusion, to a plan that resolved issues of strategy, how they're going to do it, funding, governance, staffing—the whole thing. So, that's at the planning end, a collaborative planning and preventative end, before things heat up.

At the other end of the spectrum is a case that I'm in the throes of finishing, which involves a series of interlocking lawsuits between a developer and a group of environmental advocates over water withdrawals and golf course impacts from a proposed development on the Big Island. They're in litigation. They asked me to be a mediator, and I've been working with them over a number of months. We have a settlement. Now we're just finalizing it. That's what I mean by the two ends of the conflict spectrum.

I love my work because I like participating in important dramas. I learn a lot. I like helping people get unstuck if I can possibly do that. I like people finding both intellectual and emotional solutions to things. I love problem solving. I love watching people take something that's either broken, or that has the potential to be broken, and doing something productive.

The Native Hawaiian Gathering-Rights Case

Now, this "gathering" case grew out of a Supreme Court decision that granted Native Hawaiians the right to go onto private property to exercise their customary gathering rights. "PASH" (Public Access Shoreline Hawaii) was the name of the lawsuit that the Supreme Court had heard.

So, Native Hawaiians, for example, will go into the forest and gather certain kinds of medicine and certain kinds of flowers for certain kinds of ceremonies. Or they will go take certain kinds of fish out of certain portions of a stream. These are part of the exercise of their traditional culture. These are things that they traditionally did.

The developer proposed to actually fill certain kinds of small ponds—they're sort of a brackish water pond, and in these ponds grow small shrimps that Native Hawaiians would very often harvest. The developer was basically going to develop a property there, and the Native Hawaiians said, "We'd want to be able to come to that property and gather those"—but the developer, essentially, didn't give them access.

They went to court and the case rattled around the court system for a number of years, and finally the Supreme Court said, "You have to do that. You have to give the Native Hawaiians access to exercise their customary rights. It's in the Constitution—these protections for Native Hawaiians, protection for their culture. You cannot just deny them access. Developers, you cannot just extinguish these rights that the Native Hawaiian people, in general, hold. And planners, you have to give consideration to that when you do your permit hearings and your permitting processes. You can't just say, 'We don't have to account for that.' You do have to account for that."

So, that had huge reverberations in the community. It was an important issue symbolically for Native Hawaiians—and for the business community. All of a sudden they were left in a position where they said, "We don't know how to write mortgage titles anymore. We don't know how to finance properties. Because what happens if a Native Hawaiian comes on my property, exercising those rights, and gets injured? Am I on the hook for it?"

So, if I'm a lending institution and you're a big developer, and you want financing, I may say, "I'm going to exclude some things from our financing, or I'm going to hold you liable for certain kinds of things."

This was a very volatile issue, and it also fit into the context of a resurgent Native Hawaiian culture, with Hawaiians pursuing lots of new political arrangements. For example, there's a bill pending right now in Congress to confer on Native Hawaiians some version of a sovereign state, a state within a state, such as many Native American tribes have.

In the aftermath of the Supreme Court decision, there were several bills, one of which was particularly irritating to the Native Hawaiian community, which would have required Native Hawaiians to register their rights. The Hawaiians said, "What are we going to register? You mean every time I want to go up to the forest to pick a flower or gather tea leaves to do a tradition Hula, I'm going to have to register?"

So, the legislature said, "Well, let's think about it." When they got a lot of protest, what they did was that they required the state office of planning to convene a process that would take a look at the PASH decision and how it should be implemented. The legislature had tried to remedy what they thought was a problem, and they got a lot of backlash, and then they said, "We don't quite know what to do. Let's do some kind of process."

They turned to the state planning office, and they said, "You come back to the next legislative session and tell us what to do."

I was retained by the state office of planning to help them figure out a process and help to facilitate that, potentially. What I did was spend a bit of time talking with some very smart planners at the state office, and in a series of widening conversations, I talked to different Native Hawaiians and business people. I asked, "If we were to have some intelligent conversation about this, to try to work on this issue, who should be at the table? Who could we bring to the table? What would those conversations need to look like to be comfortable for you? What are some of the specific issues?"

So, this was an analogue to conflict analysis even though we didn't do a formal written analysis. But there were a series of interviews, all of which were designed so I could come back to the office of state planning and say, "Here's a process recommendation."

Having been hired by the state office, I was received fairly well when I went around talking to people. I think there were some suspicions that the state office was part of a cabal of people trying to do bad things. But one of the things about Hawaii is that people pretty well know a lot about one another. This is a very small, intimate community. People's reputations are quite important, and people's relationships are quite important.

45

The initial exercise with the state office people was to develop a list of stakeholder voices. It wasn't so much trying to figure out every Native Hawaiian group or every business group, but to ask, "What are the critical voices that would need to be at the table if we're to try to work through this issue in a fairly disciplined way?"

Some of the ones that came up were lending companies and escrow companies and the landowners association—people who actually own large tracts of land, the developers. There were different Native Hawaiian interests. There were formal organizations of Hawaiians—for example, there's an Office of Hawaiian Affairs, which is a state agency. Then, there were a number of cultural practitioners of one sort or another, who are not necessarily organized into formal associations.

The Hula Halau teach the schools of Hula and think of themselves as "cultural practitioners." That's not a term that I particularly like, but it's their term. There are other Hawaiian groups who do other kinds of arts. There may be fishermen, for example, who have fishing groups and practice making nets and throwing nets and doing that. So, there are different cultural practice groups. A lot of this is in the context of the last 25 years of a reviving of Hawaiian culture.

The legislature had been vilified for even coming up with some of the ideas that they'd come up with. The Native Hawaiians were so pissed off. When the Senate suggested that all the Native Hawaiians in the state go register their rights, the Native Hawaiians went down to demonstrate at the Capitol and beat the drums for 48 hours down there. If you're a legislator sitting down there, listening to Hawaiian drums going—this sends a message. It sends a big message.

So the Native Hawaiians were outraged. Meanwhile, the business community was saying, "We still don't have any more certainty that will allow us to write titles, and make loans, and conduct business, and the effect of this will be that we're going to discourage any kind of people from coming to this state."

So when these people came together, I don't think they were angry personally at each other, but it was a pretty hot button issue, pretty high on everybody's agenda.

So on the basis of that first brainstormed list, I went out and started talking to people. That set the stage to come back and propose some kind of process. I'd talked with everyone about what a process would need to look like to be safe and comfortable.

"Let's Have a Study Group"

What I suggested was that we not call it anything like "mediation." We do not call it anything like "facilitation"; we do not call it a "round table," which are words that I've used in many other settings. So, we called it a "study group." I said, "Let's have a study group."

So, we had a study group, and we were to study this issue. We were to hold disciplined and rigorous discussions over a period of months, and that became the strategy—to lower the expectations of it.

If I called it "mediation," it would sound like there were deals to be made, and my sense after these interviews was that we didn't want to talk about deals. We wanted to try to think this thing through and better understand the needs, the interests, the "drivers," if you will, and the politics of this particular issue.

We assembled a group and had an initial meeting of roughly 15 people. I held most of our meetings initially at the state office of planning. They had a nice, big conference room, easily accessible to everybody.

The initial meeting is always quite important in my mind because it's all about managing expectations and tone setting, and much of what happens is chartered at that initial meeting. Basically, we did some stories. I explained to people what the purpose of this was, that we were looking for a way to think hard about PASH, its contradictions, and its implications.

We wanted to do a longer-term discussion, as opposed to doing three meetings and then wrapping it up. I was hoping that it would be rigorous but low-key, and that there would be great tolerance for people to explore the issues.

So, we had stories. I asked people to talk about their connection to the issue—personally, not so much institutionally. People took that as a chance to sort of speak at a personal level and say, "Well, the banker feels this way, but let me tell you how I feel, and I feel like as a citizen of this state—you know, this is me, personally, John Doe—this is what I think."

I was asking people to do something—that turned into, actually, a ground rule of etiquette or protocol for the whole thing—which was that all the formal hats were off. In other words, unless someone formally told us that they were at that moment representing their group, we would always assume they were speaking personally. So, that really allowed a lot of running room for conversation and immediately took a little bit of the pressure off.

That first meeting was all about trying to have some primary discussions, understand the questions, and understand the issue—to go back through this, but have people talk first at a personal level. It was a long day and a long meeting. At the end of that, we chartered a general strategy of how the group would work. The strategy that emerged, and then got perfected in later meetings, was that this study group would spend a number of meetings thinking through the issues, talking about the issues, gathering information about the issues, and trying to build some understanding, and, also—if there were recommendations to make—having a proposed set of recommendations, or at least an analysis. But that was going to be Phase One.

Phase Two would be to take these recommendations out to community meetings, to the rest of the communities that weren't in the study. Phase Two was to have the study group itself be presenters and have bankers sitting side-by-side with Native Hawaiians saying, "We've been talking about this, and here's some of what we've been talking about. Here are some provisional conclusions. Do we have it right?"

Then, in the third phase, we would return to the table to try to conclude our conversations and come back to the legislature with a report. That turned out to be the strategy.

In that initial meeting, I wouldn't say that it was charged, but I would say that everyone was suspicious, very suspicious. They didn't want to lose any ground. They're always comparing, "Can I do better privately in the political realm that I can do around the table here?"

I think the reason people hung around was because the answer was that they probably couldn't do any better politically. There was no place else to go. Then I think there were other things that developed over time. I think a respect and a fondness for each other developed over time. As in some of the best of our processes, people actually start to like each other. It's not just respecting each other, but they start to care for each other, to take care of each other in little ways.

There were some very interesting intellectual conversations. One of the things the group did was add some members. It wasn't "Peter's decision"—it was more of a rolling, aggregated decision about the group's composition. Because, as I told them in the beginning, "I don't know if I got it right. If we have people missing, let's get them in here—if there are voices missing."

One of the things that happened was that this developed into a very interesting, intellectually challenging case. These were very smart people around the table. These were professors of Hawaiian Studies. These were people from the attorney general's office. These were some of the best in the business community and some Native Hawaiians who are deeply respected as teachers.

Managing Expectations

To move this process along, I think much of what I was doing—and I think the hardest part—was managing expectations. I was trying to do a funny kind of balancing between getting people curious, committed, motivated, and enthused about actually trying to solve problems: getting people excited about accomplishing something, but on the other side, trying not to create expectations that, if we don't solve the problem, we've failed.

I think that's kind of difficult because, on the one hand, I'm trying to prod people and push people along and encourage people, but on the other hand, I'm saying, "Let's take our time. Let's just kind of work on this."

So, there's a bit of paradox and an ambiguity. I'm working with that, which I don't mind, because I think that's what much of this is.

I can't explain the moment-by-moment analysis that says, "Now's the time to push hard," "Now's the time to lie back," "Now's the time to be analytical," "Now's the time to be focused on feelings," "Now's the time to think about something conceptual," and "Now's the time to think about something practical." But there is a to-ing-and-fro-ing, a back-and-forth between these things, that takes place and that took place in this particular case.

When it's going well, I have this feeling that there's a momentum to things—that a group is interacting in a way that little windows of "ah-ha!" open for them, options start to open for them. There are clarifications; there are understandings about things. Some of their own assumptions tend to be disconfirmed, and those things sort of open possibilities.

One of the ways I've tried in practice to encourage that to happen is by preventing people from talking about solutions very fast—in other words, deferring that stuff. There are a number of different ways I do that.

For example, one of the things that I did this morning with this group was in the face of people who wanted to do a linear problem-solving process—"First we'll figure this out, then we'll figure that out..."—is to say, "No, no, no, let's do this. Let's do a pass at A, take another pass at B, let's take another pass at C, and see how these things line up with each other, and we'll loop our way along. Let's do this rather than first figuring out C, and then we'll go to D, and then we'll go to E."

So, I get people to stay patient with a bit of moving around the different elements of an issue or a problem—rather than trying to think that there's an A-to-B-to-C approach. I really try to set some expectations—I'm trying to get a group to work in that mode. I can say that it is frustrating for some people, but most people, most of the time, seem to like that.

If someone says, "Look, I don't have a lot of time here. I've got a lot of other things to do—I don't want to fart around. Let's solve the problem," I'm probably going to say, "What I'm going to ask you to do, Joe, is to be a little patient with this thing through this meeting, and at the end of the meeting, why don't you put out your solutions. But, for at least the purpose of this afternoon's meeting, if you would be patient before you go to that, I want to hear a number of things that will set the stage for everybody's best ideas."

De-Emphasize Agreements, Frame Shared Questions

Another thing that I will do is de-emphasize agreements. In other words, I really try to differentiate the front-end business of trying to achieve clarity from the more back-end business of trying to push for "agreements" or "consensus" or "resolutions." Again, this means deferring solutions for a while and saying, "The first goal is just clarification. It's understanding."

So, I might say, "Joe, Bill's been talking about similarities and differences and the overlap between the Native Hawaiian view of land and the conventional Western views of land. Do you understand that? What do you think about what he's saying? I know you want to talk about your resolution, and we'll get to it, but in the meanwhile what do you think about what Bill said?"

So, I will tell people, quite upfront, that the goal here is clarity, early on. We're not interested in agreement, yet. Maybe we'll get to that. In fact, I'm sure we'll be able to talk about those things, but this is like preventing premature negotiations, just not letting people get preoccupied with solutions too fast. So, some of this is about looping; some of this is about setting the goalpost on clarity as opposed to resolution.

Another piece that I love—that I have a big predilection about—is trying to put information on the table and getting questions framed. What I mean by that is, "What technical, scientific, economic, legal, or political information is lacking around the table? For us to talk more intelligently about this issue and be more informed, what information don't we have?" I'll ask it just like that, "What information don't we have?"

I won't ask it right away, not until we've done some things, but I will ask the group, "What is the information that is missing for us to have a reasoned conversation, or a good conversation, or a thorough conversation, or an intelligent conversation?" Inevitably, no group has all the information it thinks it needs. So, can we figure out some common pieces of information that are most crucial for us to have a second discussion? Who's going to get that, and how can we get it?

So, someone says, "Well gee, you know, we really don't have any data on how many Native Hawaiians actually go to Hula Halau. What's the registration?" Because, presumably, they're all going to go up in the forest to gather materials.

Well, I don't know if that's an important piece of information. Probably it's not—you won't find it in the resolution here. But what's interesting to me is getting people to agree on questions, questions that they think are important, and also to take the initiative to go out and bring jointly conceived information back to the table. I like doing that.

That's also part of what leads me to my interest in managing scientific information in these processes, particularly in science-intensive cases, where people are battling over models or scientific facts or theories or methods. I like working on those kinds of problems. I like trying to pour some new information on the table—if there is some new information to be brought in.

There are a number of strategies to get this working. People come and say, "Bill, you work for the attorney general's office. You would have access to some of that information we need. Would you go get that for the next meeting?"

Or they might say, "Well, nobody's got that. We need to commission a $500,000 study on this thing."

"Well," you say, "nobody's got an extra half million in their pocket, so we're probably not going to be able to get that. What can we get that's a proxy for that kind of information—not for perfect research, just for our discussion, since you say it's important." There are those kinds of things.

The Learning Curve

One of the things that happens as the conversation develops is that a group gets on a learning curve together. It's a "study group." They're asking questions, and they're trying to frame questions together, which is nice, because it means that we may get some common answers downstream. It also gets them actively engaged in the information or data gathering, if there are data to be gathered. I think it helps them circle around a problem, as a group.

Everyone comes in with their own predilections about what's the issue, what's the question, and what the answer is going to be. Everybody's got that. What I'm trying to do is defer that answer for a while and see if there are joint questions to which they can seek a joint answer, and set the stage for that over a period of time, over a period of meetings. This changes them from their original presumptions that they're walking in with and their original mindset.

My assumption is, they all come to a public issue like this with a lot of answers—but we don't know the questions all the time. It's a little bit like Jeopardy: "So, you've got your answer. What's the question that that's designed to answer?"

So the banker says, "I'm trying to figure out how to create stability in the mortgage documents that lenders give out, or in the escrow documents. I want to figure out how to clear title from land and transfer titles—and I can't do it if there are these Hawaiian rights and encumberments, and so on."

So, he comes in with his answer to that.

But if I'm a Native Hawaiian I might not even know what his question is—all I hear is his answer. And similarly all the banker's hearing is, "I want to come onto your property. I want to come onto any property any time I want."

What I'm hoping is that people will be able to understand the questions that are driving people. I'm also hoping, as they look for kinds of social or political answers to some of these problems, that they will develop some additional questions that they want to jointly answer. So, they might say, "Gee, how many properties are there that are in jeopardy?"

That's a legitimate question because it turns out there aren't that many.

It turned out that the problem was a big fear, but there wasn't a lot of evidence that was really going on. But still, that was a huge fear of the business community—that they would discourage local investment and offshore investment. But there wasn't a lot of evidence that people were being denied a chance to get their title to their properties or to transfer title, or that Native Hawaiians were being summarily excluded from coming onto land. It happened a couple of times. Was it a widespread problem? Not really.

So, you can create these very heavy-handed legislative answers to stuff like that. This is not to say that there aren't any problems—that there aren't issues to be talked about.

So, I'm saying people are walking in with their answers, but they've got a lot of different questions. Their questions are their worries and their fears and their hopes. They are worried about a lot of things that don't necessarily pan out. So in a process like this, we're trying to ask, "Can we figure out ways to meet these fears?"

In other words, if you're really afraid that Native Hawaiian culture is going to be either enhanced or reduced by what happens here—then that's another way of getting at interests and getting at some of the fundamental drivers and the general needs that underlie the specific positions that people are taking. It's sort of a back-end way of getting there.

Getting them to ask questions together is partly recognizing each other's concerns. But they also start to circle towards things that look like solutions to the problems. Part of this is so that as they start to circle towards things that look like solution to the problems, that they're doing that with a much fuller and better understanding of what's brought the other people in here.

So I can't just answer my questions. There's got to be an answer to your question—and, it's a question that we've jointly studied and jointly thought about and tried to inform with more information.

It's the difference between having a law professor come into a process like this and tell everybody the history of customary gathering rights in the mainland and how that's worked in other states—versus having a group go to that professor and say, "You know, we're studying this, and we really need to hear a little bit about how this has worked in other states."

So, I'm really interested in the group deciding what information it wants to acquire and for what purposes they think they're going to use it. So I'm facilitating a negotiation that's about what information we need and how do we learn about a problem, rather than facilitating a negotiation about a solution. In the later stages, we'll talk about solutions. We'll get at that.

Getting them to agree on the information they need is a very, very useful device, particularly when people are fighting over very different kinds of facts or they have different understandings of the situation. It's a way of jointly thinking about contentious problems rather than "you think about it, then you beat me over the head with your answers, and I'll think about it, and then I'll beat you over the head with my answers."

Our next step in this particular case was to try to pick apart some of the elements of Native Hawaiian gathering rights and to ask a series of questions about who needs to gather what, where, and when. Could we begin to paint that picture and answer the question about how Hawaiians can go about that? Because pretty soon what happened was that people were agreeing on some of the principles. People were saying, "Well, sure, Native Hawaiians should practice their culture," and, "Sure, people ought to be able to transfer title."

So, we've converted some of this stuff into a kind of "How can we?" question. If you agree with that and I agree with that, then the question is, "How do we do the best job of giving you access to your cultural practices?" If I'm the banker, "How do I make sure that I can transfer title?"

So, the problems are now joint problems. You've got to help me solve mine, and I've got to help you solve yours. Problem definitions now have some legitimacy with each other, which they didn't necessarily have when people walked in the room: "I don't give a shit what your problem is—let me tell you about my problem!"

Checking With Constituencies

In this particular PASH case, we wound up doing a fair amount of detailed work—really looking at this issue from a lot of different perspectives, coming up with some very preliminary kinds of conclusions, and taking those back out to these community meetings, which was that really volatile second phase.

We'd been studying this issue in a kind of quiet, deliberative, contemplative, informed, respectful way. All of the sudden the group is now going out to these public meetings and saying, "We've been studying this, and what do you think about it?"

The Hawaiians are rolling out, screaming and crying. Business people refused to talk about it in public because they'd just get beat up when they went to these kinds of meetings. So, from my perspective, there was this huge venting that went on.

What's that like for me when there's such venting going on? You take a lot of lumps—you get beat up a lot. I mean, there's a white guy running this process about Native Hawaiian stuff, and I hear, "Who are you?" and "How come you're doing this?"

It's hard to handle this. The public venting on issues like this is real difficult to handle because most of the people are not coming with much information—they're coming in with slogans, and they're coming poorly informed, and they're not really interested in sitting still and getting informed. It's that classic hot-button issue.

I'm always hoping that people will come away with a little bit of information. I'll do everything I can in these meetings just to simply allow everybody to talk, but also to allow people to get informed about what's going on. But I also have very low expectations of public meetings. One of my goals as a facilitator is to try to make these meetings a little better and a little bit more respectful. But in terms of either coming away with more clarity or with information or something closer to resolution, I have fairly low expectations.

A Surprising Outcome

Now let's go to the third phase. My job is the same: trying to help the study group finish its recommendations and ask, "What did we learn from those public hearings? Did we learn anything that changes our preliminary conclusions? What, if anything, that you heard would cause us to finalize our strategy in a different way or change it?"

What was so interesting was that the group hadn't fully come to its conclusions by the third phase, so the public process actually did lead to what, I think, is the actually pretty amazing outcome of this process, which was that the group went back to the legislature and said, "Do not pass any laws."

The business guys who had first gone in and said, "We want laws to regulate this," came out of this and said, "No. No, don't do that."

Everybody held hands on this and said, "If you pass a law right now, you will exacerbate the issue; we're not sure about the extent of the depth of the problem, and it's way too premature to have any kind of law on this. Their rights are so particular—the gathering customs and practices are so particular to different areas—that the conversation needs to be at a locale-specific area. You can't pass a law that 'umbrellas' over all this stuff."

The legislature listened, and they didn't pass a law. I wouldn't say that the issue has gone away because Hawaiians are still very excited about practicing their culture and acquiring land rights and water rights and all the things that they're pressing for. But, in fact, the legislature didn't pass a law on the advice of this group.

I'm saying there was a change, particularly in the business community. I think the business community now took a different view of this. There was also some continuing discussion between some of the Native Hawaiians and the business people. They formed an ongoing discussion group that went way beyond this process and didn't involve me.

Choreographing Stories

I like to think about some of this work as an addition to managing meetings and trying to strategize processes. I think of it a little bit as choreography. I'm trying to choreograph what is in the end a negotiation or a communication. I mean, an ongoing communication and negotiation process are problem-solving processes, so, I'm trying to help say, "You know what? Before we dance this way, let's dance this way. Before we move here, let's move here."

I'm trying really hard to do a little bit of stage management, but I don't mean that in a manipulative way. What I'm trying to do is not trying to micro-manage everybody's outputs. I don't really care what the outcome is. I mean, I get attached to having something, but I'm hoping, by designing something — even in the naming of a process, and by the kinds of meetings that they are, and the kind of expectations that get set in the beginning, and the kinds of exchanges that take place both emotionally and intellectually — that people will move through a process in which they are acquiring new understandings and information about each other, their views, and their positions. I'm hoping that they will be able to stay pretty tolerant for a while — as opposed to acting on their instincts, which are to do drive-by solution seeking. It's a drive-by, hit-and run: "We're all busy people. We've got to get it done. There's a big political issue. What's your solution? Ah, this is never going to work," or, "Gee, let's start hag-gling over this stuff."

So, I'm trying to figure out a pattern for this group of stakeholders, or this group of disputants, interacting with each other over a longer period of time. I guess that's what I mean by choreography. I'm trying to say, "Well, here's what I hope the tenor and impact of the first pieces of our meeting are going to be. Here's what I'm hoping is going to happen in these different stages of this process."

Part of responding to the drive-by mentality is managing the expectation of how much time we're going to be working on this. So, if people say, "I've really only got this afternoon," that calls for one kind of choreography. But it's different if we've set this up as, "This is a study group, and we're going to meet for four months and really deliberate about this."

The commitment was for people to say, "We need these voices at the table! Are you able to commit to a string of discussions over four to six months?"

If they said, "No," well, then we asked, "OK, who could represent your voice or this perspective and do that?" — because otherwise people are just going to bash on each other. They're going to beat on each other, and maybe they'll stumble into a solution.

In addition to getting them to loosen up, to slow down from the drive-by syndrome, I want them to have both a set of intellectual and emotional un-derstandings. Actually, it starts with the emotional side and then goes to the intellectual side. Because, again, that's part of having people talk about how this issue touches them personally and kind of staying patient with that.

Someone says, "You know, my family goes up into the mountains, and we gather olapa leaves for this particular Hawaiian ceremony." Or someone else says, "I'm a lawyer here, but you know what, I grew up in this community, and it pains me that Native Hawaiians hate me because I'm not Hawaiian."

Stories start where people are personally. But I don't want it to turn into personal therapeutic talk—I don't want to stay there. So, really that's a jumping-off place. I'm hoping that people will understand that this is not a just a theoretical problem—that it's a problem that touches them, touches people personally. The only way that you can get at that is by asking the question as innocently as you can and letting them talk in the way they want about how this issue comes into their life, personally.

I found you couldn't go wrong by asking that. I mean, I've asked that all the time, and I can't remember a time when somebody's run away from that, done something wrong or bad. Usually it becomes revealing of things and humanizes discussion.

Now, if we ask how do people change or what are the changes we see, I mean, I'm quite happy if people have more traction on the issue and they've talked about it in a reasonably respectful way and if they've proposed some solutions or hit a break-through moment. To me those are changes. The changes are more about political chemistry because these are public cases as opposed to private ones.

The parties sometimes develop different feelings about each other. I see that happen. That happens a lot, but that's not my primary goal. I'm much more interested in that as a vehicle for doing things than as an end goal. I'd rather do the transformative work without talking about the transformative work, if you will.

Probe, Don't Presume, or Learn Before Deciding

I've talked about the importance of people not hitting each other head-on, but somehow being able to learn from each other or about each other. Getting people to think about what other information they want is another version of that. At one level you can think of that as a distraction because my experience is that people dream up all kinds of information they want, and they don't know why they want it. So, thinking about what are the common questions and the common information they need—and actually going out and deciding what's worth actually putting some energy into—is a different piece of it.

Maybe somebody will say, "Well, we've already done all that, we already know all that."

Then we'd say, "Terrific! Could you bring that to the table next meeting so we can talk about it? You've got the answer to her question? That's fabulous: Let's get it on the table next time. Will you make a presentation? Can you do it in 20 minutes?"

So, if people will say, "Yes, it would be good to know that," I'm having people address their uncertainty together to say, "Yeah, we would all be better off if we knew this."

So, in a way, posing an uncertainty brings them together. Now, people are brought together because their common enemy is ignorance—but you've got to get them into that mode where they are willing to entertain that and where they will sit still and be patient with a discussion that asks, "What are the questions that we should be asking?" or "What is the information that we need to gather?" But if someone's sitting there saying, "Who needs all that? I've got the answer," and we're still in that mode, it's tough.

If we're still in the mode of, "I've got the answer, so we don't need to ask all those questions—we don't need to gather that information," I might talk with them privately, or I might deal with this right in the spot. I might call a break, talk privately with them, and say, "You may have an answer, but can you sell it?"

I might "talk turkey" with that person, "You think you can make it work. Do you think you've got enough horsepower in here to make it work by four o'clock today? I don't think so." I don't mind telling people that.

All in all, this case was unusual in its outcome because it's actually a case where the legislature asked a group to make a recommendation, and the group responded, "Don't do anything," and the legislature agreed and didn't.

It's interesting because one of the criticisms of mediated negotiations or "alternative dispute resolution" is that when something is proposed, it's only a question of how, not whether, to do it, and here's one where the proposal's on the table, and this group worked very hard, did some very good intellectual work as a group, and basically said, "Don't do anything right now. Don't do what your impulses are—which is to pass laws. Take another tack."

Afterword

Looking back at PASH, I am struck again by the remarkable group of people that convened to quietly, deliberately, and productively attack a complex and highly emotional set of issues centering on the conflicting needs of the Native Hawaiian and business communities. Three thoughts hit me.

First, in his fine book *The Wisdom of Crowds*, James Surowiecki argues that groups in conflict will outperform individual experts if they are well organized and have a true diversity of opinions, independence (meaning opinions are not determined apriori by those around them), decentralized and localized knowledge, and a mechanism for aggregating private judgments into collective decisions. The PASH study group had all four of these elements, created more by instinct than by rational design.

Similarly, the PASH group turned into what Warren Bennis and Patricia Biederman in *Organizing Genius* call "a great group." They argue that these kinds of collaborations are not everyday affairs. They document numerous examples in the business sector where small, nimble groups of talented people accomplished monumental things. The secret ingredients, they say, are leadership that "stewards" the process and the people, a powerful sense of mission, an articulated enemy (in this case, the legislature), and a sense of exhilaration at attacking the challenge.

Finally, when I look back at the process, which must seem idiosyncratic to some, it actually struck interesting balances between emotion and intellect, chaos and order, Newtonian and quantum analyses, and functions associated with right- and left-brain thinking. There is no purely linear pathway for challenges like this. A shaman I once spoke with told me, "Only demons walk in straight lines." PASH discussions took a circular, looping route. At the end of the day, it succeeded. I continue to be proud to have been a small part of it.

Chapter 4
From Nightmare to National Implications: Off-Highway Vehicle and Parks Regulation

Lisa Beutler

In the context of cases involving very little trust and a good deal of acrimony, Lisa Beutler's story provides powerful lessons for planners about convening stakeholders with no love lost between them. We learn about framing problems to de-escalate tensions, about harnessing anger as fuel for change, and about recognizing the accumulating costs of ongoing conflict. We see realistically how many public disputes involve messy and contentious histories—and how those histories do not need to paralyze planners' work.

Several groups of stakeholders, for example, may not think it's worth their time meeting with each other. Each one is angry about what "those other people have gone and done." They each suspect others will only act selfishly, and if getting what they wanted from the courts was possible or wasn't so expensive, they'd just "go and sue the bastards," as the expression goes. We see this all too often.

In this case, off-highway vehicle (OHV) users wanted to ride on state lands for recreational purposes; environmentalists wanted to keep the loud and smoky vehicles out of the parks—and for the better part of 20 years representatives of both sides fought each other in the press, in the courts, and in the halls of the state legislature. Efforts by a state agency to bring the parties together at last to settle all this didn't go so well: after a couple meetings with a state mediator, the parties called it quits.

Another try led to the Center for Collaborative Policy in Sacramento where Lisa Beutler had been working on environmental disputes. Lisa's story illustrates not just the deep differences dividing parties but the practical elements of problem-solving processes that she introduced to enable OHV enthusiasts and open space advocates to figure out together what to do and how to do it. Using techniques that have great promise for other cases, they created not just a strategy for regulating land uses but a standing roundtable adopted by the governor to monitor and deal with future issues. —*JF*

***

The only thing that I can work with today is the reality of today. And the reality of today is that this situation isn't working for you—period—for all of you. If there were anyone in this room that thought this situation was working for you, you wouldn't be in this room. So, your big question that you've got to pick up your mirror and ask yourself is, "Am I willing to not be in this situation anymore, and if I am willing to not be in this situation anymore, what am I willing to do about that? Am I willing to take the risk to be in a conversation?"

The original vision in this case was to convene an advisory committee of interests that wanted to oversee the management of OHVs in California. In California there is a special fund that supports off-highway use, and it funds federal and state operations. It comes down through gas tax money. There was a great deal of contention with regard to the administration of the program and how OHV use was occurring in California.

The environmentalists were very concerned because they weren't sure that the land management was being done appropriately. The OHV users were concerned because they didn't know that they were getting the level of support or the funds that were going into this. These are special, protected funds.

There is a third group, recreationists, who have an interest in access to recreation lands, and their concerns were not considered at all in planning for OHV recreation. They're fishermen, hunters, equestrians, bikers—a whole sector of recreationists—all of whom, by the way, have dramatically different interests. Then there was just your basic staff that administers programs, both federal and state. The government agencies that have been involved in this particular collaborative process are regional councils or rural counties, the State of California Department of Parks and Recreation, the U.S. Forest Service, and the BLM, but no federal EPA, because this is a program orientation rather than an environmental orientation. These are land managers. The people at the table were land managers—and, it's a very large table. There are about 55 people involved in the process.

This started in 2000—and once again this was a special program of the State of California Department of Parks and Recreation with a special funding source that was gas tax money. Part of what was interesting about this case from the very beginning was that the division deputy director had a vision that instead of the ongoing contention that had been classic and well known and well described for years and years and years, perhaps the parties could all come to the table together and begin to think in a more collaborative way—and talk about the best way to manage this program. That would be a much more preferable approach, he thought, than having the usual thing that happens—which is that land managers go do something and get yelled at by everybody.

The deputy director is an interesting guy—he came from Ducks Unlimited, and he had negotiated some agreements with the "enviros" and hunters and various land agencies to do some massive wetlands set-asides for habitat through Ducks Unlimited. So he had some experiences negotiating and also was a former legislative staffer. He came into this process really thinking that there might be some benefit to getting people in the room. His basic approach to things is more like what you would see from a legislative staffer—which is to put together strange bedfellows and build coalitions. His approach was quite political and extremely astute, and he was very experienced with such coalitions and agreements.

They had called a person who typically provides facilitations for the department of parks and recreation, and they had two meetings, at which point, according to the stakeholders—if you were to interview them—they nearly ran the first facilitator out of town on a rail.

I took a look at what the first facilitator had done. It was a disaster. So the deputy director had gotten into a conversation with one of his friends from the regional council for rural counties, and that guy had also worked as an intern with the Sacramento Water Forum. So, he said to the deputy director, "You should call this center for collaborative policy because they know how to do this stuff. But these regular facilitators—they don't know how to do this stuff."

So the guy calls in and says to the person answering the phone, "I have this case with off-highway vehicles . . . ".

At the time, I had literally just arrived—I mean moments earlier—and there was no one here that could do a case like that except me. And the reason I could do it is that I actually have an extensive background in OHVs, and I had worked for Parks and Recreation at one time, and I had been an OHV ranger. I was the first female motorcycle state park ranger in California.

So, I called them back and I said, "OK, there are a couple of things here that we need to have a conversation about. One of them is that I absolutely have knowledge about this topic, so we need to make sure that the parties would be comfortable that I am *not* biased because my role had been as a park ranger."

Inheriting History and Assessing the Conflict

Both the enviro and the user groups were willing to sign off on that. Then I said, "The second thing is that one of your staff people used to be one of my staff people," and so we had a disclosure issue there. He'd actually worked for me at one point. So, we worked through all of that stuff, and everybody signed off with all the full disclosures.

So I came in, and I did some initial evaluation of the situation, because they had already started. What happened in the first two meetings was that the previous facilitator had come into the process with a classic seven-point problem-solving model that you might see if you were to go and get a book on problem solving.

It had a complete step-down process, and so he was just going to go through the seven steps of problem solving. He just approached it like he would approach any other normal thing he might do. By the way, he's very capable—and I think this is an important piece of this story—he has been very effective in working with the organization and solving problems that had popped up all over. He was their guy—he had worked for them many times. He had helped them with many things, and he still works for them. He still comes in and helps them with little issues as they pop up—particularly workplace-related issues. So, he was using a very standard kind of approach. I looked at his material. I recognized it from textbooks that I had.

Well, here you had this really high level of contention in a room, and I had people who weren't even speaking to each other. Asking them to begin to define the problem just immediately put them into saying, "The problem is the other guy is a jerk!"

That was going nowhere very fast—plus, you've got 55 people. Plus, you've got a guy that was used to working with maybe six to 12 people. It was a complete mismatch. So, in looking at what he had done, I was saying, "You know, perhaps this was a bad match," but this wasn't a case of a person being incompetent—it was just the wrong tool.

Did they know at the beginning what they might accomplish? Oh, no, they didn't know what the agreements would be. They had no idea. They didn't even have a single topic to discuss. One of the first things I had to do was assess what could even be negotiated. I mean, I didn't even know—no one even knew what could potentially be discussed.

I think what the deputy director was really looking for was some way to get people in the room and change the quality of the dialogue—to go to a more civil dialogue. He intuited that there was room for agreements because he had experience crafting agreements—that is what this guy did for a living. So, he didn't know what it was, or where it would come from, or how it might look, but he intuited that there was definitely room for some agreements here.

So he had this intuition—but what did I do? Well, we had to undo the damage first.

Getting Going: Convening and Reframing

What we had to do there was start with a classic reframing. We sat down and we said, "We're not here to do problem-solving work. We're here because it's in everyone's interest for this program to operate at an optimum level. Can we agree in principle that the effective optimal operation of this program is in everyone's interest? We spent the first two meetings in that conversation—to reach the agreement that it was in everyone's interest to find an optimum approach to physically managing this program.

To give a little bit of background here, if you're an environmentalist, there is a philosophical perspective about OHV use—which is largely that people don't like them. I mean that's just the way it is. However, what they do know, and the environmental community would confirm, is that managed use is infinitely preferable to unmanaged use.

The environmental community in particular realizes that the potential for environmental harm with an unregulated use is far greater because you can mitigate for regulated use. So, this was an important piece of the conversation to say, "OK, we're going to stipulate that you enviros don't like off-highway vehicles—we'll stipulate to that. But that being the case, are you willing to agree that an optimum management of this program is in your interests?"

They said, "Yeah, we're willing to agree to that."

And also, "You equestrians, do you agree to that?"

"You bike people, do you agree to that?" And so on and so forth.

Everyone agreed with that. For the OHV community, they agreed that better use of their funds was an optimum state. So, everyone agreed in principle that that was the case.

From there what we did was a "mind map." We said, "If we were going to write a book about this program and what the elements of this program are, what would be the chapters of the book? What would have to be in the book—in a conversation about an optimal program?"

And we spent a meeting building this book. A mind map looks like a sunburst. In the middle you have your concepts, so it would say "optimum program," and then shooting out like a sunburst, there would need to be a chapter on funding; there would need to be a chapter on mitigation for x; there would need to be a chapter on soil; there would need to be a chapter on sound; there would need to be a chapter on . . . whatever. From that, once you have those major arms labeled, the subheadings or subchapters of those would go on accordingly.

So we drew a picture—we took a whole wall, and we drew a picture of what would need to be in the book, and then I had the group prioritize what they had energy to work on in writing the chapters of the book. So, they multivoted and picked through these.

Multivoting works like this: You take a mind map, and you take the number of arms and divide by three and you add one. Then everyone in the room is given that many dots, and they can vote where their energy is.

In a situation like this you color-code your dots so that the interest group is knowable to you—so if you're the enviros, you're one colored dot; if you're a recreationist, you've got another color. This is because one of the things that I would be looking for—if I were going to move into a conversation by caucus—is to have not just one group with an interest in talking about it, but to have a joint perspective. So I actually let them vote on where they would put the most energy, where they thought the most return would come from.

We picked out a couple of important topics. One of the topics we felt there was some room to be in conversation about, for example, was "Soils."

Mindmapping and Agenda Setting

What the mind map does is help you describe the universe: "What is the universe that I'm working with here? What is the universe of issues?" That's the broadest picture, and then from there, understanding this universe of issues, we ask, "Where is your energy? Where do you have an interest in paying attention and doing some work?"

Then people can look at it and say, "OK, it looks like all of us have an interest in taking on this particular subject."

When we had some priorities set, then I could move into a lot more classic things, like doing "issue and interests statements," figuring out what it's all about. I was dealing with a full universe—there was no topic even defined. We were just in the process of trying to begin a conversation with parties that wouldn't even speak to each other, hardly.

So the first thing was, "Can we get an optimum program?" "Yes, we can." "OK, so, if we're going to talk about this program, where would your energy be—what would we want to talk about relative to this program?"

So we came up with about five or six things that we thought might be useful to talk about. Once we had defined those things—one of them happened to be funding: about the management of the funds, where the funds went, how they were allocated—then we moved into an "education phase" where we began, based on the topics that had been identified, to learn what was involved, to learn what the parameters were.

How long did that take? Well, we did one meeting for each of the topics. In the beginning we met monthly. It was pretty intense. For example, when we got to "Sound," we called the U.S. EPA, and we had their "sound expert" come, and he spoke to the group and explained what the federal laws were.

So the mind map generated relevant issues, and the dots here and there told us one group feels really strongly about this and another group feels really strongly about that—and for some topics there were mixed colors, shared concerns.

I was looking for a space where there was energy to work collaboratively, where the colors were mixed and there were a lot of them. Where there were a lot of votes, there was a lot of energy to pay attention to this, and that it was mixed meant that it was a shared interest, and that they would be willing to make a commitment to spend some time investigating that.

The mind map did a couple of things that were very helpful with the contentiousness of the process. The energy was directed to the wall, not at each other. So, by having people focus as if we were writing a book—what would the chapters be?—it was completely value neutral. It was content based and all the attention was on the wall.

But if I had asked about their issues instead of about the book, they'd have spoken about "their beefs." When I'm writing a book on a program, one of the chapter headings is not "Joe is a jerk." But if I ask you what your issues are, one of your issues might be that Joe is a jerk. It's a way of framing the conversation to make it value neutral—it's less adversarial.

When you're asking someone, "If you're writing a book about this program, what would the chapters have to be?" and, "What would you have to talk about?," the questions are neutral in the sense that they don't suggest what's bad or good or issue-oriented. If we're going to write a book about an optimum program, that book would have to have a chapter called, "Soils," and you would have to have series of things about soils in that chapter. And one of the subheads would be "Mitigation;" another subhead would be "Erosion;" and another subhead would be "Trail Grade," and those would have to be in that book.

That's what that conversation looked like. So, it allowed me to be in a conversation—not me personally—but if I'm an X, it allows me to talk with a Y and talk about content, and to talk about the "it," the subject, not about my beef with the way it's happening. So that's why it's laid out that way.

I did this for two reasons. The first was that I needed to understand what the universe was—and I wanted to build that as a collective picture. This happens to also be very fast, because you can get a lot of information very quickly using a room full of people—and this is a very common large group technique—to have an entire room inform the process and build the picture, and I was able to do that in a day—in a couple of hours, really. And once we built that picture, we could start talking, "OK, where is there energy?"

It doesn't even matter why people have the energy because we're going to have to spend some time together. We're going to have to do this work. This wasn't like a case where you have a very specific dispute, and you're walking in the door and you're attempting to resolve that dispute. That was not my situation—I was asked to come in and work with a highly contentious group of people to build relationships, a very different kind of task.

This program had continuously, for every single administration, been a complete thorn in their side and a source of all sorts of chaos and problems, and typically it was a source of bad press—and litigation—and a million other things. The program director and the governor both had said to the deputy director, "You get this frigging under control: it's a nightmare for us." So being this person with the Ducks Unlimited background, he intuited that this was the approach.

Education

From the mind map we identified the topic areas, and then we moved into education. So, as I said, like in the case of funding, we spent an entire day where people came in, explained it, explained the funds, explained how the funds were expended, explained the whole thing. We went through each of the areas where we had identified some energy. "Grants" was another one.

So we spent a lot of time—probably the first six months—in education, going through some of the critical program areas that we'd identified as priority areas. Then we did "issue and interest statements," after we had done this education stuff. We asked people to talk about what their issues were and what their interests were in approaching any of the particular items we had laid out.

To get the issues and interests statements I gave them a set of questions to work on and asked them to finish the sentences, "Thinking about this topic area, the areas where my constituency or my caucus has deep concerns are these kinds of areas…". And, "If we think about how to make this work correctly, the way we would describe a correctly working function would be such and such…". And, "The reason I think that this will really solve the problem is…"— and that, of course, is a real interest, when they explain why they think this is the optimum solution. It's not what they actually present—it's their reasoning that provides what their interest is, because you can't get them there directly. So, you have to walk them through it.

So once they had done that, each of the caucuses shared with the others their perspective. I took away the "solution" and talked only about their reasoning—so, "This is an issue, and we explored the kinds of things that we thought would respond to that."

Why can't we get them there directly? When you ask, people typically think in terms of a proposed solution, not the underlying assumptions or premises that led them to a solution. I think that the reason for that in our society is that people are actually trained to propose only solutions. So people are always told to do the completed staff work and to come forward with a proposal, "I know the solution to this problem. This solution is X."

I think it is language and conditioning. So, you need to hit a "pause button," and you say, "OK, you've proposed a solution, but you have reasoning behind that. What are you thinking about when you propose a solution?" Because typically what people are reacting to is not one another's interests—it's their proposed solution.

Like most of my work, this is about expanding, contracting, expanding, contracting.... So, what you do is open up the range of possibilities. Then you find ways to collapse them down to single points, and you open it up again, and then you close it down again. It's like layering—so I started at the bird's eye view, the 1,000-foot level, with the map, and then I began closing down....

To see what expanding and contracting means, we can take the issue where we have an agreement because that will take it to a conclusion. So, what would make an optimum program? An optimum program, if you were going to talk about it, would mean you would have some way of addressing sound—so we would have to have a chapter about sound.

OK, so that's the opening. So then we say, "Let's learn more about sound—let's find out about that: what it means, what causes it." So the next thing was that we spent the time—we went deep into that. We had gone wide, we multivoted and got to "sound," and then we went wide again: "What do we know about sound? What can we learn about sound?"

So, we took that teeny point of agreement—to talk about sound—and then we blew it out again, and we created 27 issues associated with sound.

Responding to Actual Interests

So then I'm saying to the group, "If you were going to think about what you might do about sound, what might you do?" So, they would, perhaps, propose a solution as a caucus, and I would say, "All right, so you've proposed that solution. Why do you think that that particular solution would somehow get at what you need?"

Then what comes out of their mouth is their interest. "This solution will get at what I need because of this, and this, and this…".

OK, so now I know what those things are. And I've learned about what all the other caucuses think, too — so do we have common ground anywhere? Do we have a space where we can see that this conversation has room to continue, where we can go a little bit farther on this? What we learned is that the industry, the users, and the enviros all said, "We think we can talk about the level of sound, and we all have very different reasons for thinking we can talk about that, and very different reasons for thinking that serves our interests, but we do believe that we can talk about that."

So, for example, if I'm an OHV user, the reason that I care about sound is that whenever there are impacts from sound, the OHV fund has to purchase buffer mitigation lands. So that actually reduces my use opportunity, if I have to have larger buffers. So I have an interest in reducing the sound on a specific piece of property because if I can do that, I can increase my use to a wider area.

If I'm an enviro, I have an interest in sound because I care about birds, and I care about wildlife, and I believe there are negative impacts from sound. And also, there are health and safety issues associated with sound.

If I'm a manufacturer, I have interest in sound because I need to make sure I have a sellable product. I'm also interested in making sure there's more use, because if I have a loss of opportunity for use, eventually I'm unable to sell motorcycles — and I also need to make sure that if a standard is crafted, I can physically comply with it.

If I'm a user I have a concern that I have an old motorcycle and somehow my old motorcycle has not been accommodated. So, we went through a whole bunch of things, but they were all able to articulate what their concerns are. It helped that we had ground rules. One of our ground rules was that you're listening for understanding and that a person's truth is their truth.

When someone didn't follow these, though, we would just remind them of what the ground rules were. We had two ways in the physical process of doing this. I had them develop their perspectives by caucuses, but then I put them into mixmatched groups — again, these are all things you can do with very large groups — where they discussed their issues collectively at their tables, and then they reported them to the larger table — and one of the obligations was that the person who reports says what they've learned from the conversation, what they've learned about what so and so cares about.

One of the ground rules is that you're never under any obligation whatsoever to agree with anything that anyone says. Just because someone has a truth or a belief system, you're not being asked to subscribe to that. You're not being asked to defend your point of view; you're not being asked to do anything but listen for understanding—and be in this conversation long enough and deep enough that you can understand the perspective of the other person. That's all that was being requested.

Threats to the Process

Did it ever fall apart? Of course! I just tried to stay calm and to remind the people of what the ground rules were. At one particular point we had a situation where a person who happened to be an environmentalist, Mary, had gotten up with some very passionate sort of statement that caused everyone to get a little zipped up.

There was a particular person, John, in the group who was about 6 foot 8—and I don't know how much he weighed, but this guy was a giant. He had a habit of wearing black suits and white shirts, and he had sort of a gangster look—he's a big guy, and he would laugh if he heard these statements.

He actually enjoys projecting himself as a tough guy—that's his nature and he enjoys it. He's a lovely person, as most people like that are. So I said, "John, would you please restate for the group your understanding of what Mary just said?"

I knew he listened—he always did. So John got up and very succinctly re-stated what Mary had said.

"Oh, OK, that's what she said."

And I said, "Mary, did he accurately represent what you said?"

And she said, "Yes, that actually represents my concerns and my interests."

And so everybody just calmed down, and we just worked. I think the piece that's important is to say, "Unless we reach a point where I am specifically, com-pletely transparently, and absolutely asking you to agree or not agree, you are un-der no obligation to ever agree or not agree, unless we've reached that absolute point about process." That allows people to just listen.

Did we ever have to intervene outside the process because of things going on in between meetings? Yes, we had a couple of blow-ups, and there was a situation where one of the sectors did a hit piece on one of the other sectors during the process: they broke a big front-page story. They released a big report and made all kinds of accusations regarding other parties in the process. We had a ground rule where people were supposed to inform each other if they went to the press, but they didn't.

What happened? I met all the parties beforehand. The particular person who committed the violation basically knew he had to make an apology to the group for the violation of the ground rule—not for what he said, but for the viola-tion of the ground rule.

The particular piece that came out was an anti-OHV piece. In the past when these sorts of things happened, the other side would get all crazy, carry on, and this and that. But I'd received about 12 hours' notice before it was in the papers. I'd had a call, "This is going to be in the papers tomorrow. A reporter just called to ask us about it."

So I called a caucus, and I said, "There's going to be a story, you know — it's already been released. I want you guys to carefully think about what you're going to say." And so the OHV community said to the reporters, "We understand that this group has concerns with these issues, and we are involved in a process to be in a conversation about this, and we think there is room for people to disagree about this, and we're in a process of trying to talk about how we might move forward on this issue."

That was not only a way of keeping things on track, but this was a surprising lesson learned for them — they looked great, and the story got no legs, because in part, there's only a story if they carry on. There's no story if the parties said, "We can understand how they have concerns."

So, the story lasted one day. I had asked them to think about the value of the process — and what they learned was that this story got no legs: There's no story if there's no story. That was a great lesson learned for them. They'll never forget that. It's ironic because the person who had sent out the story had completely changed the rules of engagement we had adopted — because that was the old way of doing it, the "shot across the bow" — and so they didn't try that sort of thing again: There was no purpose to it. They still did one other hit piece since, but they had the same reaction — it didn't go anywhere. It didn't even make a ripple. The first story made the front page.

Breakthrough

Now, the place where the big breakthrough came was on sound. The EPA guy came in, talked about sound, and said, "You know, you can't do anything about the manufacturing standard."

The group was really disheartened because they wanted to move forward — they felt it was in their interest to move forward, and they didn't have any room here to move. So we just went back at it and said, "There's just got to be another way to go at this."

Because of my background, I was aware that the state could impose "point of use" standards. The state has a right, for example, to say, "You cannot use alcohol on state property."

Now, it's not illegal to have alcohol. You're not breaking the law — and if you're a certain age, there's nothing wrong with drinking. But the state has a right to impose that restriction—so somehow that came into the mix. So the next question related to that was, "Could the state impose a similar type of a standard for other uses?" That was a legal question, a question of fact. We investigated that question, and the answer came back, "Yes, you can."

OK, if you can, you've got room to move forward. So, then, what would have to be the piece of this that we could move forward on? So then we actually got talking about numbers, allowable sound levels. It was a strict, straight-up negotiation about numbers: What could we physically do?

Some people had one number, and other people had other numbers. They all had numbers—so we asked, "What is your reasoning for those numbers? What is bringing you to that conclusion about those numbers?"

At the table I had Honda, the Motorcycle Industry Council, Kawasaki—so we had experts. People came in from the California Air Resources Board, and I had the U.S. EPA. We brought in heavyweights to talk—and what we got down to was that the manufacturers eventually drew a line, "We can't go any lower than 96 decibels. We don't know that we have technology that allows the industry to go below 96."

The Motorcycle Industry Council works by 100 percent consensus, so if you have any party in the industry council that had a concern, that's a veto for them. So, that was the lowest they could go—96 decibels.

The enviros came back and said, "Fine, maybe we don't do anything. Maybe we just go after land—because if you're going to keep it at 101 decibels, we're just going to go for bigger buffers."

That's when we started talking turkey. I did a lot of shuttle diplomacy there—and the enviros wanted 94 decibels.

The shuttle diplomacy involved saying, "Ultimately, what's in your interest? Yes, you can do this, and go after land and this and that, but, ultimately, what's in your interest?"

We had a very critical person in this process. He was an essential person, a representative from The Audubon Society. He was phenomenal. For one thing, because he was from Audubon, he actually understood sound a little bit, and he felt from the standpoint of the resource that the managed use—the reduced sound—ultimately was a better solution. The way we crafted the agreement, though, was that we addressed this problem of them not believing the industry. They're saying, "We think we can go lower," and the industry is saying, "No, we can't."

So what we agreed to do, as part of the side agreement, was a series of studies, and we negotiated the criteria for the study on sound. We actually had a negotiated agreement on what would be studied—to do further studies on sound and what's possible. Those studies are actually in progress, and the stakeholders met just a month or two ago.

That first series of studies came back to the group, and it was fascinating. They actually showed where the sound emanates from a vehicle, what causes the sound…and this was the first time these particular studies had been done, and they are going to have a dramatic impact on sound because one of the things that came out was that sound is not emitting from mufflers largely. Most of it is motor noise, and so they've started wrapping where it emanates from on the bike.

There are a lot of things going on still. The current testing process, too, for sound is a drive-by at 50 yards. You can only do that in a completely enclosed space because you can't have ambient sound. You have to be able to control any ambient sound—so the federal test is a 50-yard "drive by," but the state test on a muffler is a 20-inch test from the end of the muffler—and they don't have direct correlation. They just have a marginal correlation of some sort.

Lessons

Were there lessons here? This was an emerging process, and I think you learn every day. I couldn't have predicted or anticipated where it was going to go next. I didn't know, so it was an unfolding process. It was just paying attention and staying open to what could happen. I don't know how many times it happened in the process where I thought, "Oh, man…I don't know what to do next!"

But, yes, it doesn't just unfold. If you don't have a well-defined conflict, it's critical to create some scope. I think that was important, and I used a particular tool that happened to work—the mind map happened to be a way of beginning to start that conversation. I don't know if that would apply across the board. It's a tool that I have used in other situations, and it does work, but not in every case, and I don't always use it. Where the conflict is well stated and more defined, you don't need to use this kind of a tool. There are other kinds of tools, though, that would allow you to get to the same spot. With this particular one, if you're only dealing with four or five people, it may not be the right kind of tool.

Another thing that was important was really solidly and consistently enforcing the ground rules—there had to be an absolute commitment to the ground rules and to the commitment of the group to be in the conversation, and that had to be fairly regularly affirmed for various reasons. One of the reasons I happened to know that to be particularly true is that now that we are so far in—we've been at this now for three years, going on year four, and we met only every three or four months—I'll occasionally get new people in the room, and I'll have to revisit this. I can tell the difference in the behavior when we go for long periods of time without people being in this constant commitment to doing it.

Another thing that was absolutely effective in this process was what we call "workshop work," which means that once we got particular pieces of things defined, we would ask small groups to take off and go into "workshop mode," and do real serious work on something that would then be returned to the full group for review.

We did many, many iterations of that. It allowed us to take up more than one thing at a time. That allowed us to work in parallel on a couple of issues, so in any given meeting we might be reviewing three different issues where there had been substantial work done in the interim.

These small groups have to be mixed, really, because one of our ground rules was that we wouldn't allow proposals to come forth unless there was a full consensus in the work group to bring it forward. Otherwise, it's a waste of the group's time. So after about month six or seven, we were looking at well-formed ideas—where the work had been done, where the groups had thought through it, where seven or eight people had really spent some quality time thinking about something, to form the thinking.

You might say there's a tentative testing in the small group—before it comes up higher—so it's much easier to manage the conflict in a smaller setting because you can deal with people more easily, especially when they're working together closely. But when something gets unleashed in a room of 55 people, it's very difficult to manage—it's very easy for it to go sideways.

Sometimes the small groups were facilitated, depending on the group. Where there was a strong leader, or where the issue was relatively content based, they did not need help.

The groups actually know to get help. Unless we have something where we absolutely know there's going to be contention, we usually start the groups off with a voluntary process. They all know that if they need help, they should come get me, and I have another co-facilitator who works on this project. So, they come and get me, or they come and get her. If it's less contentious, she will usually work with it. But they have a good sense of that.

Another important thing is that we absolutely do meeting minutes, and we revisit those minutes often to say, "OK, where are we at? How did we get here? Do you remember?"—because it's very easy to forget, it's very easy to slip back to whatever your original situation was.

So the minutes create some accountability, and we use them all the time to say, for example, "This is what you said about this—this is where this language came from."

But also this allows people to not ascribe motives. So if you can take a look at what the minutes were and say, "Oh, OK, this wasn't so and so trying to sneak something under the door. No, in the last meeting, we said this, and this, and this...".

And we revisit those minutes. On more than one occasion, we've gone back and needed them.

This "point of use standard" was actually created by legislation—and that reminds me, the first big agreement that we got was an agreement to continue the program; it had a sunset clause. That was the first big agreement. The sound agreement we reached came two years into the process.

The sunset clause meant that the program was to end on a mandatory basis at the end of seven years. So we got a three-year extension to the program with an understanding that the parties would stay in negotiation, and that was the first piece of legislation. When they got the legislation to continue passed, there were no votes cast against it.

You're asking if there are some lessons here—that when public disputes involve a lot of contention, still a lot of things are possible. Yes, some people will feel that when things are so contentious, and there's so much bad feeling running around, they may want to turn around and walk. I saw the contention in the room—so how did I have the sense that, "Well, yeah, they're angry, but we can get something done." Whenever there is conflict in the room, it means there's energy to work on something—conflict is always better than apathy. So, that's where I start: conflict is better than apathy. So, now, if I'm angry, I'm angry about something, and I'm angry because I don't think something is working right—and I want things to work right.

Now maybe you're angry that they're a jerk and they lied to you at the last meeting and their boss lied to your boss—all that's true, that's the Hatfields and the McCoys. I think that there was a piece of that too—but you have to differentiate between the Hatfields and the McCoys. Which is this about? Is it, "Your brother shot my brother," or is this about, "I have a fundamental public policy concern with the way that business is being conducted"? Oftentimes, both things are true because I might have started out with my fundamental disagreement, and then "I shot your brother," or "You shot mine."

So, my job then is to say, "We're going to stipulate to the fact that you shot each other. Now, we can go on all night and day about that, but that doesn't fix the fact that you are very unhappy with the way that this is working."

Taking the Risk to Be in a Conversation

I will say that very directly to them in the room. I'll say, "I'm walking into the room today and there isn't a single thing I can do about the fact that people in this room have been shot. The only thing that I can work with today is the reality of today. And the reality of today is that this situation isn't working for you—period—for all of you. If there's anyone in this room that thought this situation was working for you, you wouldn't be in this room. So—your big question, the one you've got to pick up your mirror and ask yourself, is, "Am I willing to not be in this situation anymore, and if I am willing to not be in this situation anymore, what am I willing to do about that? Am I willing to take the risk to be in a conversation?"

Will I say that very directly? I will say that to them at least 20 times. You have to say it constantly—because that's really what it's about—is it worthy of your time, to cease your suffering?

Can that get them past the Hatfields and McCoys problem? We stipulate that it's true. That means that we can say it right now—we can put it up on a flip chart— we can do whatever you need to do to say, "In the past, I've been shot," or "In the past, you've been shot." That's not a secret! So we get it out there, we recognize it... we say this is true—Absolutely! This is true, and "Do you choose to continue suffering? Do you choose to be shot at in the future? Do you choose to shoot at someone in the future? Is that your choice?"

That's a pretty bold statement, for me to look at you and say, "I choose to shoot you in the future." OK, if that's your truth, then that is your truth, but I'm not so sure that's going to help you when you want to achieve something in public policy, when your stated goal is to shoot people. If your stated goal is to achieve what you say is important to you, the philosophical reason that you walked into the room in the first place, then my expectation is that you have enough integrity to pay attention to the things that you care about—to try to do whatever it is you say you do. My expectation is that you have enough integrity to do what you care about.

But this is something you have to work on because there's some physiological element of this—people can be like salmon swimming upstream: When you move into a particular emotion, it's like the water dripping down the mountain: you go to the place you've always gone. There are actually physiological studies and psychological profiles of victims related to their natural state of behavior in certain types of stress situations. So, you have to constantly revisit it because if your habituated pattern of response to any particular area of stress is to shoot—if that's your habituated pattern—then we will constantly have to revisit that, and the only counterbalance to that is to say, "What do you really care about?" You have a choice in your behavior, even if you have a habituated response.

So my job as a mediator is to know that they may have a habituated response to attack somebody because that would be normal. That would be normal, but you can still get them out of it to solve problems collaboratively, I believe, in most cases, if people are truly in the room with integrity—and most people are. People don't get that kind of passion around bologna—they get that kind of passion around the stuff that they care about.

So, you go to that space where people care. I guess it's my faith in humanity, but people want to do the right thing. People want to live with integrity—people want to do the right thing, people care about something because it makes sense for them to, somehow, in their scheme of the world. And so, you're speaking to that piece of the person that lives in integrity, that piece of the person that wants to do the right thing in the world, and you're saying, "This is so important, and you so care about it, so can we speak to this part of your personality which can step above your habituated response to this other person? Can you do that?"

For a lot of these guys, if you really talk to the ones that care about it— off-road use is about family relationships—they go do these things with their children. It's about the only time they have a personal interaction with nature. It's about the fact that if you happen to be disabled, the only way you may ever see something is in the seat of a jeep. All of these things are true, and that's important—a lot of this stuff is in fact value-based for them. Some of them truly believe—they have various perspectives that they bring to the table—that, "It's important for people to have fun. Recreation is an important part of what's important in California."

Whatever that is, whatever that space is, they care enough about it to be mad. And if I care about something enough to be mad, then there's room to grow, and that gives me something to work with as a mediator.

Afterword

The OHV story happened in a time unlikely to be repeated, yet key lessons can be extracted. After the story originally appeared, the flamboyant leader moved on, the featured group, losing a little focus, eventually disbanded, and advocates for both sides gradually changed. One of the original advocates now serves as a governor's appointee as chairman for the commission that oversees the OHV organization and many of the others became senior leaders in their organizations. Even with these changes and under the administration of three different governors, the state's OHV soils management standard, considered a model for the nation, was adopted.

Not all was rosy. During one shift in leadership the OHV organization reverted to more traditional planning approaches that were largely unsuccessful and combined with a few other complicated issues resulted in stakeholders demanding and receiving what turned into a damning state auditor report. In response, the leadership returned to a collaborative process to craft a new strategic plan, which was widely acclaimed by the Auditor and stakeholders alike. That plan includes such bold objectives as achieving a 25 percent reduction in the carbon footprint from management of the state vehicle recreation areas by 2020.

The Division is also working closely with the industry and stakeholders to use new technology to reduce both sound and emissions. What was once the source of contention is now considered business as usual.

So what can be learned? While a great agreement is a worthy goal, even more important is what happens in the long term when people can fundamentally change the way they approach disputes. The group became skilled enough to continue without the structure of the formal collaborative. They ask questions that seek learning and identify possibility. They understand that sustainable solutions are ultimately better even if the short-term fix is more attractive. More than one has said learning these ways of approaching conflict fundamentally changed their lives. Hardball politics remain and the more extreme polarities witnessed in the recent presidential election are alive and well in this group. Yet, ultimately, the tides shift often enough, and a win-lose victory today can be reversed in the next election. For that reason, for the things that matter, or when things are horribly broken, the group seeks collaboration.

The first step in building this capacity is building relationships. An instructive cartoon shows four people on a boat. Two are on one end, frantically bailing out water from a gushing hole. The other two are watching from the opposite end of the boat, and one says to the other, "I'm sure glad that hole's on the other side of the boat!"

Job one is helping a group understand that the boat even exists. The people in the OHV story figured out that they were in the boat together. So leadership within the groups helps. It helps a lot. I am constantly looking for those in the group able to articulate why it is important to construct the future collectively. We need to move past fixing the boat to actually getting to our destination. This leadership can come from anywhere in the group and ideally is shared by the group, but it is always easier if there is executive sponsorship that is able to take this role.

Little things matter in building relationships. Breaking bread together makes a difference as does having enough informal time to talk about shared life stages. These activities exorcize the demons. For years and years the combatants in this dispute demonized one another, but that is harder to do when you learn how much you share with the person across from you. They too are dads and daughters, and they have struggles. They are not the "other."

To an observer, these things may not seem efficient and are hardly problem solving, yet they are essential.

This case also affirmed my continuing belief that our work is foremost about change. Each time we enter these disputes, or any collaborative process, we are laying the foundation for change—change from the sinking boat or change of direction. It is probably no surprise that change more often comes from pain, not vision. It is no surprise that when people are angry, they must manage this change. No one votes for a sinking boat.

During this case I used lots of process tools (mind maps, joint fact finding, etc.). What we can learn about such tools is that if they are used properly, they can be a huge help. Otherwise, though, they can actually create conflict. I would encourage readers to learn more about these tools and use them if they can be skillfully applied. Absent that, the basics work. It may take a little longer, but that is better than sending a group in a direction that you'll all have to recover from.

Taking field trips, for example, was more than just fun. In the process of learning we got on the ground and moved from the abstract to the actual. Being oriented to place created an instant common ground. We literally walked in one another's footsteps, and we could share our understandings of what we saw.

Not least of all, leadership by outside sponsors was essential. The agency (Parks) was willing to make the commitment to support the table and work with the parties. Tremendous group maintenance was needed, particularly in the beginning, to keep people at the table as we moved through the education phase of negotiations. Many, many agencies want to short cut the education phase because they just assume people have shared understandings of information, in part because the groups themselves will almost always tell you they don't need that education—they want to jump right to problem solving. But in complex cases, there are no short cuts, so the leadership commitment of sponsors can be essential.

Finally, it's hard to convey how important it is to treat each stage of work as new work. This is about group dynamics, and even though you have built group competence, you cannot make any assumptions: each and every issue is a new issue.

Part 3
Land Use and Community Planning

Chapter 5
Creativity in the Face of Urban Design Conflict

Ric Richardson

By the time the phone rang in Ric Richardson's office, he knew that the planning and urban design recommendations for improving Albuquerque's North Fourth Street Corridor were in trouble. Now it seemed that report was seriously stalled, if not dead in the water. The city's redevelopment director wanted to know if Richardson could help.

Richardson's story begins with a serious impasse and a history of local conflict, but it ends with freshly crafted proposals for North Fourth Street that the city planning commission and the city council then adopted. Getting there involved elements of process design, leadership, and negotiation that meant learning about the street and its possibilities as well as about the many players involved: local organizations of residents, commercial interests along the street, relevant city agencies, and still others. Then, of course, there were also the questions of who might speak for whom and who might agree to meet together to create workable new plans for the corridor.

Moving beyond impasse and the local conflicts that produced it took much more than scoping out representatives of the conflicting groups. It also meant figuring out who'd have a willingness to listen, to learn, and to do more, too: to be able to think outside of the box of what we did yesterday, to be able to create new solutions, financially, aesthetically, and culturally. But what kind of a participatory design would allow neighborhood residents and commercial business owners to come together to craft new urban design and community development strategies that would respond innovatively to their interests and to those of the larger city's as well?

We see no simple recipes here, but we see how a planning team might deal practically and creatively with differences to take advantage of multiple perspectives and priorities because the different parties do all care about the same place. We see that the planning process can look forward and not just back, forward and not just past each other, too, forward by exploring carefully, and at times contentiously. "What if we did this…? What if we did that…?" We see, significantly, that the planning process here helped everyone to learn—about the place they all cared about, about their stereotypes of one another and all they cared about, and not least of all about what creative steps they could actually take, legally, financially, aesthetically, and socially to do place making in a fresh, new way that worked for all concerned. Richardson's story illuminates the many forms of expertise that can come into play from the worlds of urban design and real estate, mediated negotiations and participatory processes, and economics and sociology too. —JF

They were saying, "You know, I never imagined that we would start where we did and get here"—and what "here" meant was that "we'd been able to craft a way of agreeing and a way of seeing this area, unlike we ever thought we would. It hadn't been proposed before—and it is going to be different, and it is going to take time." And others from the merchants' side added in, "But we understand how it's going to be, and it's going to fit with both existing development as well as new."

I was in my university office one afternoon, working away, and the phone rang. It was the Director of Redevelopment for the City of Albuquerque saying the city was in the process of preparing a corridor plan that was both a redevelopment plan and a sector plan, simultaneously (a sector plan in Albuquerque is the regulatory plan that establishes zoning; a redevelopment plan is a strategy and mechanism to do redevelopment). The corridor plan had grown so controversial that it had been stopped in the planning commission, which, in Albuquerque, we call the environmental planning commission. At the draft stage of the plan, there had been so much and such well-organized opposition, both led by merchants and landowners along the Fourth Street Corridor as well as by the neighbors and neighborhoods, that the commission had stopped the review process.

The area covered by the corridor plan is called the North Valley of Albuquerque, an area containing five of the oldest and some of the most well-organized neighborhoods in the city. The North Valley ranges from quite low-income households to the first set of close-in neighborhoods, to some of the oldest neighborhoods on land in agrarian areas of the city, to some of the highest income households, with very large homes and large lots, but mixed. And this area, the corridor, spans 4.5 miles, going from the northern edge of downtown Albuquerque to the city limit, and then going on into the Village of Los Ranchos, another jurisdiction.

The plan had been stopped. There had been a two-year effort on the part of the city and its consultants to plan for redeveloping the corridor. The corridor and the street had gone through many development iterations over the years—literally from the time horse-drawn carriages traveled to communities way north of Albuquerque. There was once a trolley, later automobiles. As the road became more eclectic, more trafficked, it became a major thoroughfare for residences, businesses, and then, further out, for mixed-industry and heavier commercial activities.

So Fourth Street became a major transit corridor, in search of its new life, its new incarnation, and needed to be redeveloped into—depending on who you talked to—what it should be: either the continuation of more intense commercial and redeveloped industry, or a very small-scale commercial street mixed with residential, or an even smaller-scale neighborhood-serving street and set of businesses. The street itself starts with two lanes near the northern edge of downtown, goes into one lane as it goes into downtown, and then incrementally gets more active and broader, passes under the freeway, and becomes a pretty major thoroughfare as you go further north.

Before the corridor planning effort, I had been working in that area—this is called Fourth & Montaño by the locals—together with two colleagues and a group of students. I had been asked by the neighbors at the far north end of North Fourth Street to come in and hold a set of visioning workshops.

The intersection there has a roadway that provided access over a bridge crossing the Rio Grande to the whole west mesa, and this was the newest bridge, the most recent connection, to provide access back and forth across the river, and it was a very congested place. The neighbors wanted us to do some visioning workshops so they could get organized about what to do because the city had offered them a full-fledged design charrette to solve their intersection problem and spur development. So we had been working with the neighbors there for about three or four months. This was just at the beginning of this two-year process for the Fourth Street corridor planning.

So two years before the phone call, early on, I got to know very, very well the actors and the issues at the northern end of the corridor. That early work we did resulted in the neighborhood giving the Albuquerque Planning Department and the redevelopment agency their four major goals for redevelopment and the improvement of transit. That put them in a position to guide a charrette with professionals and city staff and others, which they did. It took a while to get the funding together and other commitments from the city and others to do that.

What's interesting is that as the consultant team for the corridor plan was formed — a very respected planning firm, together with a landscape architecture firm, together with their transit and transportation consultants and market analysts — and the consultant team began their work, I naturally had an interest, but I didn't follow it closely. I had a student who was working with us in the northern part of the corridor who went to a few of the corridor planning meetings. It seemed to be a legitimate, straightforward planning process with good technical advice, and a citizen advisory committee, a 12-member advisory committee that had merchants, as well as representatives of the neighborhood organizations and advocates for transit and transportation.

So the consultant process had all of these elements, and as we completed the work at Fourth & Montaño, our smaller project disappeared from view. I mean, life went on here. The consultant project was off and running with no controversy. There was no chatter, no newspaper articles, no visible activity, pro or con.

So then, almost two years later, I get this phone call that the corridor planning project had been stalled. The consultant team had completed their work. They had prepared a draft, and that draft was the lightning bolt for extraordinary opposition — neighborhood opposition to any more planning, and opposition by the merchants to the strategy that had been laid out — to the zoning system that had been established.

A business association that was almost nonexistent up to three weeks before the plan was published had mushroomed to 50 members and had become very well organized. Their economic activities are at a scale that can get the attention of the mayor, the city council, and the planning apparatus in the city.

Early Impressions of Possibilities: Conflict Assessment

My impression — at the time of the call — about that opposition was that it was the merchants against the neighbors, and the neighbors wanted one thing and the merchants wanted another. The proposal in the plan didn't satisfy either set of their concerns.

I listened to the Director of Redevelopment as she talked for a little while, and she characterized the controversy in terms of a lot of development disputes. It's the landowning development apparatus saying, you know, "Let's keep things the way they are," if not, "invest in making them bigger and better" versus the neighborhood who doesn't want anything, who're anti-development or redevelopment.

I just knew a couple things. One was, this is a very long stretch — it's 4.5 miles long! And it goes through some very different kinds of places in terms of the neighborhoods, the people who live there, and the street and the way it functions. I also knew from the visioning workshops that even in a much smaller area, where there were four blocks, 3,000 neighbors, and a smattering of businesses, there were many different points of view from neighbors and from property owners about what ought or ought not to be done.

So when I was asked to work on this, I said, "Yes, I'm interested in working on it, but not unless you give me at least a month, maybe a month-and-a–half, to talk to people—that's the first piece of work that I want to do."

I said, "I want to begin this process—and in fact I must begin it—by interviewing, by visiting with and meeting with a variety of people up and down the corridor: merchants and residents, the corridor consultants, city staff, others that have had a relationship with this."

I packaged that as, "I want to assess the conflict. I want to do a written conflict assessment, to give you some insight; to give us some insight into what's going on—What are the issues? What's the history? What had the planning effort been like?—and to then give some kind of recommendation about how to go forward."

She pushed back for much less time.

I said, "No, it'll take longer than that. It's going to take a month, and it's going to cost X amount of money. And we won't likely get anywhere if what we do is begin right away to have public meetings and get people talking, which is good ordinarily, but if we have no sense about what kind of forum, with which people, and under what conditions—if we're shooting in the dark, if we haven't talked enough!"

What provoked me to talk this way was actually that the city has a good land-use facilitation program. They had, when the controversy first erupted, asked a couple facilitators from the region to hold some meetings to get people together and to talk. I wasn't aware of the details, but it turned out there had been two meetings, one evening-long meeting and one daylong meeting, that actually had exacerbated the conflict.

The first meeting was an open house: "Please come. Here's the proposed plan: Tell us what you think."

I think what they didn't anticipate was organized opposition—that people who were deeply concerned, people who were afraid of what was going to happen, people who wanted to be sure some things happened, all showed up and expected to be (and, were) given the chance to speak! And a well-managed shouting match went on!

During our assessment I talked to people who said, depending where you stood, it either felt like this was getting more and more intractable, that people's positions were really becoming more and more entrenched—or that you were being manipulated, under the guise of having an open meeting, since comments were taken down, but they weren't going to make a difference.

The next meeting broke things down into zoning, streetscape, and three or four other areas—and people came and independently made specific comments about those areas separately. They got a lot of good comments, but no emerging consensus, no ideas that overlapped or made way for ways to go on.

So that's a very long way of telling you, that from what she had already told me, that just having more meetings, maybe with different people, wasn't going to help—that neither she, nor certainly I, understood the people, the place, the players, and the dynamics well enough to begin to even ask them for insights into what might or might not work. So she agreed.

In retrospect, this decision was crucial in two ways. One is that, in doing this set-up work, the first step is to do a good assessment; that is, you find out who you should talk to, and then you network with that list and find out, from people you're talking to, who else you should talk to. By talking, you simply start with their perceptions of what's been going on, their relationship both to this redevelopment process and the corridor, and its life and history, their relationship with the project, the planning project. From that you ask—what did they see as issues, both things they think are good and things they think are not good.

How'd we get this information? We—I worked with my partner on the project—went in with 10 questions and a flipchart, and two sets of ears. They were structured questions, and you do an interview, and we covered the terrain but I typically didn't go, "OK, the first question is…the second question is…."

I let people talk, and I guide the conversation as we go along by focusing their attention or making sure they address issues later in the conversation, like, "Do you think it makes any sense to go forward with a process that tries to get people together and solve the problems with a consensus around what should be done?"

For example, I try to get a sense for what it is they see in the future, what they would like to see transpire. "What do you think, the controversy aside, about what the future of this place is? What kind of character should it have? What function should the roadway play?"

So I work back-and-forth with the existing situation, which is bound up in lots of feelings about who's done what, and for what reason, and who wants what, and how we're not going to let that happen. There are lots of feelings—and those feelings are really important. Feelings are extraordinarily important because the business at this end of planning is messy.

If you don't understand, if you don't, one, allow people to be themselves, and, two, if you don't understand in an interpersonal way, on a deeper level, why people feel as they do, you can know that they're angry, but until you find out why, until you find out what it is that's driving that—it could be political relationships, it could be, literally, what they'd like to see in the future, or it could be wanting to get something in place for the whole stretch of the corridor, like a better pedestrian environment—they're not going to stop until that happens. So it's about the values people have, as well as the way they perceive and value the problem differently. So that's a part of the process to get at "What are their interests? What are their values?"—and so, feelings are important.

The second thing that we did was we interviewed people both as individuals, and then, on-and-off, in many cases, with small groups, or groups of four or five, merchants who had similar businesses, or groups of four or five merchants who were in the same area, same geography, and likewise with residents. The residents were very well organized, and always have been in the North Valley, in the neighborhood associations.

This part of the work, for me, is truly enjoyable because, I think, it is an important part of planning. You know, what I bring to the interviews is a set of questions and something to write on. When I go with a small group, I'll bring a flip chart, and often, there are two of us working with the group—and, part of the art is getting people to talk to one another, and to respond to and build off of comments another person has made, and actually to get them to talk about those shared interests they've got, so people communicate in a way they haven't before.

I mean, we'd invite a small caucus or a coalition, but they have some shared characteristics, whether that's an area, or in this case, a business type, or it could be an age group, or it could be an economic group. I would ask an open-ended question at the beginning: "So tell me about how you see this dispute. Can you tell me about how you see this plan as it's emerged?"—and we'll go from there. Again, we'll go through a string of questions that builds from the history to their relationship, to what they feel are key issues.

My mind's changing over the course of all these interviews, it's changing profoundly. My mind kept going back to the very first meeting with the business association, after they'd asked for me to meet them, after the redevelopment department said, "Oh, we've got this guy who's going to work as a mediator," and I had walked into a room, packed with 40 angry people.

She had said, "He's going to work as a mediator."

Building Trust, Exploring the Willingness to Meet

So I'm walking into this meeting with 40 merchants who were skeptical at best about another person with a planning background who's been introduced this way: "OK, we know he's a mediator, but we don't have a clue what that is, and we know that everything we've seen so far is either frou-frou or is going to make matters worse. But we're willing to all get together and give it an evening!"

I walked into the meeting saying "I'm going to do the best I can, and what I want to do is to organize and run a process differently than we had before, based on first talking with you, with your leadership, and then in groups." That night, we talked enough that they said, "Alright, we're willing to go ahead."

And I said to myself, on the way home, "I don't have a clue where this is going because this is very complicated, very dynamic, with a lot of very strong personalities and a lot of influential folks."

Then I went to the neighborhoods and the association of neighborhood associations. There was a similar reaction, but they seemed inclined to be a little more willing to listen. We met down at the city planning department. They had been burned in the past, in that they felt they'd put in a lot of effort and paid attention to the corridor planning as it was going along and now it seemed nothing good was going to come of it. How was I going to make any difference?

I said I needed their help to design a process, to go forward, that would enable them—and I think I used the term with them, "I want to *assist*—to start a set of negotiations between you and the merchants. But it's got to be based on some better understanding of the neighborhoods and the areas on both sides of the corridor."

I hadn't been saying anything different to the merchants when I met with them, but the term "mediator" had come up very quickly with the merchants, and they asked—they said, "Well, so we've had facilitators, we've had planners, what's a mediator do?"

I told them that I would spend time talking to them, I would talk to them in confidence, and that based, early on, on their insights and perceptions and recommendation, we would, together, design a process to go forward, to rework the plan, if it was worthwhile. If it wasn't, then so be it.

There was a similar message to the neighborhood group that came together although they were much more willing to say, "We want this plan to work, but, at present, the way it is going, it isn't going to work. What is it that you think you can do?"

So I talked to them again about the ways in which a mediator works, both with and between people and groups, and that I would rely very much on their insights, as well as hope to get the kind of technical assistance that we would all need to design something differently.

Learning about Interests

After the first meeting with the neighborhoods, I felt a little more hopeful, although I could see after talking with them that there were fundamentally different ways of viewing what should happen to the street. The merchants were far more interested in having the continuance of free-flowing traffic as well as the addition of transit to provide better—more and better—visibility to the businesses and commercial enterprises and industrial operations. There was not much residential on the corridor, if any. There is a bit today. The neighbors, for their part, wanted a street that was more friendly. They wanted a street that they could use—that was pedestrian friendly, that was more inviting.

This is a street that opens up to three lanes in each direction with a median and a 35 mile-per-hour speed limit, which means, in an area like this, depending on the time of day, that people go 40 or even faster. So, there were big concerns about pedestrian safety, and there were big concerns about, "So when I get to the corridor, what kind of businesses are there that serve the neighborhood?"

Over time it had become a strip with a more regional-serving set of commercial and industrial businesses along with fast-food drive-ups, and, so, I felt there were pretty profound differences. In going through the interviews and caucus meetings, the more I talked to people, the more they began to suggest that, from the property owners' point of view, if you don't jerk people around with the zoning apparatus, and you allow development to occur, redevelopment, and you provide incentives for different forms of development, that might be okay. I mean, they went that far.

And from a number of the others, the neighbors, they were saying, "We've never talked about wanting to take away someone's entitlements, someone's rights." They were sophisticated, and honest in saying, "No, we don't want to jerk the merchants around."

A Promising Strategy

One afternoon, I was interviewing a guy, one of the transit advocates, and he said, "You know what, we'd live with another lane of traffic if they would accept an overlay zone, one that brings in a form-based code."

He said, "There's a new form of zoning that's based in the urbanist/new urbanist movement." The new urbanists were the creators of a zoning code that regulates the form of a building, and its relationship to the sidewalk, to the street, to the pedestrian environment, rather than its use, as traditional or Euclidian zoning would require, where you separate multifamily from family housing, and commercial from residential uses. So this is a different approach.

An overlay zone could allow more flexibility in terms of what activity could go on in the structure, its use, and the zone would regulate, quite strictly, the building's bulk and form and height and, more importantly, its relationship to the street.

So he said, "I don't want you to tell anybody I said this." He said, "We're thinking about an overlay zone that would bring in the kind of forms that we want, through the form-based code." And he said, "We'd be willing to live with some of the traffic on the street if we could get that character of the street and the pedestrian environment regulated."

It was at that moment that I began to be hopeful. It was at that moment that I said to myself and to the folks I was working with, "You know, there may be an ability to do something here—there are overlapping interests here."

So you could see an honest insight from the neighborhood's point of view into the way the merchants looked at things. With a proposal in the guise of our not saying where we got this from, there was the feeling, "We're willing to be flexible."

We finished up the interviews. We took two months and wrote an assessment of the conflict that said that the merchants and the neighborhoods involved in the conflict were willing to go ahead with the process. They felt that there was enough promise that it was worthwhile talking in some way to one another.

Convening the Parties

Halfway through the interviews, I had begun to float the idea, "What about having face-to-face negotiations—based on a set of representatives from landowners and merchants on the corridor, and based on a set of representatives from the neighborhoods?"

It was a bit startling—people liked that idea because there had been workshops, there had been meetings, there had been studies, but now we would find a place, and there would be six representatives of each, and six alternates. The alternates could serve in the place of one of the lead negotiators, but they had to be informed, so it was a good idea that alternates came to the meetings as observers.

So we proposed in the assessment that we go forward, and the process would be based on face-to-face negotiations assisted by a facilitator, a mediator.

The assessment went back first to the people we had talked to. The assessment report was for the folks that we had interviewed first, to reflect back what they had said, without attribution. One of the principles of doing a good assessment is to tell somebody, anybody that you're talking to, that, "What we talk about is confidential, and we will not attribute what you say to you. We may use ideas that you've got, we may use suggestions that you make—we want those insights, we can build on them, but none of it will be attributed to any of the parties."

We got very little feedback after we sent back the assessment. We had done well enough that people said, "Let's try to do something. Let's keep the process moving, let's do it." That assessment report went to the redevelopment department, who in turn took it to the planning commission, and the planning commission said, "Great."

We then suggested to each group, to the leadership of each group, that we would still meet with the residents' group, or the neighborhood coalition group, and they said, "Representative negotiations are good," and then we helped them brainstorm, "Representing whom? Or what?"

Each side came up with different criteria, based on the kind of voice and the kind of interest that they felt was important in this corridor area. For example, the businesses wanted to have small business, large business, auto-serving businesses, businesses from the north end to the south end of the corridor, property owners, business managers—people who worked there daily and people who had a huge financial interest, people that went to the corridor to work or who managed the McDonalds, who saw the place daily.

The neighbors also felt, and we had suggested at the outset, that they may want to represent the geography from north to south, as well as the proximity close to the corridor and a little further away from the corridor. You may want to have people that have been very long-term residents of the areas as well as people who have recently moved in, who are newer to the areas. You may want to have old-timers, and newcomers. And, on their own, they said, "We also want to have somebody who is well versed in development."

We left it to them, to the association of neighborhood associations and the merchant group, to choose their representatives: "You can carry out a process of nominating and selecting as you see fit. Give us 12 names, and a little bit of information about each person."

It turned out that during the past month we had gotten to know many of the people who turned out to be negotiators. I said earlier, there were a couple purposes in the assessment process. One purpose is to see if it is possible for a process to go forward, and now that we were at the end of it, the other purpose was for them to get to know us. We ultimately involved others, but the assessment process itself was a process of their gaining trust in our ability to help them in an honest open way as well as their gaining understanding of what we knew and didn't know, how we could listen, and how we could feed back issues. We would actively model what it was we were going to do by facilitating the small group interviews and listening and reflecting during the interviews.

It was also a process of their getting familiar with that terrain of mediating, the terrain of assisted negotiations, because there were internal negotiations, too. That's why I wanted small groups: People didn't always agree, and they work things out, and we would help. That's why we wanted six on each side—for diverse points of view, diverse sets of values, diverse interests.

So now we had 12 people. With their help, we picked a place, on the corridor, a Center for the Arts, and they had a meeting room in the back, in kind of a funky space, a very modest room. We pushed tables together and put chairs around them, and we started the process.

The first step in the process was for us to feed back, again, in an aggregate way, many of the things they had said about issues and approaches and other things at the very first meeting. So we went around the table with self-introductions, why people had felt that they wanted to be there, and then we went through the issues. At the end of that, I took a big risk and said that I felt there were three or four things that were near agreements—proposals that we should look at, that enough people had said, "Let's consider this," which I was feeding back to them from what I had heard, of course. For example, the design overlay, the respect for private property rights, and the potential to solve the traffic problem—maybe by reducing the number of traffic lanes. The idea of reducing lanes created a little wave, but I wanted to get those initial proposals on the table as soon as I could, although it felt like a big risk.

It worked fine. There was a bit of grumbling, of course, about reducing lanes and access, and some grumbling about form-based codes because people didn't understand what form-based codes were. We started the process from there.

Framing an Agenda and the Two-Track Process Design
We agreed to meet on Wednesday evenings for an education session, weekly. They wanted to move on this. They said, "We've been at it a long time, we don't want this to take forever."

So on Wednesdays we'd hold education sessions—sessions in which they would suggest—and we would help them get access to—people who knew about form-based codes, people who knew about transit options, people who knew about how the existing zoning system worked and its implications, people who knew about pedestrian environments, or different kinds of crossways, mid-block, end-block. The negotiators helped set the agenda!

"What do you want to learn, and who should we invite to talk to us? We can ask them anything we'd like…. We'll just have a two-hour meeting."

Then on Saturdays, they agreed, they would meet for three to four hours in a working session, every week. Of course, they skipped a few weeks, but they kept at it for five months. Wednesdays were designed to get together, listen, and develop a common language so we could actually talk to one another and use the same kind of terminology and understand one another when we talked about planning for the corridor.

On Saturdays we would have working sessions. We began to work out our differences about the issues, about proposals. That was a struggle. The meetings on Saturday were contentious. There were people who really didn't like others across the table, personally. It was a time to bring out how "you" (pointing to someone across the table) had fiddled with the process before or whatever.

I have three vivid memories of the Saturdays. One was coming away from all of the early Saturdays, about halfway through the process, saying to my partner, "I don't have a clue how this is going to go. I don't know—this is like riding a roller coaster. I cannot predict, with any amount of certainty, that the process that we're running is going to produce some kind of agreement, or, you know—that it's going to work."

Taking a Walk Together

The second memory was on the day that one of the lead negotiators said to the others, "Look, let's just make a decision. Can't we work on something—what about if we just set boundaries for the corridor?"

This was late in one of the Saturday meetings, and we made two agreements for beginning the next Saturday meeting. One was, "Let's all go out and walk, if we can, up and down the corridor." The second was that, I said, "I will bring someone who will help us see the corridor and the visuals to begin to set boundaries."

The negotiators came back to that next meeting, and it was astonishing. They began, for the first time, to work together. This was tangible, a visible attitude, "Let's go down the corridor and set the boundary on either side so that we settle, How far does it go into the neighborhood? How much does it affect and bound the commercial development?"

That was born out of, in part, their desire and their frustration with, "We've been talking about this, we've got principles to guide the process, we've got principles to guide our planning—let's decide something! Something that's tangible, not necessarily easy." But there was a surprising amount of consensus they discovered.

I think our contribution was that we brought a guy in with a computer and a projector. And using Google Earth, he brought up Albuquerque and then North Fourth Street and the corridor, and we flew over the corridor at about 40 feet, 50 feet, very slowly, and talked about what we saw, what was there: "Oh, that's the old Safeway."

"Yeah, I remember when it was a furniture store."

And, from one end of the corridor to the other, and then following the lead of one of the negotiators, "Well, where should we set the boundary?"

We could begin to ask that question. And they said, "Well, how about in this area, half a block, behind the commercial?"

"How about in this area—because, look, it has all those vacant lots that are leftover when that was an industrial section—we'll go two blocks now."

And so they could actually go, section by section, and it took a couple hours, but at the end of that time they had boundaries!

Later, we went from setting boundaries to looking at a cross section of the street. There was a lot of contention about the number of lanes, the width of the lanes, access for bicyclists, the width of the sidewalk, of course, street trees, relocating utilities, making a better environment for pedestrians, and then allowing access for buses. And a big issue was, "Where should crossings be?" —because that can wreak havoc with both continued access, but also truck access because, it turns out, large trucks turning left can't cope with street crossings.

So, each of the sides built different cross sections. We had had a negotiation session in which it was clear that with facilitating, each of the sides had different ways of looking at the cross section—the cross section of the street, how wide it was, the lanes, and so on.

The strategy I took was to say, "Let's have each of the sides develop a set of proposals and talk to the other group. Rather than go line-by-line, together, through an agreement, what we would do is have a package—one each from the neighbors and the merchants telling us this is what we want out of the street and the sidewalk, and this is what we want out the street and the sidewalk."

Having that package, a whole concept, we could ask questions about what problems each was solving, and discuss that then. The packages were then combinations of lane width, sidewalk width, and building setbacks, and that kind of thing.

That, ingenious as it was, in the end, created another wave of frustration because it was clear they were sophisticated enough, informed enough, and entrenched enough that it was difficult—they got close, but they never were going to agree on an absolute package. So we were stuck. We would need to send in two cross sections, and the negotiators would let the city decide.

Taking Advantage of Differing Priorities

About this time, I got a phone call on a weekend, and this is the third vivid memory. One of the leaders said to me, "Listening to all of this that we've gone through and what's actually gonna be there, I was sitting here this afternoon," he said, "and it occurred to me that the neighbors really care about what the development looks like, what it's going to be like when it happens."

He said, "Look, I'm not very big on form-based codes." It's a guy, who'd worked with developers, and he had a long history with the city redevelopment Agency as well as a representative of the neighborhood negotiating team and a good guy. He said, "But in this case, that is what's at stake. That's what the neighbors really need, what they're really interested in—when the development happens, what's it going to"—and he used the words, "look like."

He said, "But when I think about the merchants, what the merchants care about is when the redevelopment is going to happen, and what are the conditions under which they're going to be required to do something?"

He said, "Do you suppose that we could find a way for the neighbors to begin to design this way of zoning, a form-based code, and set that in motion, and ask the merchants to design the mechanisms that will trigger use of the form-based code—instead of the existing zoning?" Ultimately the merchants came up with five trigger mechanisms, but, to illustrate, if you, for example, renovate more than 25 percent of the square feet of your building, you're going to have to renovate that in a way that conforms with the form-based code. If you build toward the street, you have to put the parking in the back and have the sidewalk pedestrian. Or if you build from scratch, and there was enough vacant land, you need to build under the new code. If you're going to adapt, to do adaptive reuse, if you're going to take an older building that you own, adapt that to a new use, and rehabilitate it—no code, no form-based code, because we want to encourage the new use of the older infrastructure. So, those are what they called the "trigger mechanisms."

We had just come off, actually, trying to do the cross sections, so that was pretty contentious. There were some real frustrations. Actually a couple of the participants took me aside one evening and said, "What are we going to do next?" And I said, "You know, I'm not sure."

I was feeling stuck when I got this phone call, so it struck me that this could be a major breakthrough. I said immediately to the guy, "This is important. Let's figure out a way to begin to suggest that there's a way to go forward. Let's shift the agenda. Let's talk about these other really important pieces."

So what we did was that we got the two groups together, proposed the idea, and they said, "Oh, that's great." They decided before anything was drafted that each side should identify "sore spots" that would be deal breakers in the part of the plan that the other side was drafting.

And for the rest of the night, for an hour-and-a-half, the neighbors had the floor, first, and they could say on the trigger mechanisms, "Look, be careful of X, Y, and Z. I'm really going to be concerned if you come back with A, B, and C."

We said, "Just talk about the tight spots—places where you're going to cringe."

Then it was the merchants' turn, and they got the floor to say, "Well, when you're designing the form-based code, you know, this idea of glass on 70 percent of the frontage of the building is a problem—remember where we are in this city. I'm going to cringe because I know this is a high-crime area, at least today, and windows are expensive to replace," and the form-based code can be very rigid in terms of entrances, glass, windows, facades—articulating how much the building comes in and goes back from the sidewalk, and other design elements.

So they went away, and I think we took some extra time, and each side came back with a proposal: What are the set of triggers and why, and how would the form-based codes work? What are the elements of that, both the design and the regulatory elements?

That watershed occurred probably three months into the five-month process, and they actually set the way it was going to be regulated, and how, who would be required to do what. That gave the group a huge breakthrough, a huge amount of momentum. They had resolved major aspects of the dispute. They were saying, "This makes sense."

They were eager to go forward, they were eager to figure out what to do next. We set the agenda to return to the cross section, and let's think about a dimension of adding some of the design elements to crossings, and sets of incentives. We've got a set of triggers and regulations. Are there a complementary set of incentives that we could encourage people to use? For example, if you come in with a proposal that is compliant with the new code, you go straight to a building permit. After you review it with the planning director, there's no internal departmental review, no sets of public hearings. If you comply, you go to building permit. This was a major move!

But at that point, the neighbors said, "This makes so much sense—because we know what we're going to get: We can see exactly what that's going to be."

The developers said, "There's the time cost of money. This is a very big incentive to me. I probably knocked six months to a year off my development process."

I had personally not appreciated enough how much accelerating the review process matters—and it does. It matters a lot.

The other piece of the puzzle was that they came back and reconsidered the cross sections. They agreed—let's say 80 percent agreement—that they couldn't agree to the remaining 20 percent because of stuff they just didn't know, like, "Well, how wide is the corridor once it gets to this spot?"

The corridor width matters because of the street right-of-way. That matters because if you're going to make it a little wider, or if you're going to make the sidewalk wider, whose hide does that come out of? Is it a property dedication? Or is that in the public right-of-way? And the existing right-of-way varies a lot along the street, making things even more complicated.

Once again, one of the other participants said, "You know, when they did this redevelopment over here in Nob Hill, in another part of the city, before they finished agreeing on the design of the cross section of the street, they hired an engineering firm to do a 30 percent design study. So then we suggested, "Why don't you talk with the city?"

Bringing In and Guiding Additional Expertise

We suggested that when it came time, hiring an engineer was a good idea. Everybody said, "Oh boy, that makes sense. We could actually see where things are, what's going to happen, and who's going to pay, potentially."

We said, "Let's have that process guided by participants from this process—a cross section of this group." So they all chimed in—selecting the engineer, good engineers and not-as-good engineers in transit and traffic, designing the RFP, the scope of work, and then guiding the process. So a subcommittee of the representatives did that, and that helped with that last contentious piece of the puzzle. They met—this was now in the last part of the negotiations, months after the assessment reports. You know, this was an intense schedule, a weekly schedule.

My partner and I said, "We have pieces of stuff here that we've all agreed to. There's a map here, the boundaries, there's the basics of this and that and the form-based code and the triggers. How about if we draft a white paper for the negotiated agreement? We'll write the first draft of a white paper from the committee to the city."

They said, "Oh, that's a great idea!"

And after they had reviewed and edited—after we spent the next meeting carefully going over the white paper and this set of agreements they'd made, they forwarded that. They approved it, signed it, and forwarded that to the planning commission, via the redevelopment department. They asked that the old draft plan be rewritten based on the white paper's recommendations.

The engineering report had been a recommendation, not yet funded and not yet carried out. It was a proposal in the white paper, about which the city had said, "We'll provide the funding."

There actually wasn't major tweaking of the white paper. Other disagreements didn't surface because we had been pretty careful along the way to reflect what it was they were saying, and they had made good agreements. It was a test, though—to see it as a full 10 pages. That white paper set the stage. The planning commission said, "Wonderful—rewrite the plan."

So they bounced it back to us. The planning commission said, "The white paper's good. We agree with what it set out—the ideas seem good. Go ahead and rewrite the plan"—the one the consultant had done before, the one that had stopped the whole thing. "Go ahead and redo it."

But who was going to redo it? We proposed that we work with a technical consultant who knows about writing form-based codes, that we have access to transportation information, and that we would take the leader of the business-merchants associations and the person who had emerged as the leader of the neighborhood organizations to sit down, together, with the consulting team and a mediator.

And again, this team met weekly throughout the summer. We continued as the mediators, I continued. That became an extraordinary process, and it was line by line through regulatory code, being very careful of what was going where.

My concern, and what I kept encouraging and urging these two representatives to do, was to stay in contact with their various colleagues and the groups they were representing. Because, you know, as Louis Kahn said, "God is in the details," or the devil is in the details—and surely there were some very, not heated discussions, but thorough discussions about what went into that, because we were designing a regulatory plan. By the time the rewriting process was over, they were able to sell it to their own constituencies.

Public Review

They had sufficiently stayed in touch. I got a few calls about being a little closer in touch, but nothing upended the process. Then the plan went out for public review. Another draft!

The city posted it on its website, and they had a couple of open-house meetings all along the corridor, and they invited everybody to invite anybody else who was interested to come.

The first open-house meeting was astonishing. Very few people came. But as the evening wore on, we had an open house, with display boards, and people by boards showing different parts of the corridor and different pieces of the land-use regulation and the urban design that was going to happen. We had a timeline of events, and what happened was that the negotiators themselves, who all showed up, began to talk in a reflective way about what they had done, back and forth across the room.

They were saying, "You know, I never imagined that we would start where we did and get here"—and what "here" meant was that, "we'd been able to craft a way of agreeing and a way of seeing this area, unlike we ever thought we would. It hadn't been proposed before—and it is going to be different, and it is going to take time," and others from the merchants' side added in, "But we understand how it's going to be, and it's going to fit with both existing development as well as new."

They talked about the fears they had at the beginning, but now they could joke, "Oh, what you want is four-and-a-half miles of coffee shops and bookstores, and it ain't going to work!" The neighbors said, "Ah, no, we don't want Snob Hill down here—two-and-a-half miles of coffee shops. No! We want things like a grocery store."

When I heard that comment, "I never imagined we'd go from where we started to here," I took it as a huge compliment to the process that had been carried out. It was a way of saying, we all have gotten a lot out of this. We all have benefitted, and we were able to solve problems that we thought were insurmountable—and they were, at the time.

How'd that happen? I think that first they developed a way of talking with one another that they didn't have before. I mean this idea of a common language was important in that.

Then they used that in a way that allowed them to see things and to create things that they didn't know before. For example, they created a place, a redevelopment strategy, and the regulations to make it happen that they had both imagined in much stricter, much more polarizing ways. Together they created something that served the interests of property rights and commercial activities, and would make a more habitable, friendly street.

Beyond the Fixed Pie: Creating Value or Joint Gains

They didn't imagine that earlier—they imagined that in an old, conventional wisdom way of viewing the world, as they came into the process imagining, "This is four-and-a-half miles of property that's owned—it's a fixed pie. The only way I'm going to get what I want is through what you give up—your boneheaded way of looking at the world. As a merchant, the only way that I'll get what I need is for you to get off your high horse about making this into a boutique area."

They were then able to say, not only is there a way for the elements of those things to happen but also that adaptive reuse was a pleasant surprise along the way. Not all of those old buildings are up at the edge of the street. Not all of them conform to the form-based idea, but the neighbors said, "No, no, no! We don't want to tear down old buildings! Wait a minute. In fact, let's get the city to do a thorough inventory and find out what really is there that we ought to be conserving and building on."

Well, that was not on the table. So I think that's what they were saying. They invented a plan that met their needs and pushed beyond the boundaries of this "fixed pie"—that not only says, "I only get something when you give up something," but says that if I want something, if I want X, if I want three lanes and I know that's the minimum to serve my business, that I have to insist on four lanes because I know that you're coming from the neighborhood, and you're not going to give up until you see two lanes!" So, you know, then you go tit-for-tat and design something in the middle—but that strategy makes no sense. So this process provided an alternative to that kind of bargaining strategy.

Would I do it this way again, using the Wednesdays and Saturdays as we did? I would. Having access to technical expertise, access to those outside of ourselves, who know stuff, who can come in and talk to that—while we're not going to negotiate with them, we're going to listen, and we're going to ask questions, and we're going to be able to try to understand things— that was really key. Because it gave people—who a) didn't like one another, and b) were tired of fighting with one another, and c) had huge things at stake—it gave them time to sit in the same space, sit in the same room and listen to somebody else. And they alternately got to pick the topic and the research. Sometimes the topic, zoning, would have two or three different resources: "Here's this form-based way, here's the conventional way, here's performance zoning"—here are different ways to think about that. It gave them time to learn about things and to mutually question another expert who, they agreed, was a good resource.

So they didn't have to do that on the Wednesday evening sessions. They weren't negotiating—they were learning, mostly, and sometimes they both had problems with ideas that were on the table. There are so many things in this project that I had not done before. But there were a couple personalities on each side that were great. And this is true in many disputes, and it was true on a level here that I hadn't seen before.

There were also a couple people who really had a lot of history, who really did not like one another, personally, or their approach or their ideas or what have you.

There were at least two events, two meetings, in which one of the participants just blew—he just blew and started waving his arms and shouting at another person who just looked at him stone faced and then got up and blew right back! I let them go for a minute, as long as was appropriate, and then I made some kind of comment like, "Whoa! That was extraordinary; can we return to the subject? Can we try to keep from going down the road of repeating those comments?" I acknowledged whatever the problem was and asked if we could keep talking.

And then after a couple of incidents, I began to talk to both individuals, but particularly with one participant who had a real tough time dealing with his temper, and a real tough time dealing with the other person. I would have coffee with him, and ask him what was going on and why was he so aggravated? What was the explosion about? And I'd just listen to him. I'd get a torrent of stuff.

Over time, I suggested that he switch with one of the alternates and try the role of leading from the side. This was a very knowledgeable person, a very worthwhile resource, but not a very good negotiator, and he was really getting in the way of himself. The group had begun, in fact, to isolate his obstructions, isolate his temper.

I would say to him, "You know, when you allow this other person to drive you nuts, and then you explode, they are not going to listen to you! They're not hearing what you're saying about how the problem should be solved! They're not hearing the good ideas you've got, or any ideas you've got!"

He could hear that, a little bit. It took a number of times of sitting down and having coffee before he actually pulled back from the negotiations and took the role of an advisor to his team, an effective alternate. And he actually was happier. And later he said, "This is a whole lot easier on my blood pressure. This is a whole lot easier on me—these meetings were just taking time from the family, my work, and this is better."

So I said, "And I think you're getting your ideas in."

Managing the Drift

What also helped me work in the face the contentiousness over time? I was getting used to an extraordinarily high level of uncertainty. Part of the terrain of mediation, part of the terrain of being a good mediator-facilitator, is not only being able to sense and to guide the group and to accomplish the group's will—but to help the group make good choices, good decisions, informed decisions. I came away from many, many meetings saying, "I don't know! I don't know, precisely, what to do next," and I expected myself to provide that leadership. Process advice! That's part of the terrain of our skills, our profession. I guess I relied on my ability to listen and to ask for others' suggestions, and to listen again to what they were saying as the pieces of the process unfolded, as the pieces of the puzzle become apparent.

Part of my being driven, you know, is to say, when I start here, at the beginning, I need to lay out a process that goes there, and here are the steps in between—but to actually create those steps along the way is a very different animal. I was having an internal conversation—part of me thought I should know the steps, but in fact, it was unfolding in an evolutionary way, step-by-step, and I was getting more comfortable with that uncertainty.

What this reinforced, and what I know, is the importance of that pre-process step, the importance of the pre-process conversations, the assessment: The importance of doing a situation assessment, a conflict assessment, listening well and using that as the basis for design. Also I was, maybe, becoming more comfortable with uncertainty, the kind of uncertainty in designing the process that we were talking about—not being quite so compulsive. A colleague of mine, Carl Moore, will say, "There's two things that are important in processes like this. One is to start, and the other is to manage the drift."

This experience taught me that and hammered it home—that "process" by another name, or "managing the drift," is creating or co-creating the process that you put forward, co-creating what to do next with the participants. Actually, it's not so much what I'm saying, but about listening to the participants. There were some powerful suggestions made along the way, and one of my roles was to recognize the ideas that can help narrow the differences—and respecting that and using that artfully, the suggestions, as a way to proceed. Giving credit where credit's due, protecting ideas where ideas need to be protected, and taking responsibility for what I do. So, it's a creative process!

Afterword

The North Fourth St. Corridor Plan's mediated negotiations challenge the conventional wisdom in which planners and designers assess existing conditions, seek citizen participation, propose options, and select the most promising regulatory approach. In the North Fourth St. case, this approach had resulted in a seemingly intractable conflict.

The city redevelopment department was the driving force behind preparing the North Fourth St. Corridor Plan. The corridor was not entrenched in economic or class conflict, nor was it a blighted, neglected part of the city suffering from environmental and economic injustices. Although area residents and their city councilor had expressed concern about shabby strip development along the corridor, there were no large development or redevelopment proposals that sparked concern, nor were landowner or business interests asking the city to make significant investments in the area. The neighborhood coalition and the district's city councilor wanted the corridor to function better. The city's municipal development department had programmed investments along North Fourth St. and supported the idea of preparing a corridor plan to guide capital improvements.

While the outside consultant's original draft of the corridor plan contained a history of development of the corridor from the turn of the century to the present, the mediators focused on understanding the concerns of the parties and their historic relationships to the corridor dispute. During the assessment involving 50 or so groups and individuals associated with the corridor, the participants focused on the current dispute, not who had done what, when. The mediators took what they learned in the assessment at face value initially—without trying to reconstruct the corridor's history.

After assessing the conflict, the mediators proposed a process of learning about alternative zoning and urban design approaches, and in the informal educational sessions that followed, the negotiating parties were advised by legal and regulatory experts, consulted with urban design and development practitioners, and investigated transit and transportation options. The negotiating parties were responsible for identifying what they wanted to learn, and the mediators then helped to recruit experts with differing points of view on regulatory or design approaches. In land-use and urban design conflicts like The North Fourth St. case, mediators of such land-use and urban design conflicts should consider using joint-learning and fact-finding processes to help participants learn about options and explore solutions that fit the social, economic, and physical contexts at hand.

Regulatory flexibility can be key in resolving land-use and urban design negotiations. Encouraging flexibility works especially well when there are clear regulatory requirements that can be complemented with incentives to adopt them. The centerpiece of the North Fourth St. Corridor Plan was a form-based code that is optional except under certain circumstances. Without debating endlessly the strengths and weakness of New Urbanism or the wisdom of landscape urbanism, the negotiators met their principle to respect existing entitlements and property rights by proposing a set of simple "triggers" that would enact the new code. It would not be implemented on a wholesale basis.

The negotiators created incentives to use the form-based code by offering higher densities, mixed land uses, and an accelerated development approval. At the same time, the existing zoning could be used unless the property owner wanted to develop vacant land or redevelop his or her property. The landowners were also required to use the form-based code if they proposed a use not in conformance with the existing zoning.

To avoid disputes after agreements have been made in principle, mediators should help negotiators propose how they can actually meet newly implemented regulations. In North Fourth Street, the lead negotiators from the merchants and the lead negotiator from the neighborhood coalition, together with the mediator and representatives of the city, worked with a consultant to craft form-based zones that would be responsive to conditions along the corridor. They created appropriate zones of intensity and transition to fit with development opportunities and proximity to residential development.

The revised draft corridor plan was posted on the city website, and two open houses were held to review the plan. After the plan went to the Albuquerque Environmental Planning Commission, where participants and the public testified in support of the plan, it passed 8 to1 and was then forwarded to the city council.

The Albuquerque City Council Land Use Planning and Zoning Committee held two hearings and recommended the plan be reviewed and approved by the full council. The council held two additional hearings and then unanimously approved the North Fourth Street Corridor Plan. Subsequent to approval of the plan, a single property owner who did not like the uses permitted on his property filed suit in protest. His suit requested that the complaint be mediated in an attempt to avoid trying the case in court.

Chapter 6
From Environmental to Urban to Intermunicipal Disputes

Bill Diepeveen

Bill Diepeveen's story traces the evolution of his professional practice from what we might call "pre-participatory days" though instructive examples of mediating complex multiparty land-use and transportation cases to his work of pioneering provincial or regional institutions that enabled innovative intermunicipal mediation and dispute resolution. Along the way, we see the risks of giving up mediated solutions and going to court instead. We see the dangers of reducing conflicts or disputes to arguments that others should decide, in contrast to the opportunities of enabling the parties intimately involved in a case—hospital officials and neighbors and transportation staff, for example—to diagnose problems and to craft workable solutions together.

In a striking light rail dispute, Diepeveen shows us the dangers of the wars of "My expert versus yours!" We see instead a viable alternative, joint fact finding, that can at times not only move us beyond adversary science but also combine excellent, trusted scientific advice with wholly new senses of problem reframing. In joint fact-finding processes that are well done, we see we have not only excellent expertise brought to bear, but also we have members of the public then solving the right problems as well. Joint fact finding might help us avoid ever having to say, "The operation was a success, but the patient died!"

Not least of all, Diepeveen makes a strong and compelling case against this editor's early work that found that city planners might well play "shuttle diplomacy roles" between contentious local parties (Forester 1987, 1989). He argues persuasively that shuttle diplomacy can sometimes do more harm than good when it preempts the face-to-face work of perspective taking, gaining understanding, developing mutual respect, and building lasting relationships among contentious parties.

Diepeveen helps us to think strategically and practically about ways to convene disputing parties safely early on, so that their initial conversations can lead to wider and more problem-focused conversations later on. Building working relationships between parties step by step, coffee by coffee, or one meeting at a time, he argues, can take advantage not of the planners' distance and filtering of ideas but of all stakeholders' knowledge, familiarity, authority, creativity, and ownership. Here's a planning role bringing expertise to bear, perhaps on tap more than on top, where planners act practically as facilitative leaders rather than as solo technicians prescribing solutions. —JF

One administrator involved in a mediation all of a sudden said to me, "Until I realized that I could divorce my wife easier than I could divorce my municipal neighbor, things weren't going that well. But when I realized that I had to have an ongoing relationship, all of a sudden the incentive to negotiate with the other side was there.

The program that I manage in Alberta is called the Municipal Dispute Resolution Initiative. It's tied into the Alberta Municipal Affairs Department, which oversees municipal governance in the Province of Alberta. The program was designed specifically to give municipalities the mediation support to resolve disputes between themselves.

Those disputes can range from issues such as land use, where one municipality approves a land use on its border that could affect the neighboring municipality, or annexation, where one municipality wants to annex land from another municipality. Both of those are disputes where municipalities can also appeal to an administrative tribunal, but mediation is seen as something beforehand.

Other intermunicipal issues, however, do not have the administrative tribunal route available to them. For instance, issues like cost sharing, where residents of one municipality use recreation facilities in another municipality, or road realignments, where one municipality is involved in a situation where the only way to access a school in their municipality was to use the road in the adjacent municipality.

I was brought in to set up the program in late 1998. The funding comes from the provincial government, which in the U.S. is equivalent to state government. I have a total budget of $500,000 (Canadian), excluding the salaries of myself and one other worker.

Entry to the Field: A First Nations Environmental and Economic Development Case

How did I get into the field? I got a Masters of Social Work degree in community organization and development from Wilfred Laurier University in Waterloo, Ontario. Actually I was working as a probation officer and then got my community organizing degree. After getting my MSW, I went back and worked as a probation officer for a couple more years, and then I went to the Environment Department of the Province of Alberta. There I was organizing community groups, getting involved with community groups that were being subject to environmental impacts.

I'll tell you this story because it relates to how I got into conflict-resolution. I was doing a fair bit of work up north in the northern part of the province with the Fort McKay First Nations Band. They are on the cusp, the edge, of where all the heavy oil-sands developments are.

And they had a lot of concerns about the impact of the tar-sands development, the oil-sands development, on their community, both in terms of environmental concerns and social concerns.

On this particular occasion, one of the companies, Syncrude Canada, had made an approach to the regulators for "de-bottlenecking." They said, "We want to streamline our process and increase our capacity to process the oil sands into heavy oil."

So they put an application forward. The tribunal that reviewed the application, the energy resources conservation board, had a hearing, and one of the first persons that came up to address the hearing was Chief Dorothy McDonald, who was chief of the Fort McKay First Nations Band. Dorothy McDonald began by saying, "Mr. Chairman, I would like to begin by talking to you about the health impacts of this particular facility on my community."

The chairman of the hearing said, "I'm sorry, Chief MacDonald, but health is beyond the purview of our board." Now that was fully understandable because administrative tribunals are set in legislation and have specific terms of reference. If they go beyond that, they're subject to legal challenges.

But I heard from her a plea saying, "Our health is important to us, really important to us. It is critical that we address it."

But the chairman was saying, "I'm sorry, this is not the forum for it."

So she walked out of the hearing—very upset, of course. This was a critical issue that was very, very important to her community.

At that point I realized there was something amiss with the system. If, as a regulatory system, we cannot deal with the issues of prime importance to the people who are going to be impacted, then something is wrong. My response was, "There has got to be some way to resolve this, I'm going to check this out," and as a result, I began to take mediation courses.

This was 1985. I took the mediation courses while I was working for the environment department.

What was really fascinating was how the chairman of the tribunal responded—because about a year later, Syncrude approached the Board with the request, "We want to expand our facility."

The chairman's response was, "You know what? We need to find a way to deal with the broader issues here."

And he used his office and his status as chairman to set up a collaborative process that was facilitated by an independent facilitator. It was a quasi-mediated kind of thing that brought not only the Fort McKay First Nations into it, but also the urban white community in the adjacent city, Fort MacMurray, as well as representatives from the federal government, and the provincial government, and, of course, the company, Syncrude.

He brought them in and said, "I want you to deal with the broader issues— all the issues that are associated with this particular application. It doesn't matter if they fall into federal, provincial, municipal jurisdictions. I want you to deal with all of it."

He recognized that Fort McKay, as a community, needed a venue to look at the broader issues, the whole project, and its impacts, and that the existing regulatory process didn't allow for that. So he was saying, "We've got to find a way of doing this."

He did that by bringing these agencies together in this informal collaborative exercise. A year later, the board convened a hearing on the matter, and the agencies and municipalities that were part of the collaborative exercise came together and actually made a joint submission to the board. The important thing to note here is that the joint submission addressed only areas that were within the board's purview. They were very careful not to introduce information or topics that were outside of the board's jurisdiction. However, in their year of work, they had addressed a myriad of other issues, but those issues were not presented to the board because, had they been presented to the board, they would have compromised the board.

They had talked about health, employment issues, and a variety of things beyond the scope of the board but very relevant to the community, and they were able to come up with a plan to address all those issues. Because they had a plan to address those issues, they were then able to address the technical issues of application in front of the Board. By addressing those broader issues in a side forum, they were then able to come to the board with a unified voice and say, "In regards to the matters that can be legally brought in front of you, this is what we found." I was part of some of the side discussions.

The area that I was particularly dealing with was environmental education. The neat thing was that while the company saw it as an opportunity to educate the native community in terms of what they were doing, the native community said, "You know, it is important for us to educate you as to how we see the environment."

It was really a fascinating exchange between two communities. I was representing the provincial environment department as a community worker. My job was to do what I could do to ensure that the dialogue process continued.

And one of the things we did was develop an environmental education package for all of Northern Alberta—an environmental package that recognized aboriginal culture. I also worked with the community to obtain financial grants to do environmental things important to the community. This whole experience—from the first hearing to the end of the second—was a trigger for me to say, "There is a better way."

It led me to begin to look at more active mediation in environmental issues. Some time later, a situation occurred where I was working with a community being faced with a sour-gas facility. Sour-gas is natural gas that comes out of the ground with a high degree of hydrogen sulfide—very poisonous. They extract the sulfur from it and pipe the gas off.

The company had to apply to the ERCB, the same board that had dealt with Syncrude, to put this facility in, so, there was going to be a regulatory hearing. In my role with the provincial environment department, I was working with the community, helping them get ready for the regulatory hearings.

I had already taken my mediation training by that time, but it was hard for me to put the organizing and mediation together because I was working for the provincial government. This is fascinating because I was representing part of the regulatory system and at the same time I was saying, "There's got to be a way we can talk and use mediation to resolve some of these things."

The community went to the hearing, saying, "Hey, we want higher standards for sulfur recovery, and we want the most advanced technology for sulfur recovery in this facility." In spite of the community's concerns, the board ruled, "The company's proposal is fine, it meets the standards."

The community responded by saying, "We're going to take you to court. We'll appeal your decision and see what the courts have to say."

It was at that point I said, "You know, we've got to try something different," and I talked to my boss about bringing in a mediator.

This was a new role for us as a department. We hadn't done it before, but he was OK with it, provided I got the regulatory agency on board. So I met with the board and said, "This is what we'd like to do. We've got this issue: the community is going to take it to the courts. What about trying mediation?"

Their response was positive.

I decided that if we're going to make this work we needed a very experienced mediator, so I invited Gerald Cormick to come up from Seattle. I had taken a course from Gerry previously and had heard of his reputation—plus he is Canadian. That was, I think, from my recollection, probably the first time we sat down and had a formal mediation on an environmental issue in Alberta.

What was that like? It was awesome for me. We had to go to both Calgary and Edmonton for meetings, and I had picked Gerry up from the airport. So I had an opportunity—I was a novice in the field at the time—to sit with Gerry, who had done some fantastic work over the years, as he interviewed all of the parties in the initial assessment. I drove him around, sat in on interviews, and was also able to debrief the situation with him.

I learned a lot from the simplicity of the stories—they were profound, yet simple, responses in answer to his "Tell me your story."

He sought the "story" from the president and the CEO of the oil company, the chairman and staff of the regulatory board, the various government departments, and the local people. The interviews were all very similar. He was very passionate in terms of his desire to hear where they were coming from.

I guess the other thing I learned was that even though he might have known what the answer would be, it was important for him to hear it from each of them. In other words, I might have heard about this situation from someone else, but it is important for me to hear it from you.

In these first meetings what was really important to them was to explore, first, the issue, obviously, but second, the process and how that was going to work.

One of the fascinating things that emerged was that, for a variety of circumstances, we could meet with the community group only at the end. I drove Gerry to the meeting. We drove up into somebody's farmyard and I introduced Gerry (they knew who I was from previous encounters), and then I said, "Do you mind if I sit in on this particular session?" It's a question that had to be asked because I wanted to respect them—this was going to be their session with the mediator.

Their response was, "Yes, we do mind."

And I looked around and said, "But I brought Gerald here and I need to take him back to the city."

"Well, we can take him back to the city."

"But, I know which hotel he is at."

"We'll find his hotel."

Finally, they said to me, "Bill, you know, it's nothing against you, but it's who you work for that we have a problem with. You are a provincial employee. You are essentially one of the agencies that's going to have to give them a permit."

And I had to swallow hard, but that was another thing I had to respect, and it was a learning point for me: the hat that I wear or who signs my paycheck could get in the way of my doing effective mediation work.

And so I left.

In the end, it was a fascinating mediation process. They negotiated an interim agreement. When the larger community sat down to review that agreement and to ratify it, however, they said, "You know, this has a lot of good stuff in it and it's better than what we had before, but we feel that we have a better chance to stop the project totally if we go to court."

So they rejected the agreement, went to court, and eventually lost in court. Not only did they lose in court, but also the negotiated agreement was lost. They had negotiated some really innovative things in that agreement, innovative things that were "leading edge" and hadn't been done in the province before. Now, even though I was disappointed in their approach, I had to realize that the actions that they took were actions that they believed were best for their community.

Was I soured on mediation after this experience? No. This was an important lesson in terms of realizing that people have to be able to go the route that they think will give them the best deal. They honestly believed that by going to court, they were actually going to be able to stop the building of the facility. And stopping it was key because the mediated agreement had still allowed the facility to go ahead, albeit with some very, very stringent requirements on it.

So, again, it was a reminder to me that, as much as I may believe in the process, the process still belongs to the people.

Could we as mediators have done things differently in that case so they would have had an agreement with greater controls than ultimately it did? I'm not sure because in talking with the community representatives later it became very apparent that they had spent a lot of time and energy reviewing the mediated agreement, and at the end they really believed they had a case they would win in court. I mean, they did take the time to get a legal assessment and based their decision largely on that. You know, I always encourage parties to take any agreement they reach back to their legal counsel, and that's what they did, so I'm not sure much more could have been done.

From Neighborhood Disputes to City Planning Issues

Parallel to all of this I had started working as a volunteer mediator with the City of Edmonton doing neighborhood disputes—the barking dogs, the hedges, all that kind of stuff. Then one day I got a phone call from the Community Mediation coordinator. A proposal had come forward by a hospital that wanted to expand in the city. They wanted to purchase an actual city street to expand onto and then realign the street. The city council had held either the first or second reading of the bylaw, and suddenly all hell broke loose. The community realized what was going on and said, "Forget this." So the city council said to the hospital and to their own planning staff, you go back and negotiate with the citizens. See what you can come up with here.

They had previously had some meetings, but things had gone from bad to worse. People began calling their ward alderman, came to council chambers protesting, that kind of stuff.

That is what caused the city council to say to the planners and to the hospital, "See if you can work this out." They specifically told the city planners, "We want you to go out, meet with the community residents, work with the hospital to see if you can reach a deal there, and make this thing work."

The city planning staff attempted some sessions. They didn't go anywhere. Things were going from bad to worse in sessions, and the planners became increasingly frustrated.

So they came to community mediation and asked, "Can you help us?" Because of my interest in the multiparty stuff, the community mediation staff asked me if I'd be willing to do this as a volunteer.

My response was, "Sure," and so with a friend of mine who was also involved in mediation, we said, "Let's do it." It took us 10 meetings over the period of a year.

What did we do? We brought the city planners together with representatives from the hospital, including their architect, the chairman of their board, and the chief administrative officer of the hospital. We also brought in the community group that had formed in response to the hospital proposal and representatives from the actual community league, which, in Canada, is the equivalent of a neighborhood association.

It was important to recognize that within the community there were two factions. There was the community league, whose board had been elected by the community at large, and then there was this more ad-hoc group that had opposed the expansion. You would call them a single-issue group. So we brought them all together, and we began with the whole question of issue identification. What are the issues here? We then moved to talk about interests. Then we began to ask, "So what are the options?"

Some interesting technical considerations came up as we considered the options because the hospital was located on the edge of a ravine. So people asked, could you actually expand the hospital in this area? Is the bank stable enough? In order to get answers everyone could accept as technically accurate, we had to bring in some resources.

And at the end of the day, we came up with an agreement that allowed the hospital to expand, but it included some physical changes to the proposal. Specifically, by increasing the hospital's footprint and allowing it to go to a sort of zero lot-line (that is, expanding the property to the edge of their lot lines as opposed to having setbacks), they reduced the height. They didn't have to build higher, and that was important because this facility was located in a neighborhood of primarily single-family bungalows. The community was saying it would rather have something lower than higher. And since the hospital was right beside parkland and the ravine, having a 10-foot setback or a one-foot setback, wasn't going to make a big visual difference.

A couple more things were of interest in this case. The biggest one was that a member of one of the negotiating teams was connected politically to the party in power in the province. Some of the funding to expand this hospital was provincial dollars. So we had to be aware of that scenario and to deal with some of the political dimensions.

That was one of the first times that I had to sit down and say to the parties, "How are we going to deal with political lobbying?"

How did that affect me as a mediator? Well, number one, once we, the two mediators, had discovered it, we realized that we're going to have to get this on the table and have the group talk about this. So we raised it and we said, "You know what? It strikes me that you all have different access to elected officials both provincially and locally. How are we going to manage this?"

The group decided that the way we're going to manage it is that, even though we know people have different access points, we're all going to agree that we aren't going to use those access points. But because we do know that those people at the political level are all interested, we will issue joint statements on a periodic basis to these people advising them as to where we're going. And we will write a letter to them right up front explaining the situation and how we intend to keep them informed.

Ultimately, the mediated agreement went to the city council, and the city council adopted it, and it became part of the bylaw.

Learning from a Light Rail Case

A couple of years later I got a call from someone who had been involved in negotiations with the City of Edmonton on behalf of his community league. I was still working in the provincial environment department and volunteering as a mediator. The city was in the process of wanting to expand its light rail transit, and hoping to solve some traffic congestion problems as well. City staff had negotiated the deal with the traffic subcommittee of the local community league, and the city council had passed a bylaw based on the agreement.

City staff had sat down with that community group and negotiated the widening of the road because it was a traffic bottleneck. The agreement also allowed for at-grade light rail transit adjacent to the roadway. So they were effectively going to double the expanse of the existing roadway and were doing it through the heart of an older, well-established community.

When news of this agreement came out, members of the community were livid and said to their own negotiators, "You have betrayed us! This is not right. You've allowed this roadway to be expanded, but you've also given permission for the train, the LRT. Something's wrong here! Houses will be torn down, and our kids are going to have to cross an even busier and wider roadway to get to school."

So they formed a group to file a legal challenge to have the Bylaw overturned. That's when a member of the community league called me: "Bill, can you come in and mediate between me and my neighbors? We have to do some healing in the community about this."

My response was, "Yeah, I can understand where you are coming from, but let me talk to your neighbors," the other group that had formed in the community. I went and talked to them, and they said, "We're not interested in healing right now. We're going to court. This thing has got to be stopped. We're not prepared to talk about healing."

So, unfortunately, I had to go back to the guy who called me in the first place and say, "You know what, I'd love to do it, but the time isn't right. They're not ready to talk."

So the community went to court, and the courts agreed with the community and overturned the city's bylaw citing procedural things that were wrong when Council passed the bylaw.

The city's response was, "Well, we're just going to do a new bylaw," to which the community responded by saying, "You do a new bylaw, and we're going back to court again."

And at that point (it was about a year after I had received that first call), the mayor said to the community groups, "Enough' s enough. Can we talk?" After getting some agreement that a meeting might be worthwhile, someone from the mayor's office called me and asked, "Would you be prepared to take one day and see if you can mediate this first discussion? See if there's any hope for ongoing discussion?"

I agreed to do that first meeting. I didn't have the luxury of meeting with each of the parties beforehand. City staff made all the arrangements, though I did insist on a neutral location. I wasn't keen on having the meeting at city hall or in the community hall.

I walked into this room full of very irate people—it was tense. I mean, here are senior staff from the city's transportation department, the mayor's executive assistant, the two ward aldermen and their executive assistants, and 12 or 15 highly suspicious, well-educated, and very sophisticated community activists all saying, "OK, well, now what are we going to do?"

My job for the day, as had been agreed to with the mayor's office, was initially to facilitate those discussions to see if there was room for ongoing discussions. So our focus for that day was simply to say, "Are we going to talk? If so, what is it that we're going to talk about? And how are we going to talk about it? At the end of the day we'll make a decision if we're going to continue."

But before we could even go to that first question, we had to find a way to create a level of trust in the room that would allow for a healthy conversation. Trust was a huge issue because the last time many of these people had faced each other was in the courtroom, and the lawyers had done the talking there. So that meant putting this question forward, "If we're going to talk, how are we going to talk?"

We were trying to set some ground rules. Knowing how contentious the issues were, and with no, or very minimal, trust, we had to set a framework. So we agreed upon some very, very brief rules of behavior. And then it was a matter of people telling their story, telling what was important to them, what brought them to the table, why they were interested in it. We were allowing those stories, in a kind of venting process, to begin to answer the question, "If we are going to talk again and continue talking, what is it that we're going to talk about?"

How did I try to respond to the venting, so that things didn't simply escalate more—so that people simply didn't get even angrier toward each other? Let me confess that at that point even though I had mediated numerous neighborhood disputes, I still considered myself green, a novice, and I'll have to admit that there was a real feeling of going by the "seat of my pants."

We had negotiated some rules—I call them "rules for engagement"—but my focus was to manage the discussion. Sure, I was doing some reframing and those kinds of things, and generally encouraging people to listen, to work through issues. But I had to recognize that these people had had a number of previous interactions with each other—formally in the city council's chambers as well as in the courts and in different settings. So they were not new to each other; I was the new person.

Even though they were not new to each other, their previous experience had not been facilitated or managed much. Well, it had been controlled in court, of course. There are all kinds of rules there. But I guess the key thing for me, what I think I brought to the process there initially, was that I was someone who was prepared to help them talk—and keep them civil as they talked—and help them to have a focus to their discussion.

So that was the role that I had there—to keep focus on the discussion and to keep them civil. But also to build on their desire because certainly there was a desire on the community's part to see if they could work something out. They wanted to work something out. The community knew that the road widening and the light rail transit were critical to the city. They were advocates for public transit, in many ways. So they were, to some extent, warm to the idea of the LRT, but they weren't happy about the way it was being set up.

We had the meeting, and the meeting led to an agreement to continue to meet. At that point, then, we went into a much more formal mediation process where we negotiated our conditions of mediation. What is it we were talking about? We talked about the issues, and then we began, once the issues were identified, to explore interests. From there we looked to see if there were some solutions that we could develop. The community wanted technical expertise to make sure that the options were sound, and they didn't want to rely on the city's staff. So we were able to get funds from the city to retain an independent traffic engineer who worked with the committee to provide independent traffic advice.

I was mediating this one by myself, managing the whole process. The city had gone ahead and passed this new bylaw, and the community had a 90-day window in which to file an appeal in order to maintain their standing with the courts. So, we had three months of very, very intensive work. If we didn't come up with something, the community would go ahead with the legal action—and everyone knew that.

And actually, what happened was that at day 85, we realized that we weren't going to be finished within 90 days. So the community did file with the courts but asked that the matter be put on hold to allow the process to finish. The point was that everyone realized that the community could not be asked to give up their right to go to court while the mediation process was still underway.

An event that took place during this pre-agreement hold period turned out to be a real learning experience for me. A couple of days before we were done, I got a call late at night. I had just come back from a meeting. A senior administrator of one of the health care facilities in the vicinity was calling and asking, "Are you the mediator working on this LRT issue?"

Now one of the key issues that we had been dealing with was where the LRT would emerge from the underground tunnel and begin running at grade: where was the entry portal going to be built? This official said, "I see that you've just made this agreement, from what I read in the paper, that appears to indicate that this portal is going to be on *our* land."

I was quite puzzled and taken aback by his comment, and I said, "But it's going to be on the street, the public roadway."

To which he replied, "But we own that street!"

So, a little sticky issue came up as the whether the city owned the street or whether the institution owned that street, meaning the city might not be able to actually commit to building the portal, the tunnel entrance, on the agreed-upon site.

This was a real learning process for me because it was the first time that I had to deal with the issue of new parties wanting to come into the process. We had made some real headway and were just about to sign the agreement when that telephone call came. At that point I raised the issue with the negotiating commit-tee and asked them if they could find some way to modify the agreement, without losing its integrity, so that the new parties would not challenge it when it came to the city council for ratification.

That's when they came up with the idea of proposing a corridor, as opposed to a fixed point, where the tunnel portal would be. It still ensured that the portal would not be adjacent to the residential community, which made them happy, and it gave the city administration enough certainty to allow them to go ahead with it.

After about three meetings to determine the exact location of the portal, the group decided they'd better ask me back to come in as a mediator. Some of the trust issues were still there, and the group had been expanded to include, I think, three health care facilities and the university, as well as two new com-munity leagues and the provincial government.

This wasn't cookbook mediation—there were a couple of key lessons for me. Part of it was that I had to realize that I had a tendency to show a little more deference to the CEOs of the academic or health care facilities than to some of the others in the group.

The deference that I showed them meant that I let them get away with things more than I would other people. So it was a matter of me being aware of those tendencies and realizing that it wasn't acceptable. Most of the stuff related to behavior—I was less likely to challenge them on the issue of interrupting, for instance, and I think the group as a whole had an initial reluctance to challenge them on their opinions and expertise. It was a growth process for me as a mediator to address my own issues and for the community members to develop the comfort that they needed in order to negotiate effectively for their community. Everyone gets angry, everyone to some extent will challenge the process and the ground rules, and I as the process manager, as the mediator, had the responsibility to call each of them on that kind of stuff without being influenced by their status.

From "My Expert Versus Yours" to Joint Fact Finding

The other lesson related to the "my expert versus your expert" routine. We were debating one issue: The impact of the LRT on the nuclear magnetic resonance imaging (MRI) machines that are in the hospitals because the trains, which are powered by electricity supplied by overhead lines, go by and create a magnetic field that interferes with the operation of the MRI. You've got a person getting an MRI, or you're in the middle of this really complicated experiment, and a train goes by; what's going to happen to the machine's readings?

We had a big debate about that. The institutions were saying that the train needed to go underground because the concrete tunnel and the steel rebar in the tunnel will dissipate the magnetic fields. The city's saying, "Absolutely not. It's too expensive to put this thing underground. We've got to keep it above ground."

So for me, this learning experience was about, "Well, how do you deal with these conflicting opinions?" We weren't getting anywhere in the argument, and each group had their own expertise to support their positions.

As a group, they had to realize, first, that they were stuck and, second, that as long as they remained fixed on those positions, they weren't going to get anywhere. Now one of the things we had talked about at the beginning was that when the negotiating group members took the agreement back to their various organizations for ratification, they would be able to do so in the full confidence that the information on which the agreement was based was sound and defensible. That meant that they wouldn't have to go away and say, "We agreed to this because so and so in the negotiating group said it would work."

What this situation did was force us to say, "Well, let's see if we can get some information jointly, something we can all agree on."

So we sat down as a group and asked, "What's the question?"

We jointly defined the question clearly and got agreement on it. Then we asked, "Well, what are the skills that are needed in order to actually answer the question? What kind of skills does a person need?"

After we readied an agreement on that, we said, "OK, who's out there?" Subsequently, we did a request for proposals and ended up agreeing on a European consulting firm. We were able to send all the necessary information out to the consultant, so it meant that they didn't have to come in.

So, in fact, what happened was that this consultant became a servant of the negotiating team, the entire negotiating team. It wasn't your person, it wasn't my person, it was our person. That was really important because it gave people the comfort they needed in order to take the agreement back to their constituents with confidence.

The consultant then came back with a recommendation that said, "In this particular case, above ground or below ground, it's still going to impact the MRIs. You're going to have to protect the MRIs. You are going to have to put a shield around them." As a result they ended up talking about putting one-foot thick lead walls all around these machines.

But because it was independent, the city people could go back to their political bosses and say, with confidence, "This is what we have to do."

The health care and academic reps could go back to their boards of governors and say, "You know, yes, we thought that going underground would solve the problem, but technical expertise says that it's not going to make a difference." This group in particular was very concerned because their issue had been not only about the impact of electromagnetic fields on the MRIs, but also aesthetics—they wanted to keep the power lines and tracks and train underground.

We started out with my expert vs. your expert. What turned the corner was a realization by the parties that that wasn't going to get them anywhere. They realized that they could talk until they were blue in the face, and the other wasn't going to convince them. So now it was a matter of asking, "Guys, how are we going to get around this? What do you need in order to get around this?"

They all said, "Sound technical information that's independent. As a community guy I'm not making my decision because you, the health care reps, say it's a good deal, or because you say it's not going to have an impact. And the health care reps aren't going to make their decisions because the city rep says it's not going to make an impact. We're going to make a decision based on sound technical expertise that's coming from the outside, that is defensible, that's independent, that's from someone who's not working for you, not working for me."

What made this even more fascinating was that each group had very competent technical people. One of the things they had to do was to ensure that their own internal technical people who had been advising them up to now would not feel put off by this new approach, and that the new approach wouldn't cause problems for them within their organization when the consultant's report came back. They realized that if they didn't, they'd be stuck on this my expert vs. your expert hamster wheel that would just keep going, going, going. So what the group did was give themselves the time they needed to get internal support for the consultant they eventually chose.

Ultimately, about a month after the three-month prescribed period for reaching agreement, the city and the community came to their agreement.

Creating a Municipal Mediation Capacity

This was in 1990. I was developing a mediation practice, but I was still working for the government, for the environment department. There's a little aside here that I would like to explain because it ties into all of this. It is the event that links where I was at that time to how I got the position I'm in now.

About a year after the LRT case, and this is totally unrelated to LRT, the city found itself in a garbage crisis. The City of Edmonton had a landfill capacity problem and needed a landfill. Now in spite of—and this is commonplace right across North America—their best efforts and attempts to locate a new landfill, they weren't getting anywhere. Finally the province, the premier, said, "You know, Edmonton, you've got to sit down with your neighbors. These other neighbors are also going to need a landfill at some point. So, let's sit down on a regional basis and look at this."

The province brought together the 22 municipalities, their mayors, and their chief administrative officers to discuss who gets the landfill and what's the best approach to take?

Some time later, a couple of people who I knew told me of the increasing sense of the frustration that the politicians on the committee were having because they were just talking past each other. They weren't getting at what was really important to them and were feeling that this was a big waste of time. Some felt that they were going to have the landfill foisted on them, so they were slowing down discussions, and others who needed a landfill were getting frustrated with the lack of progress.

So I stuck my neck out and approached some of the senior people in my department who were working on the project, and said, "You need someone like me in there who can do some mediation and get them to agree to what it is they're going to talk about. You need to get some protocols in place. There is no trust in the room and no way in which they can safely have the frank discussion that needs to happen."

The response was, "Well, if we can sell it to these municipal politicians, fine."

At the next meeting, they put the proposal on the table and concluded the meeting by saying, "Look folks, I think you should talk to Bill. I think he's going to help you sort some things out, and if he doesn't, I'll buy each of you a case of beer."

I'm not sure if the free beer opened the door for me, but I do know that the Edmonton officials related my experience with the LRT project to the group, and so in the end I was invited in to do some mediation.

Now the only reason I mention this story is because in 1997 (this was a few years

120

after the landfill mediation), we had a provincial election and one of the new MLAs (members of the provincial legislature) was the former reeve (the chief elected officer of a rural municipality) of a rural county that had been intimately involved in the landfill discussions. Well, she became the minister of municipal affairs.

When she came in, she was faced with three contentious disputes between municipalities. One was over annexation. One was over revenue sharing, where there was a power plant in one jurisdiction, but the main way for trucks to get to that power plant was by driving through the other jurisdiction on the roads their taxpayers had paid for, but all the taxes from the power plant were going to the jurisdiction where the power plant was. And the third involved one municipality planning development around a lake that was within its jurisdiction, but that lake was the water supply for an urban community. So the urban community was concerned about it.

This new minister said to them, "You know—why don't you try mediation? I've had some experience with it. Why don't you give it a try?"

While the province does have an administrative tribunal to resolve some intermunicipal disputes, she wanted to avoid that process and have the municipalities resolve the matter between themselves.

They agreed, and it worked. She brought in mediators, and in all three cases the municipalities involved reached an agreement.

I have to give you a bit of history here to set the context. In Alberta, in the latter 1980s, there was a significant downsizing of provincial government services. Regional planning commissions responsible for coordinated land-use planning in large geographic areas were abolished.

So with no regional entity to coordinate intermunicipal land-use planning (by the mid-90s), the Alberta Department of Municipal Affairs was beginning to see a rising level of frustration among municipalities. Internally, the department staff were saying, "We've got to do something." It was at that point that they began to look into alternative dispute resolution, ADR. It was the coming together of the minister's initiative to try mediation and the department's own thinking that resulted in the decision to try mediation.

Ensuring Municipal Ownership and Control

This was 1998, and I was hired to develop the program. One of the first things I did was make a point of asking, "Do we have the support of the stakeholders, of the municipalities themselves?"

In Alberta, we have two municipal government associations—one that represents rural municipalities and one that represents urban municipalities. I said, "We've got to get them on board. Since mediation is voluntary, if you want municipalities to participate, their associations need to be on board. They need to realize that this is a good idea."

I invited representatives of the associations to sit at the table. I said, "This is what the minister wants to do. We want to set up this program. Would you be part of the design of this program?"

I also brought in the Alberta Arbitration and Mediation Society because the decision had been made, prior to my being hired, that any mediation services would be provided by external, private mediators, not by government. And so I wanted to make sure that we included the perspective of private mediators as we set up the program.

I was faced with an interesting scenario as soon as we started. You have to understand that in Alberta, for many years, the elected councilors for the rural municipalities were also the local school board. So they had a dual role. They were governing the municipalities, and they also oversaw the local school system.

So when I mentioned mediation, they immediately related it to their only previous experience with mediation, which was labor mediation in school board settings, and that generated the image of the traditional role that labor mediators have, which is very, very formal, with a lot of shuttle diplomacy. They had been exposed to situations in the past where labor mediators write a report at the end of negotiations in terms of what happened and what didn't happen, and that report can go to a labor relations board that can order that a particular agreement be implemented.

Based on that understanding, they were very reluctant. They were fearful that someone was going to come in and make decisions for them. All of a sudden I was dealing with people who said, "Hey, we have been elected to make decisions. Are you telling us that someone else is going to come in and make a decision for us? We don't want that!"

My response was, "No, that's not what we're doing. Let's go through the mediation process," and we explained what it was and walked them through previous cases. Eventually the committee members gained a better understanding of the interest-based approach and how it could work for them.

I assured them, "You are still maintaining control. There is no way that any mediator in this program will write a report. There's no way that the mediators will communicate with the minister. This is simply between the two municipalities to cut a deal to work together, to negotiate an agreement. They're not reporting to the minister. They're not to report to the minister and not to me — it's between the two of you. And if it doesn't work, that's fine — it's your process."

That assurance was good enough for one of the associations, and they endorsed the program. But the other one, the rural municipalities, said, "No, we won't go with it. We're not sure yet."

It took our minister going to their fall convention and, in her keynote speech, addressing this very specific point. They needed public assurances that this program was something they were going to be in total control of, and if they didn't like what was happening in the mediation, they could walk away from it.

It was only after she gave them that assurance that they said okay.

The next issue was the mediators. They said, "Hold on, we need to know who the mediators are." My response to them was, "You can choose any mediators you like. I'm not going to dictate who the mediators are." And they said, "No, no. We want to make sure that the mediators who are going to do this stuff are going to be competent and qualified. Otherwise, we don't want to recommend this to our members."

My initial thought had been that we could be much broader. If you were a qualified and experienced mediator, you should be able to handle these kinds of disputes. But they wanted things a little tighter. So they—I don't want to say "forced" me—but they put us in a position of having to create a roster of mediators. We jointly laid out some criteria in terms of basic mediation training, but of greatest importance to them was familiarity with municipal governance and familiarity with intermunicipal relations.

We sat down as a committee and developed criteria, and then went through a whole advertising process to see who was interested in mediating these types of disputes. The committee reviewed all the applications, and this resulted in the roster. We have nine mediators on the roster today.

Even though we have the roster, municipalities can choose whomever they wanted. The roster's simply there if they're looking for some comfort. But to a large extent they are choosing mediators from the roster. So, the roster reassured them about the quality of the personnel—that the people coming into the room were going to have familiarity with municipal law and municipal governance and intermunicipal issues. They didn't want to start from scratch by educating the mediator.

The next step in the program's life was even more fascinating. The minister became so keen on mediation that she said, "I want to make mediation mandatory"—in two areas: land annexation and intermunicipal land-use planning.

As I mentioned before, we have the municipal government board, which is an administrative tribunal, set up to arbitrate the two types of intermunicipal disputes. The board has been in existence in some form for a long time. The mediation program had been set up to divert cases from them.

The minister was saying, "Before you can go to the board for a hearing, I want you to go to mediation," and she was going to make it mandatory. There was a big debate about it, and at the end the act was amended to require an attempt at mediation.

From my perspective, mediation is voluntary, and coerced participation in mediation just didn't ring true to me. While the minister understood this, she was aware of another challenge the program faced, and she really wanted to do whatever she could to encourage municipalities to use mediation.

Intermunicipal mediation was new, and many municipal politicians had been around a long time. The challenge was that we were asking them to try on a new pair of boots, and we were hearing in response, "It's not going to work. But we know what will happen if we go to the board.... Even though going to the board is going to cost us a whole bunch of money because you're bringing in lawyers, you're bringing in technical expertise, etc." In short, the board process was something that they knew well and, like an old pair of boots, had grown more comfortable with age. They were reluctant even though we were telling them mediation probably would be cheaper because the province is prepared to pay up to a third of the cost of the private-sector mediator. We also told them that mediation gave them a forum to try to negotiate a deal by themselves.

My argument was to keep it voluntary, but the language ended up calling for an attempt at mediation. To ensure that it was a serious attempt, the legislation stated that if the mediation didn't work, you needed to file a statutory declaration as to why the mediation didn't work.

Creating a Track Record: Municipal Annexation Cases

How did I respond to these seasoned politicians who were reluctant to try new things? I did a lot of handholding, walking them through cases, spending a lot of time with them, just explaining the process.

Here's an interesting example. We had one case, a land-use dispute, where an urban municipality was appealing a land-use plan that an adjacent rural municipality had put in place. Now this was just before the legislation was changed making an attempt at mediation mandatory. I tried to convince them to go to mediation. The minister tried to convince them to go to mediation. They said, "Absolutely no way!"

They eventually went to the administrative tribunal where it became a very, very acrimonious hearing. I think they probably both spent up to a quarter of a million dollars on outside resources on that hearing. And then just before the hearing concluded, the urban municipality said, "Well, we'll solve the whole problem, we're going to apply to annex that land, and then we will have control of it. We want to annex the whole chunk of land."

Their annexation application came in just after the Act was amended to make an attempt at mediation mandatory. So they tried mediation, and it took just under three years—but it cost them a whole lot less, and they eventually got a deal. Instead of spending a quarter of a million dollars on legal fees and technical fees, they ended up each spending $20,000 on mediation. The board process hadn't been that fast either, and, even though a decision was rendered, neither party was particularly pleased with it. It was a very painful, two-year period.

In the end they saw the benefits and that was good for us because the very public dispute had sent a signal around the province that there was some benefit to mediation—benefit not necessarily in terms of time in this case, but certainly in terms of cost.

This early case was followed by a couple of smaller cases (annexation mediations) that were also successful. So it was because of the success of the program, more than anything, that it started taking off. To this date we haven't had any failures, and I think we've done over 30 mediations. They have all resulted in the municipalities involved reaching a deal. It's been successful in terms of mediation resulting in agreements and avoiding the tribunals. So people were finding out—the word got out, and they are using it.

There was one interesting occurrence for me in about the first year of the program: even with the initial successes, we hadn't had a lot of uptake. I had made my annual report to the initiative's advisory committee (these are the same group of stakeholders who were involved in the initial program design). Afterwards, the representative from the rural association (these were the folks who were initially very skeptical) said, "You have got to come and make a presentation to my board." He said, "I think they've got to hear what you've done this year. You know, the cost savings and the successes and that kind of stuff."

I made that presentation, and what was really neat was that the next item on their agenda was an issue about intra-council conflict. The association's board was hearing about an increased amount of conflict between council members on individual municipal councils—bickering and fighting. All of a sudden the lights went on with them, and they said, "Hey, could you work with us on a committee to deal with council conflict?"

"That's a question the minister will have to answer," I said, "but I don't think it will be a problem."

They wrote to the minister, and he gave the go ahead.

That was a real boost to our credibility because they invited me to work with them directly on an issue that was very important to them; that is, how to deal with conflict internally on councils.

That led to a report and further action by them, but it was reputation building for me and for the program. It's not a flag-waving kind of thing; it's just one of those events that when you look back, you say, "Hey, that was establishing credibility." And the more credibility you get, that translates into more work. It's a direct spillover.

I think there are a couple of things that have made mediation work and work well in Alberta. And these lessons can be replicated elsewhere.

One of them has been the dollars. The province committed up front, "We are prepared to ante up and enter into this as an equal partner in the cost of the mediators. So the total cost is not something that you as municipalities will have to carry." Even though it is costing the provincial government about $14,000 in direct costs per mediation, we avoid the cost of hearings and, by building better relationships between municipalities, reduce the likelihood of other disputes occurring.

I think the other thing that helped has been the close working relationship that we'd been able to establish with the two municipal government associations. We realized at the beginning that if they were going to be the users, they had better be involved, even though this was a directive at the provincial level, even though the minister could make it happen on her own.

I think the fact that we took the time initially to work with them to address their particular concerns, to make sure they were happy, has certainly gone a long way to actually make it work. The other thing has simply been the success of the program.

One of the things I did early on was to hire a journalist to actually write up success stories. I mean I could write success stories, but my focus would be on the process. I want the stories to come from the municipal politicians themselves. So we have a collection of 11 or 12 stories of various cases where we're giving voice to the participants, letting them tell what had happened. It's been our strongest promotional tool to date.

How does the program actually work? I initially do the convening work. The letter comes in, or the call comes to us, requesting help, and I will normally meet with both municipalities to talk about the program, to explain the program. If they agree to enter into mediation, I will work with them to scope out what the problem is and then help them pick the mediators. Then it's handed over to the private-sector mediators.

We had one situation where I was meeting with a municipality, and the Reeve and his chief administrative officer both said, "You know what, you might have a 100 percent success rate now, but you won't by the time this one ends. Because this one isn't gonna go. There's no way there's gonna be an agreement, there's too much bad blood between the two municipalities."

It was an annexation dispute, a small annexation. It might have only been an acre or two. It was quite small, but what made it look so impossible were the negative relations between the two municipalities—the total lack of trust.

They ended up getting an agreement, but the fascinating thing is that I have heard from both these two guys, who now have said to us, "You know what? The fact that we got this deal, that was nice. But the thing that has been beneficial to us is the fact that we have now established a working relationship that has gone far beyond this little land issue to a whole bunch of other things." He said, "That's been the amazing thing for me: the transformation that has come about—as a result of what was a small annexation has translated into a lot more cooperation in a whole bunch of other areas."

You see, these municipalities have shared boundaries for years. There are long-standing relationships. The parties aren't going away. So whatever the specific issue happens to be, it's always in the shadow of those relationships. The relationship building is critical. It really is.

And here's another example. One administrator involved in a mediation all of a sudden said to me, "Until I realized that I could divorce my wife easier than I could divorce my municipal neighbor, things weren't going that well. But when I realized that I had to have an ongoing relationship, all of a sudden the incentive to negotiate with the other side was there."

Another administrator said, "The mediation process changed the nature of the discussions."

The way it had been was that the rural municipality was responding to the urbans' request for annexation. You were asking for my land, and I was arguing with you on that. But what mediation did was to put the rurals' issues on the table, and it gave them as much legitimacy as the urbans' issues. So all of a sudden, he said, "It wasn't that we were just talking about the urbans' issues, but the urban was forced to talk about our issues as well!"

That was a real moment of transformation.

What was happening was something that wouldn't happen in front of a tribunal. The administrative tribunal looks at a proposal on the table, and everyone focuses on that. You're always attacking that annexation or that land use. It's an argument: you are trying to convince the board of the merit of your case and to destroy the case of the other.

But what happened here was that, when the mediators came in and reframed the situation, it became a situation of, "OK, so what's important to both sides here?" The rurals could tell their story, and all of a sudden there was, if I can use the term loosely, an "obligation" on the part of the urbans to respond to that, and to say, "In order for us to resolve this, you have concerns too, and we're going to have to address them."

So one of the things they agreed to was that as part of this annexation, land would be maintained in a rural state until it was absolutely needed to go into residential development. So there wasn't going to be any kind of interim use for the land. It was going to stay rural. It was going to be farmed, as long as it could. They talked about drainage and about how urban drainage could impact farming. These are things that the tribunal doesn't deal with. The tribunal's issue is, "Are you going to get the land, or aren't you going to get the land?" And if there are any taxes involved here, we'll deal with the taxes.

But all these other things that are very, very important to one of the parties aren't dealt with. The tribunal doesn't have the legislated mandate or the scope to deal with them. So when municipalities began to realize that there was an opportunity for broader issues to come to the table, and to look at them more comprehensively, they began to take the program seriously and use it.

This is some of the stuff that I raise with them in our scoping conversations. When I work with them to scope out the mediation, I'm trying to get clarity as to what it is that the parties are going to talk about. We do this in a joint session.

Let me give you an example. We were faced with one municipality that insisted that they were going to go forward with an annexation application. The rural municipality responded, "We're not prepared to talk annexation at all. We're interested in regional economic development." They were really firm in this: if annexation was going to be the main topic, they weren't going to be at the mediation table.

So the big challenge became, "OK, how can we bring the two together?"

Since both councils were so very determined about what had to be discussed, we had to find a way to use both terms, "annexation" and "regional economic development," in the actual scoping meeting.

The parties ended up jointly creating an "umbrella statement"—that the municipalities have come together to talk about issues related to regional economic development and annexation. The order of the words was really important because if the urban municipality had pushed the annexation issue before looking at economic cooperation, the rurals, would have walked away from the table. So the urbans had to be flexible in regards to the order of the items discussed, but they were not forced to take their issue off of the table. At the end of the day, when they actually did a deal, there was no annexation. There was joint land-use planning. There was revenue sharing. And there was a regional approach to economic development.

So that was part of the transformation that took place: the mediation allowed the interests of both of the parties to be heard. The question was asked, "By the way, what do you want to do with that land that you are talking about annexing?"

"Well, we see this as an area for industrial development."

To which the response was, "Well, we've been planning on putting an industrial park on that land as well."

"Oh?," and the lights went on.

"Is there some way we can work together on this?"

They ended up putting money together for an economic development officer, and there was some revenue sharing in terms of the tax revenue that was going to come from that area. So that's the kind of intricacies that we've been working with.

Institutionalized Capacity

As of today my office has been going for five years, and we've had about 30 mediations. I think the longest one in terms of actual negotiation sessions took us 40 negotiating sessions, 40 days. Now that was 40 full days of actual negotiation over probably a six-month period, so it was fairly concentrated. The shortest mediation lasted half a day.

That leads to another thing we've learned in the process—well, actually, there are a couple of things we've learned. We now encourage parties to really compress the negotiation period and to do two- to three-day blocks of negotiating at a time, as opposed to doing a day here and then waiting a month. We've found that it just took too much time rehashing old stuff when you came together again after too long an intermission.

The other thing we do now is that the mediator spends half a day with the full council of each municipality talking about the mediation process. This happens before they actually get into the mediation sessions. The mediators meet with the municipal councils to address a couple of things. Number one, they want to introduce themselves so that all the councilors know who the mediators are. But, secondly, it's not the entire council that goes into negotiation. It's only two members out of seven. So, since the entire council has to ratify the deal at the end of the day, it's important that they also have comfort with the mediators and the process—that they're also prepared to say, "OK, we know about the process, and we can trust these mediators." You see, it is important that their trust, or lack of it, in the mediators doesn't cloud their assessment of the agreement that is finally negotiated.

And another thing that we do now is that the mediators spend half a day with each negotiating team independently to give them an orientation to interest-based negotiation and to help them scope out and talk about the whole process and clarify what their interests are—to actually get them ready for the negotiation sessions. It's training and assessment, a mixture of both.

What would it take to replicate this in other places?

I think one of the key things was the coming together of a number of things that made this work for us. We were reaching a point where there were increasing numbers of intermunicipal disputes, and there was a frustration with what was happening and that the ability wasn't there to resolve those disputes. So the timing was good in that way.

I have been really blessed, initially, with a minister who believed in mediation and, subsequently, with senior administrators, both at the deputy minister and the assistant deputy minister level who are committed to the process and who know that it's going to work. So when people say that you need an advocate or a champion, I've had that. And I've been able to get advocates and supporters for the program at the municipal association level, both urban and rural, and that's been based on the work we've done and, over time, my own credibility with them.

The biggest resistance we faced was unfamiliarity with the program, unfamiliarity with what mediation was all about, and a lack of trust. Municipalities had a real fear that the province was going to be the big daddy and come down and lay the hammer on them. We also had to deal with their image of what mediation was, which was, at least for rural municipalities, thinking about the whole labor model and not wanting to get into that because they'd seen what they had done, and they were not happy with that.

Along with the lack of trust, we had to combat a sense of being coerced into having to do mediation—an "against our will." Then, too, it was important to take on all comers, not to be afraid, to be pro-active: I had to jump in there, to be somewhat aggressive in terms of promoting it to municipalities. You see, attempted mediation was mandatory in only two cases, annexation or land use, but there were a whole range of other intermunicipal disputes. And in those areas where it was not mandatory, where "attempted" is not mandatory, it's totally up to the participants if they want to use the service. So I had to be somewhat aggressive in accessing those disputes, and that meant reading the newspaper, checking out where disputes were simmering, and saying, "Hey, I see this is going on here. I think I might have something that can work for you. Can I come down and talk about it? Can I come down and explain it?"

In those cases, like intermunicipal cost sharing or service sharing, there was no onus on them to try mediation. I was being proactive in terms of going out there and talking to them and holding their hands, making sure that they got good mediators.

I also spent a lot of time talking to them about who they should send to the table as a negotiating team, and about the differences involved if you're going to go to an advocacy role or a mediating role. I was involved in helping them pick the mediators and just generally getting them comfortable with what the process is going to be like.

Then I'd call them up later and say, "Well, how did it go?" We do follow-up surveys with the municipalities after the mediation, and we are finding that, for the most part, they are happy with the process. We're still batting 1.000: they are reaching agreements. But I think we're on the cusp now. I'm not sure whether we're going to maintain that perfect record. I'd like to.

What keeps me interested, enthused, excited about work? I've had great internal support, and we've moved the program now from strictly mediation to now offering what I call a "system design exercise" for municipalities where we're giving them up to $50,000 to take a look at their internal operations, how they currently manage conflict internally in terms of themselves and ratepayers, or between administration and council, or within administration.

We explore, "Are there systems that you can put in place to manage conflict better?" So we now offer them $35,000 to do an initial assessment, and that's free and clear, no strings attached. And then we provide $15,000 to assist in implementation. They have to match the $15,000 that we give them with cash of their own or services in-kind.

We also now offer dispute resolution training to community leaders around the province, and just recently, in cooperation with a number of associations, we've started what we call our "peer-mentoring program." We've identified four senior municipal administrators from around the province, and two senior elected people, who have good conflict resolution skills, and they're now available for their peers to call up and say, "Hey, I've got this trouble developing. Can you give me advice?"

We recognize that an administrator is more likely to call up a fellow administrator or their own association, rather than me, and elected officials are more willing to call up an elected person, as opposed to me. This is another avenue of getting the word out—there are different ways of managing conflict—and giving people the resources to do it, to learn about the skills, to pick up the skills, and to find out what options there are. So, for me, it's been an awesome journey just watching the program expand and do different things.

When there's a lot of animosity, when there's a history of mistrust, when a lot of people would say there's been such bad blood that we're not going to get anything done, what helps me see past the surface anger? What gives me a sense of possibility? Where other people see this and turn around and quit, my response is, "No, no, let's keep going."

You see, there are two things here. The process speaks for itself. It's demonstrated to me that it works, number one. So having the experience helps, having seen evidence that we've been able to move beyond such anger.

But, I think, secondly—and it never ceases to amaze me—that when push comes to shove and you really look at the situation, people haven't taken the time to understand where the other is coming from and what's really driving them. It's still "Your grandpappy did this to my grandpappy." And they're fixated on that. They identify themselves in the history and the bad situation—the bad relationships—and they can't see beyond it.

That's the challenge that I see, that really gets me reinvigorated—that there is a way beyond it. If I can get them to park that for a moment, to create an environment where they can park that and begin to peek through the curtains as to what might be possible, that's what it takes. And if they can see that, then I think we've got them hooked, and we've got a way of making it work. That's the real challenge: to get them to see that it can work.

But that's all you need, you need them to peek and to see what's worked for others—and if they can see it once, I think they'll get the taste, because they know that the traditional process has not been satisfactory. Administrative tribunals are costly, and they're antagonistic. They do absolutely nothing for intermunicipal relations. They create—I don't want to say a "win-lose," but—a very distributive kind of process, and it does nothing to address what, I think, they themselves realize at the end of the day, is their ultimate desire: to improve intermunicipal cooperation and to work better with their neighbors. They're seeing that the traditional processes aren't working. But in some ways, it's hard for them to give it up because that's all they know. So, it's just an interesting observation, but I do know that it's been five years for the program now, and we're the busiest we've ever been.

The benefit for us now is that we're "institutionalized." We have a home and a track record, and I can't say enough about the benefits of that. I'm aware as I read the newspaper clippings that in the U.S. a variety of intermunicipal disputes like annexation disputes are going to mediation. But I'm not aware of any other institutionalized program as we have it here. But you don't need an institutionalized program to the same extent that we have it here to make this work. The financial support from the province is nice, and it makes it easier, but all you really need is someone who is prepared to say, "Let's give it a try. Let's look at the potential benefits of this." You have nothing to lose! You really have nothing to lose in this.

Possibilities for City Planners

My initial work as a mediator was as a volunteer, and I personally believe there are many, many excellent volunteers out there who have superior skills to what I have, who are in a position to actually come in and do this kind of stuff. So there's nothing stopping a local planning director, let's say, from going to your local community mediation program and saying, "Is there someone there who's got that interest and that skill, and are they prepared to try it?"—whatever the dispute might be.

There are many spots in which mediation or other conflict resolution techniques can be tried, for sure. And that's been one of the fascinating things here: All nine of the municipalities that we've worked with to design new conflict management systems have cited planning and development as the issue that they want to talk about. It's an area in the municipal operations where there is a lot of conflict, and where they're having difficulty managing it.

One of the struggles that they're having is actually seeing that there are options in how they deal with situations. We've been saying, "OK, yes, there is a defined process set out by law that you have to do, you have to follow the legislated procedures. But are there opportunities where you can actually interject more informal procedures that will allow you to deal with the conflict in a more productive manner? Are there procedural things that will allow you to supplement your traditional regulatory process in a way that gives you a better chance of success in resolving the planning issue?"

For instance, one municipality said, "We want to create what we call a 'conflict competent organization.'" So we're going to work with all of our frontline staff to give them, if not ADR training, certainly conflict management training. By saying they are "conflict competent" they're in fact saying, "We want to better manage conflict when it occurs. We don't want our administrative process or lack of skills to make the situation worse." They'll have basic, interest-based discussions with clients/ratepayers. We're talking about front-counter kinds of things: What can you do at the front counter to be more proactive in dealing with the tensions that are there?

There are other opportunities outside of those traditional formal channels that people can try. Part of it is simply dialogue: the planner taking the initiative to use constructive, positive dialogue opportunities. That's poor wording, but it means setting up mechanisms for the various parties to come together and talk. This is the one thing that I really believe in: it's the parties sitting face-to-face talking with each other that's going to result in the most productive resolution to the dispute. That can be painful, and I can understand why planners are reluctant to bring parties in the room together—because of the hostility that's there and the fear that they will have to compromise the development standards.

But my argument is that planners are setting themselves up in an almost no-win position if they're going to become either Solomon, hearing the various components and splitting the difference, or trying to come up with a solution themselves. It's got to be the developer and the community that have to talk together to come up with a solution that really is going to make it, and planners have to make sure that the municipalities' interests are protected. Planners are more than Solomon—they are stakeholders, and the parties have to recognize that.

My belief is that planners have to create the opportunities that allow for dialogue without each party's bias getting in the way. I'm encouraging the local planning director to go out and create a space to talk face to face. I'm definitely not a big advocate of big formal public meetings because I don't think that allows for the dialogue you need. I mean creating a space like sitting around a table, having a cup of coffee, and talking about the project.

Don't focus on the rightness or wrongness of his project yet. The question is, "What can we put in place that would allow us to move through this process together? To come up with some sort of resolution at the end of the day?" I'm not asking planners to speak as community leaders on behalf of the community, but I'm asking them to speak as people who live in and know the community.

They can do that in a very informal way. I have to reiterate the importance of allowing the people, the developers and the community, to talk together face-to-face as opposed to the planner functioning as the intermediary. I know that's risky. But I believe that it can be done if you take baby steps. You start off cautiously—with the small group first. You're working to create—I'm going to say a win-win, however poor choice of words that is—a win-win in terms of process design. The very first step is going to be an informal gathering between maybe one or two people that's going to be focused on problem solving—not so much on the specifics of the development, but on the process of how to review the development.

I'd back away from the project to ask about the process: "How do you want to treat each other? And at what point do you see a need to engage the broader community? And how can we best do that? What are your timelines like?"

Planners can take those steps slowly. I think the other thing is to recognize and to not deny the fact that planners also have things that have to be accepted. Whatever agreement is reached also has to meet the city's standards. The planner has to be up front about that—to ensure that people recognize that the city's interests, the municipality's interests, are also met.

At the end of the day, if planners don't do this, and this really pains me, there's a real chance that the planners will become the focus. They will be the ones being judged. They have tried to do the best they can with the input they have received from the various people to come up with a recommendation. But, in fact, they're playing Solomon. And at the end of the day, they are up for judgment. They are attacked. There are probably cases when this will happen no matter what they do, but I don't think it has to be this way all the time.

In most cases, the matter will have to go to someone or some body for ratification. It might go to a municipal council or a provincial minister. It might go to a state governor. Eventually someone needs to ratify the recommendation that you come up with, and all of a sudden it's you, the planner, that's in the vice getting squeezed. It's the planner that has made the trade-offs, and the parties themselves have not got the understanding of why those trade-offs have been made.

So I'm really concerned that planners put themselves in an almost untenable position of trying to filter all of this stuff out and come up with recommendations without having the benefits of the parties really understanding why you've done that, and understanding why you didn't do other things. Sure you've asked the developer for this setback or you've asked for this height restriction. But the developer's asking, "Why?" He or she doesn't know, doesn't have a good grasp of what concerns you were responding to, why they were important and who said they were important.

But when the developer and the community person see each other face-to-face, they learn something about each other, and they then become active partners in the resolution of whatever the situation is that faces them. Not only that; if they become an active partner in coming up with the solution, they are more likely to become actively involved in the implementation of the solution.

Now you might say, "But they're at loggerheads. They're not thinking about each other as partners. The developers might have nothing good to say about the 'obstructionists' in the neighborhood and the community might have nothing good to say about the 'greedy developer.'" So the planner wants to keep them apart, and here's Bill Diepeveen saying, "No, no, no, get them together face-to-face," but I insist, because at the end of the day, your ability to get what you want is, to a large extent, going to be determined by their ability to endorse it.

Sure, some might say, "Why bother? We've got a pro-business council. There is no way that they will listen to the community." But I have been in many situations where people have come in convinced that the council is going to support the developer, or vice versa, and then for a variety of reasons the tables turn. It doesn't pay to prejudge what the outcome might be; it's far healthier to work together, face-to-face, so that you can take a unified response to the council.

If you get them together face-to-face, there is a real likelihood that they won't just get each other angrier. There's going to be a high degree of suspicion, sure. But understanding can and will develop. For example, a community feels threatened by a developer coming in—a community that's also concerned about its very life. They see themselves changing. This developer had the potential of doing something that could inject new life into the community, but it's a matter of bringing the two together.

On the LRT dispute, we had a couple of very interesting things happen that illustrate this point. Two things came up. One was the speed of the train. There was opposition because the train goes at 70 or 80 kilometers per hour. The other concern was that the city had a policy that wherever there was a LRT station, they were going to rezone the area for high density—which makes some sense. But in this smaller community of single-family houses, that's the last thing they wanted.

So while the court battle was over whether the LRT should be above or below ground, the real concerns were also about the potential zoning that was going to come with it and the speed of the train. And had the traditional kind of dialogue happened with a focus on "above or below ground?," the solution would have been either above or below. But by having the parties talking face-to-face and gaining a deeper understanding of what was important to each other, other concerns came out, and we had a much richer discussion and came to a solution which truly addressed both the community's and the city's needs.

Afterword

As I read over the profile and reflected on it, one of the things that emerged was that there is some logic to how my career evolved and how I ended up doing the work that I am currently doing. I have always been interested in municipal politics, so the opportunity to tie that into my love for mediation has been great.

The other aspect is the support that has existed for the work we do. While, as with any new program or idea, there is always some suspicion about motives and intentions, once you have the chance to demonstrate that you are interested in working with people to allow them to resolve their own conflicts, doors can open. It has been interesting to reflect on how our program has evolved and how new opportunities emerged once a level of trust was built.

One of the key challenges that we have had has been to keep the program fresh and relevant, to ensure that it is still meeting the particular needs of our clients, the municipalities around the province.

We have really worked to push the envelope to ensure that we are bringing the best to the clients. One of the things we have done over the last five or six years is to bring together different experts from the field of conflict resolution, people who are not necessarily involved in municipal mediation or conflict resolution dealing with politics or anything like that to see what we can learn from what they have done. So we brought in Jane Docherty from Eastern Mennonite University and learned some things about culture and how to address value-laden disputes. Her observations resulted in us modifying our processes to ensure that the underlying value and cultural issues are dealt with before moving to the substantive stuff. Dave Brubaker, also from EMU, has an institutional and church background, and he gave us some really significant insights about things we can do when it came to trying to institutionalize more effective conflict management systems in municipalities, whether the conflict is between an elected council and its administration, council and ratepayers, or administration and ratepayers. Dave pointed out that it takes years for changes to an institution's conflict management practices to become part of the fabric and fiber of the organization. This has led us to provide more support over a longer period of time to municipalities as they implement these changes.

When I initially did the profile, the program consisted of me and one other staff person. Today it has grown to include five of us. One is working full time on our education and workshop program. We have expanded what started off as one course introducing elected officials and administrators to interest-based negotiation to now having nine different courses. The topics include a variety of workshops addressing advanced negotiation training, citizen/public engagement, and workplace conflict management. The evolution of the training has been a direct result of demand from municipal leaders. It relates back to my earlier comment about keeping things fresh. We have been able to provide new courses and to modify others so that they address current issues. Right now we are in the process of modifying a public engagement course to include a section on social media.

Most recently, we've begun to work with adjacent municipalities to negotiate what we call intermunicipal cooperation protocols as part of a collaborative governance initiative. You see, when we started the program in 1998, we were focused on the immediate need to assist municipalities through mediation to resolve immediate problems related to land use, annexation, cost sharing, etc. (we've done over 100 mediations and are still averaging about a 90 percent resolution rate). One of the things that became apparent to us was that if we could be somewhat proactive and get municipalities talking earlier, we could avoid the escalation of these disputes. We landed on the idea of creating protocols that would provide a clearly articulated process to guide intermunicipal interactions. These cooperation protocols are negotiated without the context of a specific dispute. Rather, they speak to how they will deal with each other on a day-to-day basis. They are there to frame how we are going to work with each other regarding what we do as part of our normal course of interaction. It has been a great success in that we have seen some really unique agreements come into play. Again, one of the interesting things is that the agreements that have been generated are unique to the municipalities involved and specific to their unique circumstances. We don't want municipalities to simply do carbon-copy agreements, a repeat of something another municipality has done. We are looking to them to come up with something that is really unique for them, that reflects their particular situation. They have got to live it, to breathe it—it has to be part of them if the agreement is to work over time.

We have had to push back when municipalities have asked for templates. It's going to take a lot of hard work and a lot of sitting down together to gain the understanding that will be the foundation of the agreement. This really reflects what we learned from Jane Docherty— municipalities have to understand their unique cultures and values. What makes one municipality tick and what makes another municipality tick. And with that, understanding the protocols, the agreement becomes sustainable. It has been fascinating to watch how the agreements have percolated down to the operations level as the grader driver or the public works foreman begins to think, "Hey, how is what I'm doing affecting my neighboring municipality? How can we work together at my level to improve services for both?"

Another thing, and this takes us back to Brubaker, is that we encourage municipalities to make sure the agreements are of a sufficient length, five or more years, before they have to be renewed. This allows them sufficient time to work with the agreement, and it also ensures that it will go beyond one election cycle since municipal elections are held every three years.

It's been an awesome ride. The key to it has been understanding the needs of our clients. If they didn't use our program, what would their best alternative be? The courts, an administrative tribunal? Obviously what we offer has to be better than the alternative. That means being aware of what they need from a process perspective, and in my case it means creating processes that are politically safe—recognizing that political acceptability will trump everything else when it comes to evaluating the acceptability of an agreement. At the end of the day, we have to be relevant and trustworthy, and if we are successful we will achieve our goal of providing relevant, and cost-effective conflict resolution options to Alberta's municipalities and their leaders.

Part 4
Community Development and Governance

Chapter 7
Facilitation, Ethnicity, and the Meaning of Place

Shirley Solomon

In this account of land-use and community planning in the Pacific Northwest, Shirley Solomon explores the planning issues involved in multicultural, inter-ethnic, and multigenerational settings. Such work, we see, involves not just future possibilities but the real and painful histories that inform the everyday experiences of indigenous groups and their future prospects too.

Solomon's practice story weaves together several forms of expertise as it combines sensitive analysis of land uses with careful thinking about process design. We find history and technique no less and no more important here than careful listening and respect. Where and how parties meet, for example, can be as important as any topic on their agenda. How the parties protect time to talk and listen will matter as much as the professional degrees they bring to the table. To create responsive and workable plans together, diverse stakeholders will simultaneously have to create trust and build relationships with one another.

We see here that historical, legal, and economic analysis matter along with no less practical, if complex, forms of storytelling and listening. Throughout, attachment to place matters. Place matters not for its coordinates in geographic space, but for its moral, psychological, and social coordinates: the significance that this and that place have in lived histories of this family, that tribe, these people over generations. Solomon puts this powerfully in many ways, perhaps nowhere as tersely and pointedly as when she tells us, "It's the history of the place, and it's in the recognition and the appreciation of that that reconciliation occurs. Stories have to be told in order for reconciliation to happen."

Solomon helps us to see that our planning virtually never begins from a blank slate. Parties to complex disputes—complex cases of shared opportunity—bring difficult histories full not only of feelings of being "done to," but also images of "Others" who have been the doers. Solomon asks us not so much, idealistically, to try to get the history right for once and for all, but to acknowledge that whenever planners convene stakeholders, those parties will have historically and culturally shaped images and expectations, stereotypes and presumptions of each other, as well, of course, as having animosities and fears and doubts of their own.

Solomon takes all this as a starting point, not an endpoint. She shows us how planners can work simultaneously on places and relationships, on future possibilities and historical recognition, and on newly crafted relationships and jointly produced, practical working agreements. —JF

⸎

What we were trying to do here was, again, to deal with place—place as the common denominator, place as that thing so that you would set aside some of your own personal stuff and think bigger, think more collectively around the good of the order, the good of your place.

My work has evolved from being linear to being much more circular, intuitive, and "of the heart." I discovered geography in my early 30's and developed that as a life work. I'm originally from South Africa. I have gone back periodically. It's a very difficult place, very polarized, very contentious, very ugly. Certainly much of that early experience is with me and is one of the reasons why I see bridging as being really critical to the survival of people. Finding some way to think less individualistically, less parochially, and more "bigger picture" and more "interconnected" is critical. The work here, where I have been for nine years, is as a not-for-profit, and it really does allow a degree of creativity and freedom that perhaps the fee-for-service work does not, although I did get my grounding in good solid environmental consulting. I liked that work a lot. It's much more product-oriented, much more specific, which is never a bad thing. Here we are really enabled through the philanthropic grants to see a problem and chase down the possibility of a variety of solutions. We've got a very good reputation, so we've been fortunate to have people join us in this work.

I consider myself less a mediator than a community builder. I do have the standard 40-hour mediation training. That's provided a backdrop, but I have always seen myself more in the role of an advocate for collaborative processes, an advocate for inclusive community structures, an advocate of the bridging and holistic view of things. It's a very energetic position in that there is a lot of selling of ideas, of conveying ideas back and forth, technical assistance, of ice breaking, and in a wonderful South African Zulu term, "bundu bashing," which means trailblazing.

The Swinomish Project

I want to talk about something that's loosely called the Swinomish project. There's a tribal community, 60 miles north of Seattle on the tip of an island called Fidelgo Island; it's a small reservation under 8,000 acres. There's a small number of tribal members, but they are great in spirit and heart. They have been there really, probably, forever and they are finding ways of living in this world that is quite different from the world that was theirs before white settlement. There's been white settlement all over this continent and certainly greatly in the area that they once called home. Various federal policies in the late 1800s created what was to have been their homeland forever on the south end of this island into something quite different.

Now, whereas they previously owned much land communally and even all the reservation communally for a short period of time, they now own a very small portion of their land. There's a very large number of non-Indians living on their land, both as residents and as landowners. So out of just under 8,000 acres, they probably own a fraction communally and less than half individually. That's true on the majority of the 350+ Indian reservations throughout the country. The vast majority of them were subject to the provisions of the General Allotment Act of 1887, which had as its intent the so-called civilizing of Indian people by turning them into farmers, and the government went in and carved up the communal land base. It held it in trust for a period of time, and then vast amounts of acreage passed into non-Indian ownership. The reservations were also opened up to white settlement. So it's a sad, sorry history after that, a very, very difficult history.

The legacy of that, which is what we deal with now, is this mixed land ownership on reservations and the inability of tribal governments to extend their jurisdictional control over their whole reservation because of the non-Indian residents and the incursion of county governments into the reservation by virtue of that non-Indian-held land. The tribe was much more interested in coming to grips with that jurisdictional quagmire and figured that the best way of doing that was to get into some partnership situation with Skagit County, to try to do something jointly. The county also wanted to do that.

There were subtleties here that go beyond the case, as is often true. The backdrop of federal Indian policy and law is what really governs in this situation. Federal Indian law and policy was, as many things, not a straight line. They have been very tortured and convoluted, one particular approach and then 180 degrees reverse, and then another approach. It's vacillated back and forth over time, probably every 30, 40 years in some dramatic shift, going from one thing to the next. There's just one terrible legacy left that's overlain with extreme racism and confusion and power and all sorts of different things.

One thing we know is that western civilization and by extension, western people, have little tolerance for those unlike themselves, and even less tolerance of things aboriginal. Certainly, there's an enormous amount of material that documents the efforts that were made to transform Indian people into white people: The stamping out of their religion, the stamping out of their language, the obliteration of just so many things Indian. Then there's the enduring spirit and the survival of Indian people. That is really a testament to the strength of who and what they are and the strength of their spirit, their beliefs. Their resilience is just astounding.

There's a treatise in which the author, who listened to a lot of tribal leaders from just up the way, documents the dark ages from the time of contact up through just very recently: the disease and substance abuse, the confinement on reservations, the inability to practice life the way they want, and their language disappearing, the cultural practices disappearing. But Indian people are trying to find ways to be native in the twenty-first century. Just what does that entail? And how does that play out? For our purposes, the integrity of the reservation land base is central to the survival of Indian people on their own turf.

Planning in the Shadow of the Supreme Court's *Brendale* Decision

To be a government as tribes are, one has to have a land base. To be sovereign in some undefined sense, one has to be sovereign over the land base. To be, to survive as, a land-based people, which is what aboriginal people are, they have to have a land base. The work of the tribe to extend the jurisdictional control over all the reservation and to be, in fact, the government of the reservation has been extraordinarily difficult because of various U.S. Supreme Court decisions.

The *Brendale* decision in 1989 essentially said, "Tribal government, you can have control over those parts of your reservation that look Indian and that are still Indian," without ever defining what "that" is. "And those parts of your reservation which have checkerboard land ownership and consequently have the presence of non-Indians or are owned by non-Indians, that jurisdiction will fall to the county. However, the county, in its exercise of its jurisdiction, will need to pay mind to actions which violate the integrity of tribal government and Indian people," and blah, blah, blah....

So what on earth does that mean? Who would know? One interpretation, not by one and all, but by some, is to say, "Well, what they've essentially said is that tribes and counties have to cooperate."

We started working before the *Brendale* decision. That was the premise under which the work was undertaken, that this was a mish-mash. No tribe could act unilaterally. The county certainly couldn't. We need to think about this in a collaborative sense. Hence, the cooperative problem-solving aspect of it—hence, the interjurisdictional, intergovernmental coordination/cooperation piece of it. That's the name of the game. We've done it in a million different ways, but that's the underlying work, that's the criticality of tribes controlling the reservation, the necessity for tribes to think of themselves as twenty-first century entities, not fourteenth century entities.

What does that mean? Well, it means that you do things that you wouldn't do if your land base had integrity, if these non-Indian people were not living on the reservation and owning land on the reservation. You need to think of yourself in ways that accommodate the full range of those whom you will be serving. It's very complicated and very difficult because tribes have very little money, and they depend totally and solely on the white economic development that they can muster, also on wherewithal from the feds.

The Swinomish work was one piece of a much larger project. The project idea was brought to the Northwestern Area Resources Center by one of our board members, then president of the Quinalt Indian nation, an international leader in Indian country, who said, "We've simply got to start standing on our own two feet. The only way to stand on your own two feet better is to have your own economic wherewithal. We need to have a way of extending our control over our resources, over our reservation. So, would you, Northwestern Area Resources Center, take this charge on—develop a project, get your own funding, and set forth and do this work?"

So we did. We got a small phase 1 grant from the Ford Foundation and the Northwest Area Foundation, which said just that: there seems to be a big problem here. Tribes can't do anything about it themselves because of all these other factors, and yet, they have to move forward and the world has to acknowledge that these reservations, irrespective of what happened in 1887, are Indian. They are the last vestiges of Indian land. They were promised by the federal government, by Congress, by presidents, by everybody, as being Indian. The fact that those promises were broken doesn't make any difference. These things are Indian, and those who are on the reservation need to begin to understand and acknowledge that, and everybody else needs to begin to understand and acknowledge it as well.

Also, these things cannot function as "black holes," as enclaves independent and disconnected from the state. There are ties. There are systems that need to move back and forth. So, these black curtains that have been established around these Indian land bases have got to start coming down. We've got to figure a way of linking here.

Land and Governance: Ambiguity and Safe Spaces

We worked on a number of different places. We worked on land restoration on one place, and on other sorts of things elsewhere. The Swinomish wanted to address the governance question. We did a lot of going back and forth, helping both the tribal senate and the staff figure out what they wanted to do. They knew in general terms that they wanted to extend their influence over the reservation and understood that meant reaching out to at least the county and probably other entities as well.

The county acknowledged that they had interests on the reservation, that in the pre-*Brendale* climate, they felt they wouldn't prevail in a court of law. There was just enough "grey" attending all these issues at that point in time that we could go ahead.

I like ambiguity. You can do a lot with ambiguity. My feeling is that there's no such thing as black and white anywhere. Life is in fact shades of grey. Not everybody thinks that, but I do. We worked very effectively in that grey area, suggesting to the county that the tribes had rights and interests, and that it behooved the county to get into some collaborative mode with the tribe, as a partner, not trying to prevail in a hierarchical way with the county being on top, so to speak. They were quite willing to listen. I never ever had a door slammed on me. They were reluctant to a certain extent, but reluctant only because of the appreciation that it was a volatile undertaking; it involved political risk; it would take forever; and they had no real sense of what would come of it. But they were not at all resistant to the idea of partnership.

Again, if you can create a safe place wherein people can just talk about things without it being product-driven or where there are no specific stakes, where you can just come together, talk about things, weigh some options, test out some ideas, you can do a lot.

That was really what the first phase was all about. To create that safe place, we carried messages back and forth between different people in county government and different people in tribal government. We engaged both the elected officials and the key policy staff people. One county commissioner, in particular, was willing to talk about things. The planning director was willing to talk about things. A couple of his staff people were willing to talk about things. On the other side, the general manager of the tribe and several of the senators were interested in just testing the waters and seeing what could happen.

We began laying out the premise that given the underlying land ownership pattern, no one could act unilaterally. Things were stalemated. The county had constituents on the reservation. The county felt that they had jurisdictional authority on the reservation. The tribe certainly had what they felt was jurisdictional authority. Both were essentially saying the same thing. So there was a conflict there. So these were initially very informal get-togethers, the tribal government and the county meeting face-to-face. It was people with the cloak of office. It was not as a formal get-together between two governments. It was the county commissioner and a couple of people from the tribe just playing around with notions of what could happen. We had quite a number of meetings.

Finally, they had the sense that they probably had talked through things sufficiently that they were ready to put together a Memorandum of Understanding (MOU). The MOU said that the tribe claims jurisdiction over the whole reservation, and the county claims jurisdiction over the non-Indian-owned land on the reservation. That's the way it was. They weren't going to dispute that. No one was giving up anything, but they felt that if they spent some time engaged with one another, they could, in fact, come up with something.

The Fellowship Circle Process

So what they would do was undertake an effort to look at joint comprehensive land-use planning and regulation for the reservation, in a partnership. They would set in place a planning advisory body of eight folks, four appointed by the tribe and four appointed by the county, and our Center was asked to undertake the role of chair and to provide technical staff support. They would set forth and develop a plan. It would be done through a consensus-based process. Anybody could get out whenever they wanted to with due notice. This was a one of a kind case. It's still, as near as we know, the only one that's ever been undertaken.

Tribal-county interactions are the frontier of Indian country relations and also intergovernmental coordination. The case speaks to what can happen if there are leaders on both sides and if there is a willingness to undertake those things that are, perhaps, politically volatile but that need addressing. The first phase was about a year in length and really involved conversations between those in county government and those in tribal government. The outcome of those conversations was the MOU that said, "We have things in common, and by undertaking a joint project, we will be able to develop the partnerships necessary to avert major conflict in the future."

The planning advisory body was duly constituted, worked for several years, and put together a draft plan for the Swinomish reservation that spoke to many of the issues we have talked about here. The overlay of Indianness is something that comes out and which is conserved, respected, and acknowledged.

Another MOU was developed that would administer the plan. The plan was accorded all sorts of accolades from here and there. Then, as all good things do, the thing got shelved. The State of Washington required all counties to begin a bottom-up but very comprehensive planning process that looked at resource lands, at critical lands, at all aspects of the environment, and made allocation decisions on the basis of the underlying natural world.

Skagit County was much engaged in that, and it put aside the joint reservation plan. To get things moving again in 1992, the Center was again invited to come up there and kind of "jump start" the process. At that point what we did was something that we have termed "the Skagit Fellowship Circle," which included other folk in the area. The first years of work had been just between the Swinomish and the county. The fellowship circle was designed to build support for that effort and open it up and include the two other tribes, several towns and cities, several special districts, such as ports and the public utility district, an economic development council, and a variety of others.

That particular work has gotten a great deal of publicity because of the way in which we went about it. It was not issue specific. It was designed to transform relationships and to speak to "community of place" issues. The Center initiated it, developed it, and ran it. We made a video about it after the fact, a 17-minute thing. It's just a lovely, lovely little piece. The 22 participants talk about the experience, what it meant to them, and so on.

I had thought about whom to invite in a different way, but in conversation with the project participants and those people who are sort of key players in Skagit County, we narrowed it down. I thought originally we would invite not just those concerned with government, in other words elected officials and again the key policy staff people, but also community leaders, community activists, people of influence, those who influence things in the county.

It was important to think about having all these people because I like a larger circle. I don't think everything should be vested in one particular quarter. I think that community is vested in lots of different places. I like lots of voices. I'm the lowest common denominator type, and "the more, the merrier" as far speaking out on behalf of cooperation, having an understanding for what linkages can be made.

I don't think that's a government function. We had several mayors, key policy staff people, tribal leaders, executive directors from the port and the public utility district, and other activists and community leaders. We invited them out of the county. Everybody thought that was by design, but it wasn't.

The facility that best accommodated this type of activity happened to be in the next county. People came four times over a six-month period, all day, from 9:00 in the morning until after dinner, around 8:00 o'clock at night, and did a variety of different things together, some planned, some spontaneous, some formal, some informal. But the intent was to think about their place in that place, and then their place in that place together.

The Significance of Ceremony

How did we accomplish that shift, from their place within that place to their place together? We ceremonialized the activities. To the whole concept of open space, safe space, we added sacred space. There was the whole notion of getting to higher ground. If we push our own particular agenda, if we talk about ourselves as individuals disconnected from the whole, we get into the difficulty that we're into now as a region and as a nation, I think. There's got to be a call to common purpose or to higher purpose, and what better to use as the galvanizing force or the underlying connection as your place?

If you cannot think in terms of protecting your place and of making your place better, not only for yourself but also for those who will come after you, your family, and the family of your neighbors, then…I can't think of a better connector, myself. We've done a lot of convening and gatherings, and by and large one always gets into "my view versus your view," and "my needs versus your needs."

What we did here was sweep that aside and have people talk about what that place was to me, for me, and how my life and the life of my family, both before me and after me, are in that place. I was surprised at just the history the vast majority of people had there. For instance, one county commissioner that proved to be a real leader in this effort was third or fourth generation. His people had come there as farmers way back when.

So, he felt close to the land. He characterized his feelings differently from a tribal leader, but you began to see the similarities and the common ground—or not the common ground, but the opportunity to find the common ground. I think the video we did captures it really quite beautifully, people talking to one another, and people just talking about what came out of it all for them. Anyway, so we used a talking circle, with different people opening the circle. For instance, for the very first circle, I asked one of the tribal leaders from the Swinomish to open the circle. Then, just a few minutes before the thing was to start, he disappeared.

149

Oh God, I was wondering, "Now when is he going to reappear," and so on and so forth, because I had a schedule to maintain. But he finally arrived. What he had done was to go off and find a cedar tree and take a bough from the tree, in ceremonial fashion, to use in this circle. Also, he'd found a particular rock, and he talked to people about what he did, why he did it, and what the symbolism and the significance of it all was. That really set the tone and the tenor for the initial sharing. That was then carried forward by others who used their own symbolism and used their own orientation. But we immediately created a very special space in that initial introductory event, if you want to call it that.

What you had here was essentially two worlds, two cultures. People will say though, "Well, hell, you know, I mean that's nonsense, because Indian people have been around white people for a century or more. They run their governments. Their governments look very similar to any other form of government. They know how to conduct meetings. They do Robert's rules, all these things.... What are you talking about, two worlds?"

The Challenge of Recognizing Our History in Public Processes

The fact of the matter is that an Indian world view is fundamentally different from a Western world view, and the structures that we brought with us are those that have been superimposed over Indian peoples, like it or not. Now you've got a real and pretty hefty callous that has built up. If you want to shape-shift things, if you want to shake them around and have different outcomes, then you've got to come at it differently. You've got to allow that which is not prevalent in the way we do things—you've got to allow that forward.

I also, as a woman, have had great resentment, over time, to the way in which conversation and dialogue has been just obliterated from the way in which we conduct our business. The whole relational aspect of our work has been neutered, just sterilized, I think. There's no opportunity to do anything other than speak to the topic at hand. Our public engagement processes are just criminal in my mind. A public hearing, for instance, is just an abomination because it requires people to indulge in hyperbole: You've got two minutes to speak, and you've got to be as rash as you possibly can in order to make a point. There's no opportunity for discourse.

That is what we were trying for in this fellowship circle thing: thoughtful discourse, where I had the opportunity to tell you something about me, the way I see the world, the way I think about things, and you not being in "rebut mode," where you're sitting there poised to say, "Yes, but..." or poised to use what I am saying as a way of making your own point better, but instead to really see my world, see things from the vantage point that is mine and mine alone. People on the video speak to this phenomenon.

There's one piece that just brings tears to my eyes every time I hear it. It's Jim Wilbur, who you have to sort of bend forward to hear because he doesn't articulate, he doesn't move his lips, in a way that helps you hear very easily. But what he says is, "In those meetings where it's Robert's Rules of Order, I know that I either have nothing to say, or what I have to say counts for nothing."

It just pierces me every time I hear it. That is, by and large, the world for Indian country and Indian issues. There is not the opportunity to bring forward who and what they are in totality. What you have is what is derogatorily termed, "the thousand-year speech," where an Indian person will stand up and talk about what and who they are, how they see things, what has happened to them. And people "turn off" because "the thousand-year speech" is an attempt to gain standing and status, but it's given in an environment that is unsympathetic. It's "Out of Order," so to speak. It's not part of the agenda, but it is a valiant and courageous attempt on the part of that particular Indian person, taking on the role of spokesperson, to let all these uncaring others just hear something that is different. But it's ineffective.

In our case, the intent was to get more familiar. That was the whole and sole purpose of the undertaking. How did we get people to not turn off? It involved the whole notion of collaborative learning.

There's a wonderful image. I've never seen this, but I've heard several people talk about it. There's a temple in Japan someplace that has a garden. The rocks are arranged in such a way that one has to walk all the way around in order to see every aspect of it. The principle is that no one individual could possibly know all that there is to know about anything, about this piece of art, let alone anything else. So in order for the larger truths to be revealed, all the voices that are part of whatever it may be need to be present and need to be heard.

We tried to create that mind set. When you invite people to events such as this, there's a maneuvering that goes on, and you think about who commands the most influence, and that person is invited on board first. That paves the way. That then enables others to say, "Well, alright, I'll participate." That also pulls the recalcitrants forward. So certainly out of the 22 that were there on the first day, I would suspect that there must have been a percentage of them who certainly were uncomfortable with this particular mode and also unschooled. I mean, we are not used to sitting in a dialogue situation with people. Also, and this is a very important point, out of the 22 people, 20 were men, and all 20 were middle-aged men.

So it's simply not part of their culture to be doing this; "sharing" is not a word that just rolls off many of their tongues, and especially not in rural agrarian areas. I mean, if anything, males are forced into stoic roles that may or may not be comfortable, but certainly are the prevailing personas. Seven or eight were Indian people.

Ceremony as Process Design: Beyond Argument to Dialogue

Why the ceremonial aspect of it? Think about a council meeting. Think about any of the governmental meetings that you go to, just how it's a slam-bam sort of thing. It's all left-brain stuff, and I object to that because I really don't think much of what we are about nowadays lends itself all that well to the bashing of the gavel and the speed-up of the operation. Certainly there's a place for that, but I think we also need to be carving out time to approach these questions in a different aura.

I for years have been focused on "product" and kind of moving through things and getting things accomplished and that sort of thing, so I've come to understand that, in many ways, what we've produced has been certainly quite creative and innovative, but there's a bloodless aspect to it. What I'm much more engaged in now is the transformative part of conflict resolution, or conflict management—it's not resolution. You never resolve it, but you manage it, and you manage it in a creative way.

You manage it in a way that allows it to be an opportunity as opposed to something polarizing. And in these sorts of longstanding conflicts, reconciliation is a piece of it. Your heart has not opened if you have not been able to acknowledge the past, acknowledge past history. You need to be able to say what needs to be said.

I've worked on these issues for a long time, but people say to me, "Well, hell, what are you talking about? I mean, that wasn't me. That wasn't even my ancestor."

But that begs the question. There's a cosmic responsibility that operates, and without assuming reparation, or anything like that, there is an acknowledgement that, if it is freely given and freely received, it transforms things and moves things to a different plane. You know when you see it happen. It happened in this group.

There's the prescriptive approach, where you go in with your process, and there's the elicitive one where you're the catalyst for something magical happening that is not of your doing, that you cannot claim responsibility or the praise for, and that's elicitive, where something bigger than all of you gets touched, and something new emerges.

We hit a point in the project where things were not going that well. Things were stalled. We were thinking about ways of getting things back moving and back on track again. We had some experience with relationship-building efforts and wanted to test out some of our ideas up in Skagit with "place" as the connector, the assumption being that people could find common ground in the place they lived more easily than perhaps on some bigger public policy issue. As the organizer, I was talking to different people and saying, "Things seem to be stuck again. Do you think there would be some benefit to coming together, to get to know one another better, to find opportunities for collaboration, for breaking the deadlock that seems to be surrounding you all?" There was very definitely an interest.

Convening a Four-Day Circle Process

Something that made a real difference was having a new county commissioner. Someone who was of the area, second or third generation of the area, a farmer, and very outgoing and who really felt that something like this would be a good thing, and that if it didn't achieve great things, there was very little to be lost. We said to them all, "You are all in this place together. Very clearly, there are a variety of things that are short term, and certainly some longer-term issues, that need to be addressed in a collaborative way, that you, the county, cannot do unilaterally and that you, tribes, cannot do unilaterally, or anybody else for that matter."

We said that the way of the future was to think about this in a collective fashion. Then there was concurrence with that notion and a real interest in everybody getting together to figure out how to work together more effectively. So then we designed the four meetings to help accomplish that, to help think about the sorts of things that you would want to do.

The first day was really laying the foundation for getting to know one another and a variety of formal and informal activities around that. The second day was to just develop a better understanding of differences, cultural and otherwise, communication styles, ways of addressing conflict, value differences, lots of different things around that. The third day was about trying to use the differences creatively in thinking about bridging differences. Then the fourth session was pulling it all together. In the third session, we looked at what was the unifying force: the river, and the resources of the river. The river was a foundation for what we called creative dialogue—building common ground and developing common understanding.

The sessions were very open ended. We were really creating a setting in which certain activities could occur and dialogues could begin. There was no preordained outcome. We were not going for a settlement on intragovernmental cooperation on solid waste management. We were not going for an MOU about growth management or any of those things. It was really very elicitive, I suppose—it was not prescriptive in any form or fashion. There was a setting created, and there were certain activities that were quite rigidly managed, but at no time did we have any sense of what the outcome would be. For some people, it was not tangible enough. It was quite difficult for some to go through it, inasmuch as it was so loose and open ended—or it was perceived to be loose and open ended.

The fact is that we were talking about the natural resources of Skagit County. We were talking about the land, the fish, the physical attributes of their shared place, and the fact that as a farmer you viewed those resources in one way, whereas as an Indian fisherman you would view those resources in another way. As a fifth generation individual, you would view those resources in yet another way. We were bringing together all those truths into a larger mosaic.

In contrast, traditional mediation is very prescriptive. You're there for a very set outcome. You are there to negotiate the delivery of a service or a particular regulation that needs to accommodate certain needs or principles, and you follow a set of ground rules or guidelines.

This was much different. This was an agreement to come together and talk about those things that were at the root of things, the values, the way in which individuals see their place and themselves in that place. We talked a bit about the opening circle and the ceremony aspects of that meeting, and of people sharing their stories. Anytime you set out to ceremonialize something, you've got to be inordinately cautious because if you take a ceremony of another group, then you risk the danger, as we have in the past, of being open to charges of "appropriation" or "misappropriation."

What we did do, ahead of time, is send out just a three-paragraph piece that talks about a listening or talking circle, that characterizes it as a communication technique. We just introduced that to people and said that we will, in all likelihood, use a communication technique like this one in order for all the voices to be brought forward, in order for a setting to be created that allows people to speak.

What that tribal councilman did, by getting the bough of cedar and the rock in response to my request, was one of those unforeseeables that in this instance was just breathtaking in it's symbolism, I suppose. It was quite unexpected and not programmed in at all, but it elevated that circle from a communication technique to something of tremendous value. To say I hadn't planned it misrepresents it as well because I have been in those circumstances where something takes hold of the group—it is a different life force. It's a different energy. It's something that everybody wants to achieve and it's—well, grace descends, OK? When it descends, you give thanks for it. You cannot program it in.

This is not "New Age" hype. It's not all the things that we disparage about that. There's truth here, and people who have been in those places know that truth, and when one begins to talk about those sorts of things you immediately strike a chord because that is what makes the difference. It shifts things, and then in the shifting there's got to be somebody who then takes the ball and runs with it—so that you've achieved something. It's not just a personal or a cosmic shift—it counts for something. It's translated into X number of feet of shoreline saved, or X more fish in the stream. It's the translation that's important.

It's not just a group of people achieving a personal, interpersonal, or collective breakthrough, but it's the end that counts: What do we do with it? Perhaps even more importantly, how do we sustain it? Because you can have that feeling, but as we've written extensively on this, old habits die hard, the wounds attend —these issues are huge. The pain is great, and one nice experience does not change this world I suppose. So we set the sessions up. We said, "O.K., this thing is going to be a little different, guys. We're not going to talk about 'Who did what to whom?' We're not going to talk about the development over the hill there and all the prescriptions that need to occur in order for that thing to be. We're not going to talk specifics. We're going to talk about more amorphous sorts of things."

Taking Time to Remember, to Reconstruct Histories, and to Listen

The structure was particularly good in the way we did it. We gave them plenty of time. We set the stage, and then we set the stage, and then we set the stage again. We made it quite clear what we would talk about and what this thing would be. We were not there to resolve all the multitude of problems and issues that were waiting for us outside the door. What we were trying to do here was lay some groundwork, create an opportunity for some relationships to evolve that would enable us when we opened the door to be better equipped to face the world, so to speak. All the days went from 10:00 to 7:30 or 8:00. Long days!

The setting was quite idyllic, very comfortable, rural, quiet, no telephones. We had to drive a distance to get there. When you were there, you were there. There was a large room with lots of windows, a very nice open deck. The weather was always good, so we sat in the large communal space. There were comfortable chairs, and this for me was very important. You've got to get comfortable. There's got to be a comfort factor, a safety factor where there's not a lot of outside activity occurring, where you're not bumping into people as you go to the bathroom. The bank of phones isn't there for you to make your way to. In fact, people had to take their beepers off and all that stuff because you couldn't have called anyway. There was one phone, and it often got locked up.

But the morning light, the light in the room was a factor. There was wildlife that would sort come out of the woods, and people would stop what they were doing and get up to the window and take a look at that. We had caterers coming in, very nice people from the town that the group felt very comfortable with as time went on. The food was very good. So creature comforts were attended to. At lunchtime, people served themselves and then just sat at will. Most sat outside on the deck and on the steps. Then each time before lunch, we would say all right, take a walk. Take X amount of time and pick somebody you don't know. Pick someone that you've had difficulty with. We just gave them different instructions to how to mix and mingle. We did that for the first couple of times, and then we didn't do it for the last two times. So we were being fairly directive in certain things. I set it up that way. "I will be suggesting certain things to you, and you can take the suggestion or not, but in other things I will make a suggestion, and I will expect you to go along with it."

They were very responsive. Let me go through the first day. The afternoon was just a very fine time. We had two presenters, as I've said, just to talk about creating a sense of place. I wanted to help people understand that that place has been occupied by Indian people for time immemorial: lots and lots and lots and lots and lots and lots of generations have been there and have lived there very differently from the way it was now being lived in.

We invited an archaeologist who has worked with all three tribes for a very long time to talk about the place that was. She took us on an imaginary canoe trip, a trade trip from a place that is now named the Skagit River and across the mountains to a lake on the east side of the Cascades. She talked about what that would have been like in 1520 or so and talked about what an experience like that would have been. It would have been a family that set off in a number of boats. She was just spellbinding. We had lots of props and maps of different scales.

From the way people asked questions, you could just see that it was mesmerizing, with people becoming engaged in that story and beginning to think about what life was like there for those people. But the whole thing needs caution. You've got to be really careful. You have to look for certain people to make these presentations: people without baggage. It certainly cannot be someone who has been in conflict with some of the participants at the time. It's very delicate because, again, you're dealing with a great power imbalance, great loss, great change, guilt, fury—lots of things. I mean there's a cauldron under this that you're trying to help release in a way that doesn't just blow you all to hell but starts the siphoning off of all this torture and pain. We had the professor that came from the community college in the area talk about, "And then the settlers came." So it was historical. The one talk was prehistory and the other was history. So he talked about white settlement and what and how it occurred. But his manner was just a little more abrasive, so he was harder to deal with for the participants.

But the story he told is a story that needs to be told. When white settlement occurred, the environment of Skagit County changed dramatically. There had been spruce marshes and cedar marshes, and all those ancient, ancient, ancient trees got cut down, and the area was drained and diked, and it became farmland. That brought prosperity to those who moved in and usurped Indian land, and it brought extreme dislocation to those who were displaced. That's a story that needs to be conveyed. It needs to come out. It's the history of the place, and it's in the recognition and the appreciation of that that reconciliation occurs. Stories have to be told in order for reconciliation to happen.

So, the objective of this was to create a dialogue and a sense of community that would move forward the way that people did governance together. This happened on the first of four days, in the first of four activities—to get familiar with one another, to learn something about one another as individuals, and then learn something about your place within this place—because your place in a place is quite different from what you think it is. Everybody's perspective of place is quite different.

One thing just to keep in mind is that while all this is interpersonal, it is also with the cloak of office that these people came to get together. They did not come as individuals. They came as county commissioners, tribal leaders, planning directors, and the like—but appreciating that it is an individual who holds office, and that it is individuals who create organizations, and that individual relationships really matter. But what we were trying to do here was, again, to deal with "place"—place as the common denominator, place as that thing so that you would set aside some of your own personal stuff and think bigger, think more collectively around the good of the order, the good of your place.

So the last piece of the first day set the stage for the "personal." The presentations had created a sense of place, a prehistory, and a history. Then we had the personal stories: How I came to be at this place, and what this place is to me. We structured that around slides. We brought a couple of carousels of slides in; we had asked people to bring a slide or two or three, or however many of something that would speak to either, "This how I came to be in this place" or "What this place means to me." Some people brought slides. We interspersed them. We took pains to make slides that spoke to the full range of experience.

We used a lot of historical slides. There's a historical society in Skagit County that's put out several books. We took pictures out of those books. It took a tremendous amount of time and energy thinking through what we know about people, what we know about the place, and what we were trying to bring forward.

So we put together this carousel and ran it through a number of times and thought about, "If you were so-and-so, what would you see when you looked at this slide?" We said, "OK, here are images. Some of them will speak to you. Some of them won't. But just talk about what you're seeing, what you're feeling, what story it evokes for you, what questions you may have, so on and so forth. So here's this carousel."

So up the slides went. We'd just hold the slide and start asking questions: "What does this evoke? What is this of? Do you have any relationship to whatever's being portrayed there?"

That was just a tremendous session. We scheduled it for a couple of hours, and it just went on and on and on and on, and was just wonderful—very painful, very funny, very revealing, lots of things. I've got lots of stories just about the "where" and "what" of that.

One particular story was about an Indian family in the hops field. One of the kids had what looked like a uniform on. They weren't getting a whole lot out of the slide, but I knew this slide was an important one. I said, "You know, that uniform looks very much like the uniform that I wore when I was in boarding school at the convent. I wonder what that kid's story is?" And we just got talking about what the boarding school experience had been like. That led to just an enormous amount of very, very painful information—not my own, somebody else's. I just asked the question, but then someone was telling about the Indian boarding school experience. It was priming the pump on my part, but I knew those stories were in there. I know those stories need to come out. So what did I need to do in order to help that story come along? I needed to ask the question, to put the image up, to say, "I think there's something here, what is it? From my perspective, I wore a uniform like that. Is there anything here?"

What makes the difference here, and I don't know how this translates into replication elsewhere, is that I know these people very, very well, especially the Indian people. I know them. I know their stories. They have shared things with me that they would not want the full story told. They can at least say a few words about what the boarding school experience was like, about what it really did, and not only the boarding school experience, but also what that time period was like in the lives of their families. You begin to get the feel of the huge loss that occurred at that time when you hear their stories because that was when their language was stamped out. That's when many of their religious practices were no more. There were big-time dislocations.

Social Learning and Recognition

There was a lot of opportunity for questions after the stories. "What was that like?" "I don't know anything about that." "What happened?" So there was a sort of social learning and collective sharing and the opportunity to bear witness to what had happened. There was the necessity for those who are of the group that hold the greatest power to sit in place and be with this. Most times, it was, "Oh well, it wasn't my people." Or, "Oh well, it wasn't me." Or, "Oh well, I just moved here." Well, that's true, but that's not the story. That's not the history of it. This is part of who these people are, and irrespective or whether it was you, your ancestors, or somebody else entirely, it's part of their story in this place. It's part of the ethos of this place. I mean it's what this place is all about.

Did I meet with resistance from anyone who just didn't want to hear all this? I have in other circles. But in this one, the time was right. The place was right. The people were right. It was just organic, and it just happened. It just filled the space. It just went real well. But if somebody's just sitting there, arms folded, pushed away from the table, not really looking or listening what do I do? I call it. "Let's call time out. What I'm seeing is an effect that's counter to what we're hoping to achieve here, and there's a tremendous amount of pain and sorrow, and there's resistance to that. What going on?" In that way, we're asking people to take responsibility for what they feel, to step up to what is going on inside them. "If something's happening that you're uncomfortable with, then essentially stop the show, and say, 'This is more than I can deal with here'."

Dealing with resistance is an equal-time thing as much as anything else. What you're hearing is one person's experience. The setting and the forum are not designed to debate issues or to change opinions on things, but really just to get a feel and a sense for somebody else's experience. It's a gift. It's a window into somebody else's life, how they do things, what has happened to them, how they've processed it. In most instances, what's done is that one calls a time out and speaks with the person individually to see if there's some way of moving things forward, or you just ask the person to sit with it for a while. We've had a couple of times where it's just badly degenerated.

Sometimes we've been able to pull it back up, and sometimes we haven't. Sometimes members of the group help and just ask the person to hold their critique at bay for a while and just roll with it, just to see how things go. We had a circumstance once where we invited someone with tribal affiliations, but not connections to any Washington State tribe, to act as the circle keeper. That was a hideously bad mistake. That blew up and was highly unpleasant. We weren't really able to pick up the pieces. We had to change the whole format. So it can be really quite disruptive.

The second meeting was "skills development," a standard skills development workshop. We talked about communication, cross-cultural communication, conflict communication, and we did small group exercises. So it was all skill development stuff, trying to help people understand where their differences would lie, where they would manifest themselves, and how to prepare to be attentive in a way that bridged and worked around it.

We took a number of different articles, and breaking people into smaller groups, we asked them to work at using some of the cross-cultural communications and conflict communications skills. We said, "Take the articles and then read them and talk about them, and figure out how you would come at these things a little differently on the basis of what you had just learned." We'd collected some really splendid stuff, and I just liked the idea of using, for instance, a Newsweek article, "Why We All Love to Hate," about the ethnic polarities and what has continued to feed our long held likes and dislikes, and has kept all the stereotypes in place, and how when you sit down with people and begin the humanizing process, it's really bloody hard to continue to demonize and to keep people in the "us and them" mode. It's just very interesting to use other examples. So they read these articles, and we asked questions: "What comes up for you?" "What do you learn from this?" "How did it play out in any experience of yours?"

Here's another small group exercise we put people through: "Select some personal experience, cross-cultural, work-related, difficult, uncomfortable, that had an undesirable outcome. Think about and describe the context, the circumstances, and the outcome. How did you feel? How did you behave? Analyze that experience looking at your communications style and the assumptions that you made based on the skills development stuff that we put people through. Look at your communication style. What could you have done differently?"

In many ways what you find out is that some of the assumptions you make are really fallacious and are based on a stereotype that you have of, say, a tribal government or an Indian person, and are also based on the stories that have been built up around various historical interactions. For example, the Skagit County planning department has never been able to penetrate the Swinomish planning department. You know, "They always hire people who are Indian advocates and, you know, blah, blah, blah." There were plenty of those sorts of stories. So this was an opportunity to begin to share: "Three years ago when I tried to do this, this, this, and this, I didn't like the way I behaved. I didn't like the way the outcome was, and had I known this, this, this, and this, I would perhaps have thought about it differently. Had I been better equipped to understand my conflict, my style of conflict management, and my communication style, I may have been able to frame an interaction that would have had very different results."

But there's more than skills building going on. Certainly, people were able to talk about past experiences. What they wound up saying was, "Knowing what I know now, I know now more than I knew four years ago, certainly. Had I had that information, we could have strategized internally and handled X, Y, Z situations somewhat differently. There are some tenets that I can carry forward and that I can start institutionalizing."

That was, in fact, what people did, and said, "You know, I can think about these things in a slightly different way. Not only as far as we here go, but in general terms, these are universals. These are problems the whole world is having, and they have their roots in this, that, and the next thing, and they are maintained by all these different things. But if I want to be able to work with you, and if we want to be able to clean up Skagit Bay, or if we want to be able to get that new road in, or whatever it is, then we better strategize and figure out some institutional approach here that accommodates and attends to and addresses all these potentially polarizing circumstances."

Reconciliation and Fundamental Differences

So, there are different things going on, on different tracks. You've got 20-some people, very different styles and levels of awareness and position. Everybody's not tracking in the same way, and reconciliation is something that takes a lifetime. What we were trying to do here was pierce the skin, the crust that holds everything at the status quo. It's like a pie really where you have to break the crust to relieve the pressure. Some steam comes and so on and so forth, but you also want some left, so that there's some dynamic energy.

There's no reconciling the differences that attend these issues. They are fundamental differences, and no matter how many times you sit in circles, no matter how many times you experience greater understanding and transformation, the fact of the matter is that I see things fundamentally differently from the way an Indian person sees things. I always will because I am not an Indian person. But now, what we are trying to do throughout the course of this is to find an overlap where we are identifying commonality, where there are places that there is an overlay of interests, and where we can start small. We're trying to do this "crawl, then walk, before you run" routine where you're developing some habit of working together in a different way, where you begin to see the opportunities that collaboration may offer.

A lot of this is just done on "a wish and a prayer" because you're looking at truly different orientations toward, certainly, their use of resources. There's an onslaught in the form of all this growth that's occurring that does not cease to be and has the weight of law behind it, since the law is permissive: people are allowed to do this.

I suppose this is no different from anything else. I've heard teachers say that if you reach one kid a year and that kid goes on and does remarkable things, then over the course of your career you will have done something. The problem that I always have—and this is a personal problem—is that I just don't know if that's going to be enough, if it's fast enough, if it's enough to conserve the resources because the resource loss is happening at an accelerated pace. In most instances, that is where there's criticism of this sort of approach, not the circle approach, but the slower, plodding approach. That's where people get tired of it and go back to the power play in the legislature and the mode that we know best, which is power politics. It's because the loss is at this accelerated rate. I don't know the answer to this. I know that we're experimenting, and that in the experimentation we seem to have discovered or unearthed something that has some merit. That's really about the most hopeful one can be. We're not looking for a cure. We're not looking for an antidote. We're looking for something to change the way we are in this place, this place being this whole universe of ours. But that really is quite presumptuous.

County Planning Challenges

The third day consisted of talk about all sorts of aspects of the particulars of Skagit County from, again, the different perspectives. It was quite directive in some instances, having free-flowing conversation some and then more facilitated conversation so that you're essentially being asked to think about specific issues and to think about how to talk about those issues in ways that press things forward. We asked them to be mindful of time constraints and how to get the most out of discussion, how to put forward your issues in a way that enables others to better hear and to better address them, and then in ways that sift out common concerns and common ground.

The newspaper, the *Skagit Valley Herald*, at that time had put out a series on the river. So we used that as the basis for discussion and made it quite clear that we were not there to discuss or to focus on solving anything, but rather to provide a focus whereby people could talk about the issues, their issues, and their concerns about the river.

We were coming at it from a number of different perspectives and then trying to build a "bigger truth," if you will. We had a hell of a lot of trouble that day. It just went quite poorly for part of the day. Part of it was that someone that we had invited in as a process person put together a role play, and what she came up with just didn't fit. It didn't fit right. Several of the people couldn't get into it because they just wanted to be themselves. They wanted to talk about their perspectives, their issues from their perspectives, and to represent themselves. So we labored and loped and had just a very difficult time and finally, we stopped that and got into, "You as you," and "You as who and what you are," and talking about your issues as opposed to taking these roles.

How did we realize that something was wrong? There's a feel out of a group. You know all the nonverbals, all the weird energy that starts coming up. You lose people. They get up. They walk around. They shake their heads. They do all the things that you'd never want to see your group doing. It was an excruciatingly difficult time; what I did was that I just took the group back, I guess.

It was awful. It was a very delicate thing. What I felt I had to do was to redirect the group. But the only way I could redirect the group was to take charge of the group, and in doing so, we had to pass the baton from one facilitator to the other and do it in a way that was affirming in some way.

All this is experimentation, and it's not like there's a prescription or a cookbook, and you're following it, and it all goes the way it should go. You try to think of how it will go and try to plan on, "If this happens, then I'll do that. If that happens, this is how I'll do it." But I don't know how other people do it. I run it through in my mind. I know these people, so I have a clue of who's going to do what and where, where the hot spot will be, where the good energy will be and how to help it. The role playing just was not the right technique to use because all these people were very much engaged in these issues, and it's passionate for them. They learned not at all from having to take the other's role. For instance, the Swinomish general manager was asked to be a developer. He just didn't want to be a developer, you know. So he tried to do it for a while, and then just got aggravated with it. One of the tribal leaders never got it, couldn't get into it, and just couldn't believe he wasn't able to represent who he was himself, you know?

Beginning Again

So, then we switched gears and moved it to them talking from their hearts, from where they really were at. We started to really get to some of the things that they felt they should be doing together. What we wound up doing was still talking about the river, but talking about it from people's experience with specific issues they wanted to think about and talk about, including the river, from their perspective.

From there, it got bigger. What they wound up doing was exactly what we had hoped they would do, and that was start bringing it down to the ground. What opportunities were there to be more collaborative? What were the specific things that they needed to begin to work on because, not only were there opportunities there, but also things that could really cause great difficulty if they did not come together.

One of the participants, in time for the third meeting, sent what he called a "found poem." He was looking through the meeting notes. I'm struck by the scene: "With a little sorting and not much thought, I put together a found poem." I think the poem contains at least one comment from each participant with a little minor editing. It's a beautiful, beautiful thing, and everybody's voice is represented in this "found poem" that he offered to the circle.

Actually he used this as the opening to the third meeting circle. Drawing on the meeting notes from the first and second meeting, he put this together and then used this as his tool to open the circle. We used the talking circle, the talking/listening circle as the so-called communication device, to open each of these events. The second time somebody else had done it and brought something of consequence to him.

Then this person did it the third time with this poem. There were a lot of good opportunities there. It was just, "You know, I've always thought that we would be able to do blah, blah, blah together." "I've always wished that we could think about the road culverts in a way that facilitated fish passage." "I've had a difficulty with this, that, and the next thing." "Do you remember the big brouhaha we had a few years ago?" "Well, you know, if we'd had this and this in play...."

Enduring Differences, Recognizing Opportunities for Collaboration

I think people also understood that there was no requirement that the county and the tribe get into lock step over anything. They understood that there are differences that are enduring differences, and that there are differences that make not a whit of difference to collaborative endeavors.

But it's finding those places that are potential hotspots or are fertile opportunities for collaboration. We had to figure out what to do in those instances where they may be problems. It could be something as simple as, "Don't ever go off half-cocked over something. Always check-in with your counterparts, or with others, to find out what the specifics are. Do not accept on face value what you read in the newspaper, what you hear from people, but rather get to a reasonable fact set before you decide on what it is you need to do." Many, many, many opportunities came as a result of that one particular day.

Then the last day was, "OK what are we going to do now?" talking about the different resource protection processes that they could address, golden tenets of resource protection. What would they like to see as an outcome of the circle, what tangible sorts of things? We got down to the details, and then they went off and came up with that open letter that is just a lovely, lovely thing that talks about what a wonderful thing got set in motion here and how they want to maintain it, and they want others to join them. That was not planned. And then the resolutions were not planned.

A great deal of cohesion came out of it. In hindsight, I would have continued to staff it in a more substantive way if I'd understood how fragile all this stuff was. I think you've got to nurture and squire and nurture and squire, maybe forever, you know? It's not that people are reluctant. It's that there are too many other things on the front of the plate. It's also atypical behavior; it's not institutionalized behavior this way. But no one is reluctant. It's just not their mode. It was as if people felt "create the setting, and I'll come"—that kind of thing.

I had hoped for a concurrence in which they would continue with the process and agree to meet, agree to do some things, and then meet in the future. What they wound up doing was writing an open letter to the community, and, first, one mayor, and then another city person, and then the county, offered a resolution acknowledging the tribe as the rightful government and pledging a cooperative mode of dealing and being. I never would have thought of that. It was far, far beyond what I would have hoped for. It was bigger than anything I would have hoped for. Then there was just talking about very concrete things that they would want to do with one another in the interim. It's made a difference to intragovernmental carryings-on in Skagit County. I mean, it's one of those events that stands tall.

I've been at the Center now for nine years. When I first came here, it was much more "agreement driven"—we were much more into schedules and tasks and getting from point A to point B in the straightest line possible. With the Swinomish joint plan, we had been fairly creative, introducing a notion of the reservation as Indian Homeland in language that was very clear and explicit in the plan. That was not done before. We realized technical solutions could very well be applied, but they weren't. Certainly, for social and political reasons, things weren't happening the way they should happen. What was needed was to look at the underlying issues and somehow find a way to begin to reconcile the history. It came about slowly, and the Swinomish work was the second circle I had gathered.

What I had tried to develop over the years of doing this work was a number of different tools and techniques. Some problems yield to an MOU, but others need something different. Certainly in the State of Washington, we have been playing with collaborative processes for quite some time. In some cases, they achieve what they need to achieve, and in others they don't. When they fail, it's because the underlying relationships have not been established in a way that allows a variety of different things to continue—in some instances, not even the letter of the agreement.

So what does one do in order to transform things? Well, from my standpoint, what you do is unleash the energy between people who live together. There's a tremendous cost in conflict. Sometimes it's not overt and not open conflict. Sometimes it's just a very latent hostility. Sometimes it's just a blockage of some sort where this group doesn't speak to that group or where there is a polarization. But there's energy involved in keeping that in place, and if one can use that energy in positive and constructive ways, and if you can leverage opportunity, it seems to me that you can get a hell of a lot more done. That's the premise under which we operate for the circle. The purpose of the circles was to set the stage in a way that allowed new things to happen, to set it so it was open, and safe, and finally sacred.

Can I say more about that? I'll tell a personal story. I'm going through some fairly major changes here at work. We're undergoing a strategic planning process that's very task oriented. What I'm finding is that I'm unable to stay to task. The reason I'm unable to stay to task is that underlying issues are not being addressed adequately. There's a role reversal that takes place, and I see people who I've worked with in group, that I have tried to keep to task, and they have been unable to stay because there's all this underlying stuff that just hasn't been adequately spoken to. But I have a bias. My bias is that if you don't take care of all this stuff, it comes up and catches you time and time again at times when you least expect it.

Then, if we go through the political deal making that attends so much of the mediation that I have been exposed to, all you're doing is band-aiding the stuff again. It's a power play and you're herding and corralling and co-opting and doing all the stuff that I no longer want to be a part of. But the fellowship circle and the transformative sort of work is to me a way of attending to the needs of the future by healing the wounds of the past and by releasing all the energy that has gone to attending to individual pain or collective grief or to power politics or to the Alinsky style of organizing, which I certainly have followed for much of my career. But these are such huge issues that speak to hierarchical, patriarchal systems that really are entrenched and that hold the power and assert an energy that will eventually spin us into oblivion, I believe.

Afterword

In reviewing the profile, I am struck by the optimism and the sense of the possibility of progress in that earlier time. And I am taken by the innovation of the tools and techniques that we put to use. But I have been sobered in the intervening years and now recognize that the fundamental change we sought to institutionalize occurs slowly and unevenly, and requires constant nurturing and vigilance.

My further thoughts on the matter are well represented in my chapter "Salmon Is Coming for My Heart: Hearing All the Voices" in *Across the Great Divide: Explorations in Collaborative Conservation in the American West* (Island Press, 2001).

Chapter 8
Collaborative Civic Design in Chelsea, Massachusetts

Susan Podziba

Imagine that your community goes into bankruptcy and that the state government, in a moment of surprising clarity and imagination—and perhaps also wisdom—decides not simply to ask a prestigious law firm to help to draft a new city charter to set things right, but also asks you to convene and to manage a bottom-up process in the city to rewrite that city charter. This was, indeed, the situation in Chelsea, Massachusetts, in which Susan Podziba, a recent planning department graduate from the Massachusetts Institute of Technology, found herself. Maybe this task would be perfectly clear to you, but more likely you might very well wonder where and how to begin, and how then to manage and carry through a job of this scope.

You'd have no blank slate with which to begin, but rather a history of mismanagement and varying competences in city administration. You'd have to think carefully about who to involve and how to involve them, even if—or because—you'd soon find out that many different stakeholders have even more different ideas about who's to blame for the city's past troubles. Of course, the past mayoral candidates have their forcefully argued explanations for what's gone wrong. But your job, you remember, is not to act as judge or jury, not to figure out who's guilty and who isn't, but the more practical task of helping the city and various stakeholders "from the bottom-up" to write a new, improved, workable, sustainable city charter. Your job requires you to work with local stakeholders not so much to look backwards but to look forwards, not so much to judge the past as to create a legal and political framework for the city's future.

So you'll need lawyers, and you'll need politicians, and you'll need a diversity of community representatives. How will you choose them? That's still near your beginning, for once you've assembled representatives who, you hope, will be willing and able to serve, what will you do then? How will you design a process, or parallel processes, that will help them focus on the problems they need to tackle, learn what they need to figure out, make the decisions they will need to make, and more?

Should all these questions not seem so simple and actionable to you, you'll be pleased and intrigued to read what Susan Podziba did to handle these problems, to do this job. Readers in Italy have found this story of community renewal, development, and governance so compelling that they've produced a book about it. Now you can see for yourself. —JF

～ల≫ల～

In the early days of mediation everything felt magical because it was as
if in these situations that were so stuck, with just a couple of questions,
you just opened it all up.

I studied philosophy as an undergraduate at the University of Pennsylvania. At the time, I didn't really think about future job opportunities; I studied philosophy because I loved it. I graduated in 1982, during a recession, and it was a difficult time to look for a job. Once a guy interviewing me said he'd called me in just to see what a philosophy major looked like!

During this period of flux for me, a friend of mine heard Larry Susskind, an MIT professor, speak about environmental mediation at a conference in Boston. When he got back to Philadelphia, he told me he'd found the field I'd been looking for. He was sure that I was meant to be a mediator. When a major dispute broke out at our food co-op, my friend, Scott, asked me to mediate it. I resisted because I had not done anything remotely public since I had stopped working with the peace movement.

I had led a student peace organization at the University of Pennsylvania. We had a few hundred members. In those days, I had a really strong fear of nuclear war. There was an organization at the time that would periodically announce in response to political events how many minutes we were to "midnight," which was the time of our mutually assured destruction.

At that time, I was studying with Professor Philip Rieff, a Freudian sociologist. He forced me to question everything about myself, and especially, my political work. He was very severe. He posed incisive questions that I found very hard to answer. I rejected his assertion that I was responsible not only for my own decisions but for those of people I influenced. He persisted, and I got very scared when he forced me to confront my responsibilities as a leader. I dropped out of the movement; I just stopped doing the peace work.

I had realized that I didn't have enough of a foundation. I passed off the leadership to somebody else because I didn't have answers to the questions Rieff was posing to me. I knew that I didn't know enough. In my mind I kept hearing a line from a Bob Dylan song: "I'll know my song well before I start singing."

I threw myself into studying philosophy. I just read. That's all I did. For a while I didn't even have a telephone. I read mostly Plato. I also read a lot of Nietzsche and Hobbes. I did all the reading in an attempt to forge my picture of the world.

When I couldn't find a job after graduation—really, I didn't know what I wanted to be—I went out to Eugene, Oregon, to play semi-professional ultimate Frisbee. My friend and I did odd jobs, like picking cauliflower and waitressing at ladies' garden parties, to support ourselves. After the season, I moved back to Philadelphia.

By then I hadn't done anything publicly for about four years. I wasn't keen to mediate the co-op dispute when Scott first asked. I still was reluctant to take any kind of public action. But Scott did a wise thing. He suggested I co-mediate with a woman I greatly respected. Of course at the time, we didn't know what these terms even meant. We had no connection to the field of mediation, except that Scott had met Larry at a conference. Still, Scott convinced me to give it a try.

We mediated and resolved all the issues in a single meeting. There were 12 staff members, six board members, and the wife of a controversial staff member present. It was an incredible experience. We talked to people and helped people say what was on their minds. We got people to understand what others were saying and perceiving. And for me something clicked—I knew mediation was the field I had been looking for.

I had done something in the room that led to an agreement that settled a really bad situation. People came up to me afterwards and said, "That looked like a dance." It had felt like a dance. It felt bigger than me. When people said, "It looked like a dance," I understood that to mean that I was taking in and responding to the energies in the room in certain ways, protecting certain things at different times— just being in a very natural flow with the situation.

But I wasn't quite sure how to begin doing it professionally. At the time, I was working in the University of Pennsylvania Religious Studies Department for a visiting professor from Israel. We were cataloging Sinai inscriptions, and he was plotting the paths of different pilgrimages through time, based on the graffiti and mosquitoes around wells and things like that.

About a month before the co-op mediation, he had asked me to go to Israel for a year to continue the work there. As planned, I went, but after two months the grant ran out. I had an open plane ticket and an apartment, and I'd planned on being there for a year. So the big question was, "What am I going to do now?"

Divorce, Custody, and Maintenance: Mediation in Israel

Then I saw a tiny ad in the *Jerusalem Post* about divorce mediation. In Israel, divorce is complicated because family law follows Talmudic law, which states that a husband is required to give his wife a writ of divorce called a "get," and a woman is obligated to accept it. But sometimes one of the parties refuses. Usually, the man refuses to give the wife the "get," and then there's nothing she can do. The organization I eventually worked for started as an advocacy group for "stuck women." They did things like hold demonstrations at recalcitrant husbands' places of work to pressure them into giving their wives a get.

After studying some Talmudic Law and working with some of the organization's social workers, they gave me cases of my own, mediating divorces. I didn't really have any formal mediation training yet. We mediated custody and maintenance issues.

In those cases we started by trying to set up an initial meeting with both the husband and wife. Some of these people were separated for years and years. One party was just a holdout. I'd talk to the wife first because she was usually the one that would come to the agency, and then I'd call the husband and say, "Your wife was here. She wants the get, but we need to hear your side of the story."

The husband would say, "Well, didn't my wife tell you the story?"

I would say, "Well, we heard from your wife, but we need to hear from you in order to get a complete picture." Those were magic words to some of these men. Allowing them to talk and legitimizing their hurt often made them willing to come to a meeting, and eventually to give the wife the get. In the early days of mediation, everything felt magical, because it was as if in these situations that were so stuck, with just a couple of questions, you just opened it all up.

In one situation, a man kept changing his mind. One day he'd agree to give his wife a divorce, but then he'd change his tune in front of the rabbinical court. He'd deny she even wanted a divorce, and then when she insisted, he'd say she could have one. And the process would repeat itself, over and over. Finally we got him to sign some papers in the office so that he couldn't flip back again in the court.

The work was great for me in a lot of ways. One was the results. I really felt that I was doing something worthwhile, really helping people to get out of bad situations. I also felt that I really had found my career path, which had been the big question for me, and, of course, for my parents, who had paid for my education.

I don't want to do divorce mediation anymore, but I'm glad that I did it, because as a laboratory it was fascinating. People in divorce situations are at their worst in some ways: they're really insecure, they're really scared, they're really angry, and they're vengeful. My background in philosophy had fostered this idea that every person is capable of the full range of human behaviors—good and bad. As a mediator, the question is how to get the best out of everyone so that they're willing to talk in a way that they weren't before. In divorce mediation, as in most mediation, the critical elements are asking key questions, carefully framing those questions and scenarios, legitimizing what each party says, and absorbing anger without reacting to it.

I did the divorce mediation for a year. Then I moved to Massachusetts and wound up with three part-time jobs in mediation because as someone with actual case experience I was a rare commodity in what was a fledgling field. One of the jobs was at the University of Massachusetts, Boston, where I assisted David Matz in setting up the graduate certificate program in dispute resolution.

Back to Massachusetts and on to MIT

My other job was as executive director of what was called the Faneuil Commonwealth Mediation Program. Faneuil and Commonwealth are two public housing projects in Brighton, Massachusetts, and the program used public housing tenants to mediate disputes. The tenants from Faneuil would mediate at the Commonwealth development, and vice versa, to ensure confidentiality. My roles as Director were to train them, set up the cases, and supervise the cases. Unfortunately, this job ended fairly quickly. The Boston Housing Authority defunded the program to put more money into midnight basketball.

When Faneuil folded, I went to the Lynn Youth Resource Bureau. They do community mediation, and I was the community mediation coordinator. That program got referrals from the district court and the department of social services. It entailed contacting the parties, informing them about mediation, and really trying to convince them that it would be a good idea to use mediation to settle their case. In most instances, it was a good idea because there were a lot of assault and battery cases, where if people could get restitution, the charges were dropped. So at least for the party that was arrested, there was a good reason for them to come to mediation.

My real motivation for moving to Massachusetts was to go to MIT and study with Larry Susskind. There was a Society of Professionals in Dispute Resolution conference in Boston the year that I moved there, and Scott and I met Larry and talked to him, and he encouraged us to apply to the program in urban studies and planning.

We both went to MIT from '86 to '88. By that time, Scott and I were married, and we did the program together. At the very outset, I saw myself as doing more public disputes and international work, but I did divorce mediation and the other kinds of mediation as a way to get my feet wet. I remember reading an article about how divorce mediation was similar to international mediation, which made me feel like I was on the right path. The article made sense to me because it talked about security. It talked about jealousy and sharing scarce resources. Certainly, there are some similarities. But now that I'm in public disputes, I can see that there are at least 58 more layers in public disputes than there are in divorce situations.

As a graduate student, I worked on prison overcrowding issues at the MIT-Harvard Public Disputes Project at the Program On Negotiation, and I wrote my thesis on the Israeli-Palestinian conflict. After the program, I worked for Larry at Endispute, a private mediation firm, from 1988 to 1990. When I was there I worked on affordable housing, environmental, and energy issues, and I did an analysis of the Army Corps of Engineers, use of alternative dispute resolution. I also wrote a lot of proposals. We submitted proposals to address racial unrest on college campuses, but we didn't get very far with that.

Affordable Housing and Public Disputes

The affordable housing work was the most exciting. We mediated affordable housing compacts in the Greater Bridgeport and the Greater Hartford Regions of Connecticut. Connecticut had tried to pass legislation in response to the Fair Housing Act, but there was a great deal of organized opposition to affordable housing. This was happening during the real estate boom of the eighties, and prices had skyrocketed. Teachers and fire fighters couldn't afford to live where they worked, and young people couldn't afford to live where they had grown up.

Someone had the idea of trying to get all the towns within a region to develop an Affordable Housing Compact. The idea was to distribute affordable housing fairly across the region by creating a voluntary agreement among the municipalities. Our job was to mediate the compact agreements.

I worked with Larry Susskind in the Greater Hartford Region, which had 29 communities, and with Howard Bellman in the Greater Bridgeport Region, which had six municipalities. Each negotiating team included one representative from each community and one state representative from the Connecticut housing agency. We reached consensus agreements in both regions. In 1990, I left Endispute to start my own practice.

The Chelsea Charter Revision Experience

So, how did I wind up mediating a consensus charter process for the troubled City of Chelsea, Massachusetts? It's kind of a weird story. We refinanced our mortgage, and I got to be friends with the woman who was the loan officer. She was a consultant, and I talked to her about the work that I did. At the time, she was involved with Community Reinvestment Act work in Chelsea, and she said, "Boy, they really need you there. They would really make good use of you."

She sent me a paper about the demographics of the city. Soon after that, a woman Larry had asked me to meet with told me about a project in Chelsea that was being discussed at the Program On Negotiation at Harvard (PON). After talking to a few people, I called up Debbie Kolb, who was then executive director of PON, and asked her about it. She said, "It's funny. Your name came up when we were talking about the project. We thought you might be a good person to work on this."

Debbie explained they were looking at it as a research project on cross-cultural negotiation, and it seemed to me that that wasn't what Chelsea needed. I told Debbie I was going to call the receiver (the man who makes the decisions when a jurisdiction is in receivership) to get a little more information from him.

Chelsea is a city just outside of Boston, with 30,000 people on about two square miles of land. The city was in state receivership. It had a $10 million deficit on a $40 million budget, after a $5 million bailout by the state. The city was headed for bankruptcy. It couldn't make payroll. Instead of bailing them out yet again, the state decided to put the city in receivership. The sense was that if the city went into bankruptcy, a federal judge would be in control of it, and people feared it would never be released.

Receivership means that the state has absolute authority over all decision making in the city. The local government is suspended, and the receiver makes all the decisions. He only answers to the governor.

I called Harry Spence, the receiver, and sent him some material about my firm and past projects, and then I met with him. We had a really good conversation. It became clear to me that research was not what they needed; Chelsea needed a very unique consensus-building process. The receiver wanted a process to write a city charter that would reach deep into the community to actively seek participation.

Designing a Participatory Process

He understood that in order to get a city charter that would have value for the city, it had to be done by the people who were going to live under it, not by him. He had actually been the deputy receiver to a first receiver, who had commissioned someone to write a city charter.

But Harry Spence and the aldermanic subcommittee on governance rejected that charter because it had been written with no real input from the community. That's when he went out to the dispute resolution/consensus-building field looking for ideas. As we talked, I became aware of his goals and what he needed. Most importantly, I understood that he did not want us just to call charter meetings and to expect people who had never before participated to show up. We had to come up with some way of getting to people where they already were anyway, without expecting them to come to separate charter meetings. He wanted us to actively seek participation.

I teamed with Roberta Miller, an expert in local governance issues and herself a city councilor, and we submitted a proposal in a competitive bidding process. We were interviewed by the receiver and the aldermanic subcommittee on governance, and we got the project. We had proposed identifying and training people from Chelsea to function as facilitators and run community meetings at local clubs and organizations. Eventually, we went to clubs and organizations that had regular monthly meetings and asked, "Can we borrow an hour of your meeting to talk about charter issues?" In the first round of community meetings, we had a Chelsea person go to each meeting and ask three specific questions about local governance. I think we got the project because we had a way of going into the community and getting participation from people who ordinarily wouldn't participate in a political meeting.

We went to churches, we went to the sisterhoods of synagogues, and we went to the strong social club network in Chelsea. They all had monthly meetings where they would talk about their future events, fundraising, and that kind of thing. We also went to elderly housing developments and condominium board meetings and high school classes, all as part of the initial outreach outlined in our proposal.

Roberta trained the facilitators for the community meetings. Initially, I interviewed the "community leaders" of Chelsea: people who were identified as the formal, elected leaders, and informal leaders or opinion makers within the community. I talked to everyone from past and current elected officials to the city Santa Claus. Harry and his chief of staff, Steve McGoldrick, provided me with an initial list of people to speak with, and I found the rest by asking each person I interviewed, "Who else should I talk to?"

The interview part of the process was great because I was doing what I love to do: talking to people and hearing their life stories. These were informal interviews. I wanted information about Chelsea. I needed reference points of the city. I wanted to know why and how they thought they wound up in receivership. I wanted to know what they thought their new government should do. What were their ideals of a new government, and where did the last one fall short? And what I got were people's stories.

Chelsea is an immigrant city, so everybody's got a story about how they wound up there, where they or their families came from, and what they've been doing since. Eventually, we'd talk about the governance issues as a part of their story. That's very much the way I work, and it really fits in the Middle East context: First you talk to people about themselves, their families, and their lives before you talk business. It was great for me. I got these stories, and I got the information that I needed for the project. For six weeks, all I had to do was to go around to different people and hear their stories. It was fascinating. Chelsea's fascinating.

I was getting the information I needed while I was building relationships and trust. I was also letting people know about me. I was an outsider. And in a city like Chelsea, I was really an outsider. They're very suspicious of anyone from the outside.

Chelsea is an incredible fabric of different cultures. It's almost Third World-ish: everything travels by word of mouth, and information gets out in a minute. I needed to build a rapport throughout the community, and during the interviews, as I learned about those I was interviewing, I also shared information about me, and I described the process in very specific terms. I knew the information about me would spread throughout the city, and I wanted as many people as possible to have first-hand experience of meeting me.

From Meetings to Representatives to a Draft Charter to Ratification

We used a process map that laid out every step of the process to explain it. First, we had all these community meetings. Then, we would identify people to serve as the decision makers. I'd mediate their negotiations as they'd draft the city charter. Their proposals will come out to the community, which will have an opportunity to provide input. Then the decision makers will revise the charter, based on that input. When it's done, there would be a special election.

Having the process map and explaining it to everyone in the community was critical for the project. In Chelsea, people aren't used to people actually doing what they say they'll do. I know this now, but I didn't know it quite as clearly then. Just being very clear on what they could expect, what we were going to do, and how they could play a role was crucial in those early interviews.

During the interviews and the community meetings, we asked people to identify individuals to serve on a charter preparation team, who were to be the decision makers. The facilitators ran the community meetings throughout Chelsea while I conducted interviews.

The first phase of the Chelsea process included 25 to 30 community meetings, and 40 to 45 community leader interviews. At the end of phase one, we had community objectives for the new government and various opinions about why they wound up in receivership. We developed a rapport with people in the community, and we had a list of 70 people who were nominated for the charter preparation team. We'd also gone on cable TV a number of times to explain the process, and we'd circulated Spanish/English newsletters to all households in the city. We had a charter hotline that people could call with their thoughts and ideas, and to find out about meetings.

There were some surprises in that first phase. One of the surprises was the level of distrust. People in Chelsea really see a lot of things in terms of conspiracy. Some people thought that the receivership was the result of a state conspiracy to build an airport parking lot. The fact that they had a $10 million deficit was lost on them. Some said, "We have no problem." I also learned a lot about politics and the existing political structure in Chelsea from the interviews.

One of the hardest parts about this first phase was compiling all of this data. We also had significant time constraints. We were supposed to have 12 months for the project, and we now only had nine months because of contracting issues. The receiver and the state just didn't know the hoops they had to jump through to contract. Phase 1 took about three months.

To begin the second phase of the process, we needed to appoint the charter preparation team from the list of 70 that had been generated during the community leader interviews and community meetings.

At that point I called a lot of colleagues in the field of mediation and asked for advice. I knew that this was a crucial lynchpin in the process because it would determine whether the charter preparation team would be viewed as legitimate in the eyes of the community. But I wasn't sure how to do it.

I'd called a lot of people, and I got the best answer from Howard Bellman. He said, "If it's hard to chose 20, maybe it's easier to choose three." What he meant by that was to choose three people in the community who would then choose the 20. So that's what we did. That was ingenious, in my opinion. The receiver, his chief of staff, and I agreed that we needed people in Chelsea who were considered highly moral and whose ethics could not be questioned by anyone in the city. Believe me, that was a tall order in Chelsea! We wound up with a local pastor, the editor of the local newspaper, and a woman who had started an alternative high school program. The three of them and I took the list of 70 and chose 18 people. We made our decision based on criteria: Each team member had to have an ability and willingness to learn about governance, an ability and willingness to learn about operating according to consensus, and an ability to take the long-term view of the city's interests, rather than having a narrow agenda. The final criterion for the team as a whole was that the team be representative of the city, and also that team members be respected throughout the community. That was one tough piece.

The other tough piece was deciding what to do with the politicians. We knew we had to have them on board because eventually the charter had to go to an election. If they were the people that won the most votes in elections, we didn't want them against us. I talked to a lot of them and asked them how to handle this. They said things like, "Well, if you have too many of us, the people are going to hate it. The people will reject it," because the politicians were seen as part of the problem. So with them, I came up with the idea that we'd have three aldermen and one school committee member, in addition to the 18 citizens. Then we had our team.

We published the list of team members in the local paper with the charter hotline number and asked the community to let us know if they felt they were represented by someone already on the team. We added a few more members based on the hotline nominees. After three rounds, we didn't get any more calls. And really, it was a great group. We really succeeded in getting a group of people that were representative of the city, and probably, the best of Chelsea.

We were also trying to reflect the diversity in Chelsea. Unfortunately, two representatives from the Asian community dropped out midway. If we had had more time, we would have been able to replace them, but it was a very hard community to gain access to. During the interviews, I had met with a Vietnamese man and a Cambodian man, and both of them agreed to be on the team. In my initial meeting with the Vietnamese man, he gave me the list of demands of the Vietnamese community and thought that I could do something with it. I think when he realized that the charter was a bit more abstract than he'd assumed, he didn't really see the connection between the charter and meeting his community's immediate needs.

The process for selecting the charter prep team members was important in other ways as well. One woman was nominated via the charter hotline on all three rounds. She was rejected every time because the selection committee saw her as historically operating from a narrow agenda that would not suit the team well. When I spoke with her, she yelled, "I'm willing to volunteer my time, and you're rejecting that!" I was able to tell her of the criteria we used to choose the team members and that selection committee members didn't feel that she met those criteria. I felt the legitimacy of the selection process protected us from her rage. I suggested other roles for her in the process.

For the preliminary meeting of the charter prep team, Roberta made a timeline with some historic Chelsea moments, including when Abraham Lincoln and George Washington were in Chelsea, Revolutionary War battles fought in Chelsea, and the major fires in Chelsea. One fire in 1903 had destroyed three-quarters of the city, and another in 1974 destroyed the city's commercial district. After we put up those historic points, we asked people to put themselves on the timeline. When did they move to Chelsea? When did their families move to Chelsea? When did they become politically active in Chelsea? This was a meant to be a group dynamics/team-building exercise. Some of the charter preparation team members knew each other, others didn't. We wanted to give them an opportunity to learn a little bit about each other, to share something about themselves, because they were beginning this pressure-cooker kind of process.

After that, we developed ground rules, which is an early task of all consensus processes. We started with a mission statement, and then we addressed questions about the roles of the participants, the role of the mediator, record keeping, and dealing with the media. We also discussed the decision-making rule: Were we going to operate by consensus? Were we going to take votes? Were we going to make motions? Those kinds of things.

The decision about the media was pretty standard: You ask people not to negotiate through the media. People otherwise would tell a reporter that the best thing for the city is "X." Then that gets out in the public and either wins or loses support. Instead, we identified three spokespersons who were to talk about the process and proposals under consideration, but they were not to attribute statements to anybody. The meetings were open, so the media was often in attendance. You can't shut out the media. If they want to come, they come. We also met with reporters and the editorial board of the local paper to explain what we were trying to do.

As for the decision rule, the team decided to operate by consensus. To move an issue forward, if we had talked it out, and it was clear that we weren't going to reach consensus, the team empowered me, as the mediator, to call for a vote. If something passed by 80 percent, then it would be considered a decision. However, the entire charter had to be agreed to unanimously.

The first team meeting also dealt with technical aspects of charters. A professional charter drafter supported the team, and he gave a 45-minute talk about state requirements in city charters.

The meeting went pretty well. I'd met with most of the team members separately before the meeting. It's really helpful to go into a meeting having already established a rapport and some trust with each person. I didn't expect blow-ups, or anything like that. My hope was that they would all stick with the process. We had a couple of people who dropped off after the first meeting, but we went back and refilled those seats.

I had planned on holding meetings every other week with work groups in the off weeks, as needed. When I suggested a work group everyone on the team volunteered for it and so we wound up meeting weekly. It was really intense.

Here's an interesting thing. The first meeting was a preliminary one, and we didn't get into negotiating any substantive charter issues. At the next meeting, I began with the preamble because a preamble is generally an overview statement: What are everyone's overarching goals for this charter? The idea is to get a quick victory, an easy consensus decision, and that builds momentum.

Well, at this meeting a major issue arose over whether "God" should be mentioned in the preamble. We had one woman who felt that she was representing the atheists in Chelsea and another woman who was a born-again Christian, who insisted that God be mentioned in the charter. We had handed out examples of preambles from other city charters, the Massachusetts Constitution, and the U.S. Constitution. The Massachusetts Constitution refers to the "Great Legislator." That is its reference to "God." This issue was a real frustration for me because what I had assumed would be an early victory to build momentum turned into a mess. After a while I just tabled it. I said, "OK, we're not going to talk about this anymore; let's move on to the next issue." In complex mediations, you don't expect to settle every issue the first time it comes up for discussion.

Between meetings, I worked to mediate between these two women on the assumption that an agreement between them would be acceptable to all the others. They both agreed on language. In fact, the woman who was a born-again Christian offered some language that the other woman, begrudgingly, agreed to. It was on the same scale as the "Great Legislator," where it wasn't directly naming "God," but it referred to a higher authority through capital letters.

Two meetings later, I raised the issue and assumed we had an agreement. But the woman who suggested the language said she couldn't agree to it. I was shocked. I tabled the issue again. I took her aside after the meeting and said, "I need to talk to you about negotiating in good faith." I explained, "Natalie conceded to your language. She compromised to accommodate your concerns, and now you're saying it's not good enough. You can't do that without really getting someone really angry." She soon came to understand the situation and agreed to the language.

One of the real challenges of Chelsea was that we were dealing with lay people, both in terms of the substance and in their knowledge of negotiating. Typically, when I do a case, I'm dealing with professionals or semi-professionals who have a real handle on the substance, and I'm just helping them put it all together.

This was different because as part of the process I needed to provide information on governance and also to educate them about how to converse with each other. Ultimately, it was the strength of the process. It gave them a new way to discuss contentious issues. I had heard lots of stories about aldermen meetings where people came to blows, and the police had to be called in.

Part of the reason that I love mediating is that it's democracy in a pure sense. You get people together and have them debate and discuss elements of the law that's going to affect their lives. You help them bang out the agreement that works for all of them. That's what they did in Chelsea, despite the fact that it wasn't typical for the city.

It wasn't easy. There were some "bombs" that got thrown at us. I took some strength from my Hebrew name, Zelda. In modern Hebrew, a Zelda is an armored personnel carrier. That was what I felt like in Chelsea. The bombs were getting thrown, and I was just slowly moving through the city, feeling protected by my armor. Each bomb was an attempt to delegitimize the process of creating a charter. In every case, people start off skeptical but after a couple of months, that feeling normally fades. In this case, the bombs and the skepticism they relied on and fueled continued throughout the whole process.

Primarily, the bombs were from the existing aldermen, people who were concerned about losing power. For example, an alderman announced publicly that he had recently been at the state house and saw the charter being printed up. Of course, it was a lie, but it found its way into the local newspaper.

In response, five charter preparation team members went to the next aldermen's meeting. During the public comment period, each of them made a statement about their work on the charter. We didn't address his comment directly, but they just made statements. They said who they were, what their role was on the charter team, what issues they were tackling, what issues they felt most strongly about, and how they had been resolved. Having five people telling those stories was our way of illustrating to the community that these were the people who were in the process of writing the charter.

Similarly, another alderman announced during a televised aldermen's meeting that someone left a copy of the complete charter in her mailbox and that the whole mediation process was just a sham. The headline in the local paper the next day read, "Charter Is a Done Deal." It turned out that the charter that had been anonymously dropped in her mailbox was the charter that had been rejected by the second receiver and the aldermanic subcommittee on governance, of which she had been a member. We wrote a letter to her and the editor of the local paper explaining that. It's possible that she forgot or that she was set up. Regardless, her action raised doubts in the minds of a skeptical population. Despite a behind-the-scenes commitment to apologize, she never did.

We had another bomb from within the receiver's office that really almost blew things apart. Someone who had nothing to do with the governance project made a statement to a *Boston Globe* reporter, saying that the charter was almost done, and there was going to be a 15-member city council.

We had never even entertained that number. At the time, we had talked about seven, about 13, and everything in between. We never considered 15, and yet on the front page of the Metro section of the *Globe* blared the headline, "Fifteen Member Council for Chelsea." And the statement was attributed to the receiver's office!

The paper didn't quote anybody, but my sources told me who it was, and I was furious. This time even the charter preparation team members were shaken. I worked with the Receiver's office to draft a letter to the charter prep team assuring them that Harry was committed to their work and the process. Then I had to turn to the chief of staff of the receiver's office and said, "You've got to control your own people. "At the next staff meeting, there was a very strong statement from the receiver. He told them that they were not to speak to reporters about the governance process, or they would be gone. We had to do additional damage control. The *Globe* ran another article on the council, but it was buried deep in the metro section.

I learned an enormous amount about political power and power grabs, and how those get played out through the media. I had to focus not only on the dynamics of the governance committee, but also on how it was playing out in the larger picture. We had to respond quickly to protect the process. Ultimately, despite all the bombs, the team completed the draft charter. We published its key components in a Spanish/English newsletter that we sent to all the households in the city.

For an entire month, we had another series of community meetings. I synthesized all the feedback we got and linked each item to the section of the charter it related to. We reviewed every piece of input that we got from the community. Some were rejected, but every piece of feedback was considered. Some comments resulted in significant changes to the charter. For example, the team had initially proposed a 13-member council, and they reduced that number to 11. The draft had called for two-year terms for district councilors and four-year terms for at-large councilors. At its last meeting, the charter prep team changed that to two years for everyone because the community felt that differing terms would create a power imbalance among the councilors. So key items really changed based on the community input.

The charter prep team reached final consensus—unanimously—on the final charter. All the people on the negotiating team signed off on it. The final charter was circulated throughout the community. There were copies available at city hall and the library and local businesses. We discussed it on local TV. My work was done!

One month later, there was an election to ratify the charter. The receiver had said at the outset that he would accept the work of the charter preparation team as long as the community ratified it. It was a huge risk. There were actual campaigns: the "Yes for Chelsea" and the "Vote No" campaigns with bumper stickers and political ads and all.

The charter passed with 60 percent of the vote! At first I was disappointed that we hadn't reached a higher percentage of, say, 80 percent. But the charter drafter told me that charters typically pass with just 51 percent of the vote. He saw this as a huge success. I was relieved.

The morning after the election, I felt really powerful. But shortly after that, I felt a real strong letdown. I started thinking about the nature of work. I'd spent nine months working on the Chelsea Charter, and this was, in a way, the ultimate that a project could be, but there was something missing from it in terms of personal satisfaction. It was nothing compared to having a baby! Yes, I had done something that had really helped out a community, and I gave it my all. But there was something missing. It caused me to think about work in a different way. It was that intense. But in all honesty, three months later I was looking for the next big case. Chelsea was very special for me—it brought together my love of mediation with my love of governing infrastructure. And I wanted that intensity again.

I'd say there were several lessons one can take away. One is to stick to the basics of mediation. For example, try to link issues rather than work to settle each one separately. Also remember that personal relationships are paramount. As an outsider going in, the way you legitimize yourself is through those personal relationships.

And remember to pay attention to cultural differences. There were some Hispanic members on the charter team, and I found I needed to talk to them individually to encourage their full participation. In general, facial expressions can tell you a lot. Look for people who seem to have something to say but are holding back. Sometimes you have to encourage and to support people to participate in forums that that may perceive as somewhat intimidating.

I think public policy mediation can be a real learning experience for the participants. For example, in Chelsea we had panel presentations on different forms of government, and the team members were able to ask the experts lots and lots of questions. But the learning experience goes beyond facts. The people on the team also learned a new way to communicate and solve problems. They learned how to deliberate. Instead of simply shouting down an idea as "terrible," they learned to take three giant steps backwards and just listen a little bit before they reacted. They also became more able to seriously consider a range of options.

To make that happen, as a mediator you need to create ground rules and then enforce those ground rules. You carve out the space for people to talk, so that if someone's talking and other people are trying to jump in, you're protecting the space for that first person. Also ensure that people understand what the other has said and why they've said it. Ask them, "Did you hear what they really said, and why that's important to them?" That doesn't mean that people don't get angry or yell. It's just that you manage that, so that it doesn't become hurtful, and therefore hurt the process. People still need to be able to raise their voices at times. It helps others gauge the strength of their convictions. I'm not trying to suppress emotions, but I'm certainly trying to keep the discussion on a little more of a rational than an emotional level.

Do people learn during the process about what they want? In some ways, yes. Each person develops their sense of issues and their priorities change. In some ways, that was the scary part of it. Often things seemed to be in flux. Even where people stood on the issues changed. In one instance, a member of the charter team made an impassioned plea as a parent with children in the school system for "at-large" school committee members. She swayed a lot of people. Then, when we went around the table to state how we would vote, she'd changed her mind! It made me really scared as a mediator. I thought maybe we're asking them for too much—to learn about the issues and then make decisions that they don't fully understand.

Eventually, she switched back to her original position. I justified this dynamic to myself by seeing it as a sign that people were actually open to the deliberations and listening to everyone at the table.

Afterword

In the 15 years since Chelsea came out of receivership, it has become a stable municipality with private investment on the heels of state economic development projects. It has had two city managers, both with deep roots in Chelsea, and has consistently elected diverse city councils.

A *Boston Globe* article, "After a Decade of Change, Chelsea Dares to Dream" (10/6/2005) spoke of balanced budgets, professional governance, new schools, and its new problem—a lack of affordable housing. In April 2005, *Boston Magazine* referred to Chelsea as "a paradise for urban types." Certainly, the receivership proved to be a successful state intervention and the Chelsea Charter Consensus Process, for which the city was named a National Civic League All-American City, contributed to that success and the city's stability.

Now into the twenty-first year of my public policy mediation practice, the Chelsea Charter Process remains for me a touchstone project. I've carried many of its key lessons and affirmations into every consensus process I've conducted since. Most importantly, lay citizens really are capable of wrestling with complicated policy questions. If you provide people with unbiased, digestible information, coupled with an opportunity to have an actual impact on laws affecting their lives, they will step up and work their way to responsible decisions.

Secondly, each public policy mediation requires a uniquely designed process to account for its particular circumstances and characteristics. Projects may include similar process components, but each part is uniquely molded, and decisions about what to include and how they will be sequenced depend on the unique qualities of the situation. Chelsea has served me as a model of how to design complex processes in that I design to the elements most people perceive as barriers. For example, in Chelsea, people were never expected to come out for charter meetings, so the design required we go to the places where they already met.

Finally, Chelsea is the place where I cut my political teeth. It was where I came face-to-face with real politics. I was often told that politics is the game of choice in Chelsea and that people play hard. It served as a great training ground for me.

Some years ago, I spoke about the Chelsea Charter Consensus Process at an MIT Conference on deliberative democracy. Two weeks after the conference, I received an email from an Italian participant, who had negotiated a book contract for me to write on Chelsea. My subsequent book, *The Chelsea Story: How a Corrupt City Regenerated Its Democracy* (Milan: Bruno Mondadori (Italian only)) is used in courses throughout Italy and has contributed to a growing field of public policy mediation there.

My book, *Civic Fusion: Mediating Polarized Public Disputes* (American Bar Association, 2013), includes the stories of the Chelsea Charter Process and two other past cases, a six-year secret abortion dialogue conducted among Massachusetts prolife and prochoice leaders after fatal shootings at two women's health clinics, and a negotiated rulemaking to develop federal worker safety standards for the use of cranes and derricks in construction. It uses those cases to illustrate the dynamics of public policy mediation.

Part 5
Environmental and
Regional Planning

Chapter 9
Consensus Building and Water Policy in San Antonio

John Folk-Williams

In a rich case that illuminates Texas's water controversies, John Folk-Williams takes us through a process that began with deep political rivalries and dueling experts in San Antonio and ended with members of the city council calling the result "a big breakthrough." Folk-Williams recounts how he worked with: mayoral candidates; chamber of commerce influentials and their own up-and-coming next generation; well-organized and powerful religious, community, and environmental organizations; scientists; and representatives of the military as well. We see intense political controversy and impasse give way to new beginnings. We see apparently sensible, initial efforts to "define the problem" put off to avoid narrowing issues to produce another dead-end. We see strong personalities threatening the larger planning and analytical process—and how Folk-Williams responded. We see, not least of all, instructive differences within the team of mediators or facilitators themselves and their differing temptations about just what to do as they faced energetic and passionate local sentiments and concerns, proposals, demands, and more.

We see no magic bullets, here, but instead practical ways of handling contentiousness and controversy, debates between experts, and rivalries between politicians. We see listening and learning in the service of acknowledging deep values, histories of suspicion, and corners turned by the parties as they mapped shared concerns—all enabling the questions that followed, questions asking for workable proposals or for proposed guidelines that could help the city council move forward—to address not one but many interrelated issues of water use and conservation, equity and development, and environmental planning and regulation. —JF

‿୧୬ح

Many people can't understand that the louder and harsher they sound, the less others hear what they're trying to say. They hear aggression and attack, and that tends to evoke responses of either fear or anger. Strong emotions always trump the analysis of ideas in the mind. The emotional give-and-take has to tone down before people can hear the content of their ideas.

San Antonio had been deadlocked about water policy for a number of years. The developer community had been very, very strong in setting water policies for some time. But beginning in the early 70's, the developer community ran into some determined opposition. That opposition came to focus more and more on the impact of development on the water supply, which at that time came exclusively from the Edward's Aquifer, a very abundant limestone aquifer formation that covers five or six counties across south Texas.

Background: Growth and Environmental Quality, Business and Neighborhood Interests

The opposition was concerned in part with runaway growth taking investments in major development outside the older part of the city and developing a whole new area of the city on its north side, adjacent to a major interstate route. The business community was previously conflicted about whether to develop outside the boundaries of its old development area.

For one set of constituents, it was all about urban sprawl, about the city subsidizing growth in completely undeveloped areas at the expense of the rest of the residents. So, in part, it was the question of equity: Who should pay to support all the infrastructure for that development?

Another set of constituents was very concerned about the disinvestment in the older parts of the city. While all this new investment was heading to the north side, the center of the city, and the south, east, and west sides of the city—where the people of color lived—were neglected in terms of public investment for many, many years. And those urban sprawl critics and the inner-city critics got together to defeat a major mall proposal in the early-to-mid 70's. It was at that point, as I understand it, that the growth issue got connected with the water issue.

The question of managing the Edward's Aquifer and deciding which city residents would have access to the groundwater there had a long, long history apart from the development issue that came to dominate things in San Antonio. But the city policy clash was coming to a head starting from that period in the 70's through the early to mid-90's. One development proposal after another suggested that the city become less reliant on the Edwards Aquifer and import surface water from other sources.

The focus of the controversy became a reservoir project named Applewhite. The proponents of development wanted to build a reservoir on the south side of town that would primarily fill up with treated effluent from the sewage treatment system as well as from natural runoff. But the main rationale for the reservoir was really that it would be a holding area for water imported from outside the region. So, it was linked to a much larger plan, and it became a critical focal point for a lot of different constituencies.

It was the Applewhite project that led many groups to think developers had just gone too far. For various reasons, the project came to symbolize city hall being in bed with the developers, telling the rest of the residents what the future was going to be like. Consequently, even though the Applewhite reservoir was approved, and $40 million had been invested in it by the city council, and it actually was under construction, these opponents forced a referendum on the project. They won, even though the referendum had no binding effect. Despite the lack of the power in the referendum, it answered the question, Should this project go forward? And the answer was a resounding no.

The city council, however, didn't accept that verdict. First of all, the referendum, as noted, had no binding effect. Second, the council said, well, there's too much at stake (remember, some $40 million was already invested); we have to go ahead with this anyway. So, the city came up with a new water plan that still included the Applewhite reservoir. The city council approved the plan, which generated another referendum. The backers of the plan lost by an even bigger margin, at which point they conceded to reality and killed the project.

Getting Involved in the Case

So I got a call in 1995, about a year after the Applewhite referenda. The city still hadn't been able to do anything in terms of water policy. There were just these polarized factions. I mean, after two public referenda, with all the political campaigning, television advertising, all the slogans and sound bites, this was just as sharply drawn a controversy as you could possibly have.

But, at the same time, the city still faced a problem—they were facing increasing restrictions on access to the Edwards Aquifer, largely because of the Endangered Species Act. This case had gone to federal court. The Sierra Club had brought a major lawsuit against all the Edwards Aquifer pumpers, including the City of San Antonio. It had a federal judge from Midland who was intent on putting a ceiling—a mandatory ceiling—on groundwater pumping, forcing all the pumpers to cut back.

It became clear the State of Texas was going to have to adopt some form of regulation on tapping the aquifer. And then the state did adopt a new regulatory regime governing the pumping of the aquifer, but that was thrown in doubt by further litigation. So, you had a mess going on in terms of litigation by environmentalists to impose pumping limits as well as litigation by pumpers to declare the state-imposed limits unconstitutional. For about a year or year and a half, the opposing parties were at a standstill.

San Antonio's water policy was always central to what the whole region was going to wind-up doing about the management of the aquifer because the city was responsible, as the largest user, for much of the success or failure of any regulatory regime or any concept of conservation. And it was now clear that the city was going to be a main player in any agreement between the opposing parties.

There was a mediator—an attorney/mediator—in San Antonio who called me. He had been talking with members of the city council for some time, and he persuaded them to give mediation a try. I happened to be in Santa Fe, New Mexico, at the time. He knew me because I had taught him in a workshop in public involvement a couple of years earlier. And, actually, before this call, he had brought me around to have a talk at the law school in San Antonio with a group of people, including a member of he city council. This group wanted to hear my thoughts about the issues, including the possible use of mediation or some consensus-building approach. So, all of that early work seemed to bear fruit. He said that the city council really wanted to do something about this. They had gotten to the end of their rope, they didn't know what to do, and they were going to try mediation.

Conflict Assessment

So they called me in and gave the assignment to me and this other fellow to be co-mediators of a process to break the deadlock on water policy in San Antonio. I guess the total time we spent was two or three months in interviews and preparations, and then seven months in meetings. We had a 34-member committee on water policy created by the city council. We had done a full assessment of this process, and that committee was appointed by the city council with our advice.

We had seven months of very intensive meetings. Ultimately, the committee came to an agreement that was short of full consensus. The schedule we had come up with was a minimum of six meetings of the full group—so, a meeting every month—and then there were many committee meetings in between. By the end of January, we had at least as much agreement as we could get, which was regarded as a great success by the city. In fact, the report and the policy that we developed were adopted, in principle, virtually on the same day by the city council.

The agreement was really a very basic one. It was impossible to get specific about which water sources would be used. But this was an agreement, for the first time, to explore all of the various ideas out there. That consideration represented a complete turn around since new proposals for how to solve the city's water problems had become so politicized that it was very hard for anyone to even concede that an opponent's idea had even basic validity.

So, the city council now said, "Everything is on the table. We will study all these ideas." They came up with an action plan and allocated money for it, but then the other part of the agreement was to create a public process for using the results of that scientific research to develop all further water plans, policies, and projects. We created a set of criteria—eight major criteria that had to be satisfied for any plan or project in the future. So, this was not a bold solution as much as a solution in principle that enabled the city to move from immobility to get on a track that later resulted in a full-blown water plan five years later.

Early Stakeholder Meetings

When I got the call, I went down and had a meeting with the mayor and the city council's water committee, made up of three members of the city council. I also met with the San Antonio Water System—SAWS for short—and that was set up as a semi-independent agency with its own board of directors. So, the chair of the board and the head of SAWS were now involved.

My co-facilitator and I talked about the principles of the consensus-building process. The city council had a traditional method for creating any kind of task force or committee, and that consisted of allowing every member of the council to appoint someone, with a couple of extras appointed by the mayor.

So, we told them that wouldn't work. We needed to do an assessment and to interview all of the interest groups' leadership. From the outset, they realized that what would set this apart from previous water committees—and there had been at least half a dozen other committees, none of which had worked—was that it wasn't going to have a predetermined outcome, which was a great problem with all the others.

The city council members and the mayor were not going to be on it—to keep the elected leadership away from pushing it in a particular direction—and the most vociferous opponents of the current mayor and city policy in general were going to be at the table.

So, those were the characteristics that would set this apart. In addition, we successfully argued that there should be no appointed chairperson, that the mediation team would manage the process, which was quite unusual. They agreed to all that, and they funded the process, quite handsomely.

During the interview process, which took about eight to 10 weeks, we interviewed at least 70 people representing all the major interest groups. The Greater San Antonio Chamber of Commerce was the political voice of the business community. Traditionally, that body had been conceived as very arrogant, almost dictatorial—they wanted to impose policies on the politicians, the city council, and that was it. So, it was very hard to get them to turn around. I had to start with them, and then in this polarized situation with the other side—who were the harshest critics of the city.

One critic who had waged a successful candidacy against the current mayor had a sort of populist organization. She pulled together a coalition of anti-tax people, urban sprawl critics, and a number of the minority groups. She wasn't the only one pulling them together, but she became the leader in terms of getting out front, in front of TV cameras, because she was good at that. Then, after the referendum that defeated Applewhite, she ran for mayor, and she almost won. But that had happened before I came.

Then there was this husband and wife couple that had just devoted all their spare time to studying this water issue. They and the former mayoral candidate described many of the city politicians as "crooks." They threw that language around a lot. There were "deeply imbedded conflicts of interests." There were "crooked deals." The dam builders "wanted to make a fortune from the city's water policy"—and the Applewhite group, of course, had a field day with that because the Applewhite project had apparently been technically vulnerable to begin with.

The former mayoral candidate never tired of saying, "They want us to drink sewer water"—"us" meaning the southern part of the city, which is poorer and non-white—"and then they want to charge us to pay to pump the stuff to the far north side where the actual development will take place and where the beneficiaries of this new water policy will be." So, in trying to put this group together I had to deal first with those polar extremes.

Building Up the Middle To Deal With Extremes

Then I had to identify everyone in the middle. Ultimately, the secret to getting anywhere with this process was to build up the middle. The middle turned out to include a great number of people who had been anti-Applewhite and had been written off by the chamber of commerce as just opponents to city policy—but the coalition was much more complex than that. There was Chicano leadership, African-American leadership, and community organizing groups. There were union-affiliated groups. There's a tremendous tradition of parish-based organizing in San Antonio, and the most famous manifestation of that was called the COPS (Communities Organized for Public Service) organization, built on the Saul Alinsky model, and they were part of this coalition. The "middle" included many, many groups, including a lot of the north side middle-class and upper-middle-class people who were fighting urban sprawl. All of those groups had reservations about the extremists of the anti-Applewhite crowd—namely this mayoral candidate and a few others. They were the bitter opponents—nobody expected them to change or to concede much of anything.

So, first of all, to build up the middle we had to make sure that the chamber of commerce did not just come to dominate the committee. Now usually my habit is to meet with people one-on-one, or in small groups, and draw them out. But when we first went to meet with the chamber of commerce, it had me and the co-facilitator go into an auditorium—where they had 40 members of their group—and get up on a stage and sit next to one of the real hardcore advocates of importing new water into the region and a bitter opponent of the anti-Applewhite people. He was there to articulate all the things that he stood for. I got a little bit into describing what this process was about, and all of this anger and frustration just rose up out of the audience. They were not having any of this. One member of the chamber group just said outright, "I don't know who else you have to worry about—this is the only community [the business community] you have to worry about."

Well, mixed in there were some very influential younger attorneys and some people from the military. Even among the younger attorneys, whom I later interviewed one-on-one, some of them said, "You know, what you were hearing the other day is exactly what the chamber has to stop doing: They have to stop ordering people what to do. And if you set up this committee, you have to make sure you get business representatives who are not going to be on the phone every night taking orders from the leadership of the chamber but who are instead free to express their own opinions."

Then, when I talked to the military, I learned that the military had formed a kind of study group of their own to look at the water issue. They had chosen one man, an Air Force colonel, who was looking for a way out for the military so it could preserve its water supply, which was a key to getting funding from the defense establishment. There were five bases in San Antonio at the time, so it had always been a big military town, and this one colonel was an excellent and very reasonable guy. He said, "Well, you know, you listen to the chamber, but you also listen to everybody else. Don't take them too seriously."

When I left this meeting in the auditorium with the business community, I thought this wasn't going to go anywhere, if that's the way the chamber is talking right now. What they wanted was for the mayor to step up and declare what the policy was going to be. They didn't want the whole process to be turned over to some sort of nonpolitical public group that was going to debate the issues openly. That was the last thing they wanted. But I thought, "Well, this isn't going to work without them."

But some people got to them. I communicated what was going on to a state senator who happened to be the wife of the president of the chamber, and I talked with a member of the city council who happened to have access to a lot of business people. The mayor himself was allied with one of the very senior development people in the community, and sooner or later—or eventually—the chamber turned around.

So, suddenly, the next time, they welcomed me—I met privately with a couple of the guys from the leadership, and they basically changed their approach. Instead of saying, "This is bogus. This is the wrong way to go," they said, "Well, we think that this might work, and here is a list of candidates we would like you to consider for this committee."

At the time we were talking about a couple of dozen people—maybe a group of 34 or 35. I said something like, "How am I going to cover all these different constituencies?"

They said, "Well, here is our list," and it had about 30 names on it because they had broken down the business community into every conceivable sector—including the military.

I said, "Well, this is a lot of names, and we can't have this thing dominated. Maybe five?"

They just looked stunned. "Oh! That's impossible!" They thought, there are 30 names here—you could form a committee here without adding anyone—you don't have to look further than that.

Diverse Local Leadership

So I took the list, and I told them, "There are a lot of constituencies," and I told them about some of the other interests. They tried to argue down most of those.

I talked about some of the anti-sprawl interests on the north side because those groups had formed very influential neighborhood associations, and then I talked about umbrella organizations within the neighborhood organizations that were getting involved in politics. In fact, that political dimension of the neighborhood movement elected the next mayor a couple of years later.

But the chamber just argued, "This has nothing to do with growth." One of them just said to me, "If you think you can bribe some people into this by promising them that you're going to deal with a favorite issue of theirs, you can just forget about it right now."

So, anyway, I had their list, and it turned out, in fact, that the real hard liners in the business community were not on that list—that it was mostly young people. Like many business communities, the one in San Antonio is very clever about recruiting new leadership among younger entrepreneurs, about giving them exposure, gradually, and getting them on committees, building them up prominently for public service roles. There were a large number of very interesting young people, so we interviewed many, many of those folks. Many of them were quite moderate—and had a distinctly new cast of thinking. Some of them, I knew, would follow orders, but others would not.

There were many well-known civil rights leaders who just commanded tremendous respect in the Chicano communities of San Antonio. That's one of the great treasures of San Antonio: its history and its involvement in the civil rights movement—going back to the Mexican Revolution. One of the early calls for Mexican independence was written in San Antonio, and it was a place of exile for a lot of people who lost struggles. A lot of radical thinking came up from Mexico and settled in during the twentieth century in San Antonio.

This meant that there were civil rights leaders like a fellow who had been a state senator. He was then running for state superintendent, a member of the state board of education. Another interesting person was the first Chicana elected to the San Antonio City Council in the 80's, and she had served on the same city council as Henry Cisneros. She was a person of great principle and refused to be influenced by political offers and the business community. She stuck to her guns—at the cost of being politically isolated during that decade—but she had great standing. She had been very prominent in the fight against Applewhite, but she was a very important figure to include. There was also the leader of a major social justice group, a part of the Archdiocese of San Antonio, who was very influential in the community.

These groups were very obvious, very well organized social justice groups. They were already vocal and talking about the issues. Not only that, San Antonio had a tradition of organizations dedicated to civil rights and social equity. These groups were very much part of the fabric of San Antonio, and what gave some of them much more credibility was that they were part of the fabric of the Catholic Church. So, church leadership was involved.

COPS had come into the picture in the 70's or so. They had a principle of not cooperating with consensus-based efforts because their strategy was very much to pick their own targets. They like to summon politicians to their big meetings, giant rallies, and put them on the spot, and basically say, "Are you with us, or are you against us?" They want "Yes" or "No" answers on all their issues. That's the way they like to deal with people, and then they might send a couple hundred people to the city council to demonstrate.

In the end, they agreed—they said they were not going to take an active part in the sense of being members, but that they would monitor the proceedings. They sent two people to take part that way in every meeting. They weren't official representatives, but they were there. But that was a very important avenue of communication in the community because there were two organizations like that—one was COPS, but another was METRO.

COPS had done all their organizing in certain parts of town through the Catholic parishes, and METRO had done their organizing in other parts of town through non-Catholic, mostly Protestant, parishes. In short, the alliance of COPS and METRO was a very extensive political community-based network. So there was really no problem identifying leadership for the poorer areas—the people of color. That was very well established in San Antonio.

The co-facilitator and I were trying to put a group together, a group that the council would approve. So we came up with our recommendations, and they included hard-line anti-city advocates, the business community, and everybody in-between.

One member of the city council on this water committee was really upset at some of the choices that I had urged on the mayor. During a private session, after the committee had finally agreed on all the members, this councilwoman just gave me a tongue-lashing like I've never had: "Who do you think you are?" She was talking to me as if I had just loaded the deck totally against city interests when we were only trying to get a balanced group. Fortunately, the mayor and most other council members consistently supported having a balanced group, even though it meant including political adversaries.

The city council ultimately adopted our proposal in the form of a city ordinance with a charge to the group, a budget, and a list of the members of the committee.

Surprises After Convening

That marked the formal start of the process, but there were many problems to deal with once we had everyone together around the table. To begin with, many of the most important advocates had little interest or skill in the give-and-take of interest-based negotiations. This hadn't been so apparent in the early discussions. Some of the participants who turned out to be the most intransigent once the meetings got underway had presented themselves in early interviews in a completely different light—as reasonable and eager to have a chance to work out a new approach for the city's water policy.

There were one or two who were reluctant to let any comment go unanswered that supported a different point of view. They seemed not to trust anyone to form an independent judgment and felt compelled to respond point for point. At the beginning of a process, you always have to educate a group of advocates to change their tone and language. It takes them a while to realize that they aren't talking to a judge or the media, and that their considerable skills at argument quickly become counterproductive when the goal is voluntary agreement.

Some participants had a confrontational style and tone—quite apart from the content of their ideas—that also discouraged real conversation. That too is a common problem. Many people can't understand that the louder and harsher they sound, the less others hear what they're trying to say. They hear aggression and attack, and that tends to evoke responses of either fear or anger. Strong emotions always trump the analysis of ideas in the mind. The emotional give-and-take has to tone down before people can hear the content of their ideas.

The process has to be the equalizer and moderating influence. Getting participants to think through ground rules and follow a certain structure in getting ideas on the table are the means you have to refocus them away from advocacy and into meaningful dialogue. But when you put together people who have spent years fighting, distrusting, and trying to manipulate each other, they don't become the angels of honest discourse overnight.

We used a number of methods to enforce attention to ideas in as open a manner as possible—small groups, brainstorming, and a form of idea mapping using large wall charts, scenarios, and tours. Some participants had so much difficulty breaking out of their rigid ways of formulating arguments that it would take repeated explanations of how an innovative process worked before I knew I was actually getting through to them.

Distrust in a group also spills over into attitudes about the mediators. People pay a lot of attention to how much time you spend with members of one group or another, how much airtime different participants get, and how often you have to cut someone short or try to draw out another person's ideas. There were times when different groups would express concern that I was tipping the process toward one set of participants. You have to be open constantly to concerns of that type and spend as much time as necessary responding and building trust.

Local Knowledge and Talent

Those issues are always there, but in this case I also had a co-mediator to work with, and the fact was that we had very different styles. My colleague was an attorney who had turned to mediation late in his career. His natural style tended to be argumentative; mine is more elicitive. Both styles can work quite well in mediation, but we had not worked together before so I didn't have the instinctive understanding and trust in my colleague's style and experience that you need in order to have the best team relationship. I couldn't be sure of the impact he might have in handling a particular situation, nor could he be sure of mine. We dealt with that by carefully dividing responsibilities to avoid getting in each other's way. But there was one time in a tense meeting when his approach backfired, I had to step in, and then some in the group felt that even the mediators were disagreeing. We recovered from that, but it's the sort of worry you don't want to have in an already difficult process.

How did we design the process? Well, 34 makes for a large group, and we used a subcommittee structure to give as many people as possible specific roles. A tremendous amount of time was devoted to giving people background information on all kinds of subjects. It was a very technical area to get into. We had a number of very well respected experts, external people, brought in to give us this information.

There was a very wonderful guy from the U.S. Geological Survey who was well respected by everybody. He was a natural with groups in explaining concepts simply and directly. He put together slideshows on how the aquifer system works, and everyone could listen to him because they trusted that he had no ax to grind. He was terrific.

The group wanted to have a technical consultant work with us, and I thought that was going to be very hard to get consensus on. But in fact, there was a person who had worked for one of the river authorities, and then he had gone to work for the SAWS. I thought, "Well, this is going to poison or taint his usability in this case"—but not at all. The harshest critic of the city said, "He's been on the other side working with them, but we still respect him." I had worked with this fellow before on an earlier problem—same set of issues, different setting. So, he would coordinate with the other experts. He would find the people. He would sometimes give presentations himself. So, that was great.

The co-facilitator and I were, from the beginning, searching for basic policy elements the group could agree on. What would be the major principles guiding the allocation of resources regarding water for the future of San Antonio? What would these principles be?

For a long time, I had to resist pressure from many participants to "define" the problem. They wanted to have a discussion about defining, "What is the problem we are here to solve?" The problem with a conventional approach to "defining the problem" is that you generally end up with a definition that limits the terms of debate and forecloses some possibilities. This is especially true in a case like this where the definition of the problem had become part of the political fight. So it became very sensitive whether you said, "San Antonio has a water problem," or not.

The anti-city policy people said, "They are pretending that the city has a water problem. They are talking about drought. They are talking about all these problems, but this aquifer is the most abundant water source in Texas [which is demonstrably true, because of how it is structured]. Over time, it has shown no major decline in its elevation."

The water levels in these limestone aquifers of the region drop rapidly in periods of drought, but they fill right back up in times when rain returns. So, to characterize this as a "water-short" situation, the critics said, just created the idea that we live in an arid environment, a water-short environment, when in fact, "All they want to do is profit. They want to make you think we are running out of water so that they can build their dam and import water! Then they could control water instead of preserving this aquifer as the sole source of drinking water. They could build over the recharge zone 'til their heart's content and do anything they want."

So, of course, on the other side they are saying, "We don't have enough water. The federal government is telling us that we have to protect this species and these springs. The way the water formation is set up, water moves across a broad area about 150 miles in length and narrows, and at certain points comes to the surface in the form of very, very abundant springs, the most abundant springs in Texas. There's a whole economic world developed around that, as well as endangered species and very strong environmental interests. So, in order to keep the springs high, you have to be conservative in the amount of water you take out of the aquifer."

So, on the chamber's side and others, they were facing regulations. They said, "The state is trying to limit how much water we can take out. If the state fails, the federal government will succeed because of the Endangered Species Act. We can't pretend this isn't happening. We need some other sources of water."

Mediation as Policy Analysis

The way the problem needs to be defined in consensus groups is really by looking at interests because this is a political problem that we're dealing with—the inability of the city to make a political choice. So certain interests have to be satisfied, and all those interests were around the table. All of those interests have to be satisfied before the city can break out of this impasse. That's the problem.

The basic question was, "How is the city going to spend money in the future on water sources and water supply?" That was the charge, and that's what I limited the discussion to. The city didn't say exactly that, but they did say "water policy."

The principles came out more spontaneously because one of the structural devices we used in this big committee—an unruly committee in some ways—in addition to using subcommittees was the use of interim reports to the city council. Everyone wanted fast action, and we had to make an interim report about two months into the process.

I can't remember who suggested this. I think what happened was that the committee had been talking and identifying issues as we went through the process of looking at information and recording people's reactions and all of that. What I did was to take a huge roll of newsprint, and after one meeting I spread that out, about 30 feet long, and I had written all of the ideas they had come up with. I clustered them into groups that made sense to me. I put this up on a huge wall in this vast hotel conference room that we were in, and I started pointing out what I was hearing in terms of the clustering of these issues.

One of the big clusters had to do with people's sense of community: Whatever policy they came up with had to show that San Antonio was together, that it was unified—the water policy wasn't driving the city apart. Some people wanted that as a kind of hitch to the outside world in terms of economic development. Some people wanted that because it was a deep core value they had as social justice advocates. Or whatever.

So, community unity stood out as something that came up again and again, and then there were a few other things, like equity. The issue for some people, African-Americans on the east side, for example, was, "Hey, we are saving water. We're paying high prices for water, but then when I drive up on the north side, I see these hoses going forever, these sprinklers going forever, on these golf courses or whatever. It's unfair. We have to cut back, but on the north side they can have all the water they want." Not only that, the city had an old-fashioned rate structure under which you paid less per unit the more water you used. So that favored the commercial interests—an equity issue.

So I put up this big newsprint with these clusters of issues. Out of that I said, "Now we need to come up with a report. What are we going to do?"

Shared Principles

People really sort of looked at that and kept thinking about it, and came up with, "Well, there are some principles we can say that we agree on," and those eight core values came really to be the heart and soul of the ultimate agreement.

So, we identified those principles for this interim agreement, and it was almost a matter of course at that time—they didn't even think this was a big deal. It just seemed self-evident, but in fact it was a very big deal.

We went from clusters to principles because in clustering I brought up some of these more general ideas. I named them. I didn't try to do anything more than that. And that, I think, registered with people.

It wasn't at the same meeting, but a couple of meetings after, they said, "Ah! Principles—there they are," and they got in the habit of thinking, "There are some basic things that we share—in terms of concerns—and we need to acknowledge those."

The deadline for this report was important in making it happen. There was a lot of pressure in the process. That was very good, because for that six- or seven-month period—you can't hold people's attention for a real long time—this process became the only game in town. If you wanted to talk about the future of water policy in the city, this was it.

Now, if it were any less important than that, I don't think there would have been the pressure to agree. There was a lot of publicity around it. There were columns in the newspaper written about it. There were TV and radio reports regularly about what was happening. One curmudgeon columnist ranted in one column about how much money this was costing and how it wasn't going to get anywhere, how it was a big waste of time. So, the pressure was important.

The deadline was important because people needed to see results. The next year, the mayoral election was going to be held. So I had a mayor who was going to run on having made a breakthrough in water policy—so we damn well had better make a breakthrough in water policy! And I had the arch-opponent of the mayor from the previous election, whom everyone expected to run again—and, in fact, she did—and she was going to run on the fact that the city had screwed up water policy. So everyone thought, "She'll never agree to anything," because it wasn't in her political interest to do so.

Navigating Politics As Usual

As we moved towards the end of this process, everybody else started declaring his or her interest in running for mayor. One was this very grandfatherly member of the city council who was monitoring the whole process with us. He was in the room largely because he had a good relationship with the anti-Applewhite people and with the mayor. He was a very helpful intermediary, a kind of calming voice on the radicals. He was not a member, but he was there. He would remind them that the city council had this in mind, and it didn't have this other thing in mind when they wanted to push the scope of the process. He decided that he would run for mayor. So I now had three mayoral candidates directly involved in this.

Then another mayoral candidate—whom I had interviewed during the run up to this whole thing—wasn't at the table but was a member of the city council. He declared he would run for mayor, and he sent a letter to every member of the committee—except for the radical anti-city activists of which there were four. His letter said, "Be reasonable. Come up with a policy. Don't listen to the hardliners. Make this breakthrough—do it." He wasn't specific in his suggestions, but he was clear in saying, "Repudiate the extremists and come up with a new policy." So he was getting political points out of this "open letter to the committee," and all that was very good—because there was a lot at stake, and when there's a lot at stake, you've got to get this resolved. Something has to happen here.

To help them move ahead, the interim reports were the occasions to summarize what they could agree on, without saying, "This is a big deal," and saying instead, "This is just an interim report." In short, they realized we've got to tell them something, and here's an opportunity to summarize things we've been talking about.

So from the first meeting I had them talk about what would be achieved if we succeeded in this process and had a great breakthrough. Alternatively, What would the future look like if we did not succeed? I had them talk about that in small groups. Then, after we had many meetings of background information, bringing out all the ins and outs of the technical problems and the policy questions, I did my 30-foot spread of clustered issues and got them thinking again: "OK, here are the good things that can happen, and here are the bad things that can happen. You keep coming back to these same things."

So when it was time for that interim report, the way had been prepared for people to say, "Well, there are some things we can agree on—at the level of general principles." That was a very important step.

Now, in an intuitive way I knew that we were heading in that direction without explicitly saying, "This is the goal of the process." I didn't tell them, "We need to come up with these principles before we do anything else," but it did emerge. I expected something like that because I could hear right off the bat some of these big themes that kept coming up. I didn't tell them the themes, they told me. I wouldn't have known these ahead of time really, so from that first discussion as these things started coming up, it was my job to put the words in front of them to show, "Last time you said this, this time you say that—this is all tied together."

After this midpoint of formulating these principles, the group felt very strongly, "OK, we want a big report—a big report about how all of these issues fit together, and that will be the structure for indicating what our policy recommendations are."

I argued against that. I said, "There is no way you can do a big report. It would be a hundred pages. How the hell are you going to agree on a hundred pages? We have a lot of principles agreed upon—and that's great—and there are some more of those, but if you try for a hundred page deal...."

A Solution: Studying Competing Strategies

They would not accept that. They said, "Oh, we can do it," because, after having done those eight principles, they thought, "Hey, we can do more. We can really do something here!" So, they set up a drafting committee and in a couple of meetings—maybe it was just the first one or two meetings—the lights went on.

It started really in one of those hallway conversations with a few people who said, "Now, look. What if we just said, 'We don't make a choice about which water strategy we are going to follow.' We don't say, 'We're going to follow the anti-Applewhite strategy.' We don't say, 'We're going to follow the chamber strategy.' But we just honestly study all of the strategies side by side—we don't rule anything out—and we allocate money to make sure every conceivable strategy is thoroughly reviewed and do that in a very public way so that it's above-board." That was the key. That was the contribution of these principles.

The committee members didn't really have adequate data about the specific water projects or strategies at the time of the discussion. One group kept claiming, "We don't really have a problem of water scarcity. You can rethink your way of managing this aquifer. You can take more water out of it." But they didn't have a technical solution worked out at that point—though about four years later they did—but at that point, it was the vaguest thing. So, even if you believed it—if you wanted to believe them—there was nothing really to look at. It would take years of study to fill in the blanks. The best we could really do was to say, "We will study all of these things."

The committee that decided this included people on all sides. There were some very reasonable people from the business community, this younger generation. They could see the logic of this. The military was interested in this approach, and everybody wanted the military on their side. The military was just so important for credibility as well as economic clout in San Antonio. The business community claimed the military as one of their own, and the anti-city hall group were just as eager to demonstrate to the military that they could have a better deal if they forgot about the expensive importation schemes and focused on managing the aquifer differently.

So the committee had this meeting where it was clear as a bell to them. They said, "This is going to work—we really have the secret." Then they went to the full group, and it was a very interesting case where the committee was so excited about what they presented, but the verbal articulation of it sounded very flat, and it didn't click with anybody else. The others just said, "What's that?"

They didn't even put it the way I put it, "We'll keep everything on the table." They just said, "Well, here is the structure of a report," and they put it in a very boring format. I should have worked more with them on that.

So it took several more meetings of thrashing through the issues and getting everyone to see that they were really onto something. But in the end, it was all useful, because they struggled through it, and they really got some clarity.

Challenges of Closure: From The Groan Zone to "We Can Do This!"

We got through to a point where we said, "Well, to wrap this up and to finish up this big report, we need a weekend retreat." So, we had a weekend retreat, and we went through all of the recommendations trying to get drafts of all the language of this big report. But unfortunately—and as I feared—the drafting committee started coming up with drafts that were partisan. They just weren't able to write objectively, dispassionately.

I was helping, I was involved, but they were doing the drafting. Then I would see the results and ask, "What the hell is that?" One of them read just like a brief or a PowerPoint presentation about who was right—it was horrible.

So this started creating problems, and even though we reached a lot of agreement in this weekend retreat, it was getting into the last week and we still had this big fat report that was just too long.

What I had foreseen as a problem came to pass. They could never agree on the details of a 100-page report. The result was that they were focusing on the 20 things they couldn't resolve and forgetting about the 20 things they had resolved and agreed to already. We really got down to some hot and heavy issues during one last meeting, and they spent the first hour of this meeting just fighting back and forth, back and forth. It was just reverting to the worst behavior.

So I said, "OK, we're taking a break, and I'm going to come back and I'm going to make a proposal."

We had about two days before we had to bring our final report to the city council, and I figured that what I was going to do was strip this down, throw out most of this language, and get it down to core principles that I knew they had already agreed on. I'm not sure it would have worked if I had announced after the break, "I'm going to do this."

But fortunately the military guy, the colonel, said, "John, why don't you give me a few minutes after we come back from the break?" He was writing up—on a flip chart—exactly what I had in mind. "Here's what we have to agree on"—because he had listened to the chamber and had been to all those meetings. He had also listened to the hardliners, and he had listened to all the experts too. He saw that there were some ways in which the hardliners were right on—about how the aquifer worked and the way the problem looked to them. And he could also see where they went too far, where the facts didn't support them. So he said, "Well, look. We pretty much have to agree. We've already agreed on these things, but there are a couple of other things we have to agree to—because we can't change them." He just explained it in that way, and again, he was from the military, and everybody wanted the military on their side.

The relief was instantaneous. It was one of those great moments where we went from what some people call the "groan zone," where people are at their worst—fighting, accusing, and falling back to the original behavior that got them there in the first place—to where, all of a sudden, there was this wonderful exhilaration and excitement that "Hey, we can do this!"

So, we resolved that the colonel and I, overnight, would produce this small report. At a final meeting the next night we would notify everyone and build our consensus, and the morning after that we would take it to the city council.

The next night, almost everybody came out in support of this compromise proposal, including most of the old allies of the hardline opponents of city water policy. One by one, they came out and supported this, including some very influential people in the audience during a public comment period. But the four hardline leaders wouldn't sign off. They just refused to sign.

Near Consensus: A Big Breakthrough

The rest of the group was really at the end of its patience. I was feeling kind of bad because I knew we were going to wind up by counting signatures—as if it was a form of voting. So I was feeling bad, thinking, "If we don't get them, what kind of agreement do we have?" They refused to sign it, but everybody else signed it.

The next day, we went in to the city council, and we presented this report. I presented it for a little while, and then everybody talked about it—the mayor and all the members of the city council. They hailed it as a "big breakthrough." Then at least half of the members of the committee came up individually to offer their comments.

Then it was the turn of the opposition mayoral candidate. She got up there, and the first thing she did was to thank the mayor for sticking to his promise and not meddling in the committee for six-and-a-half months—for staying on the sidelines. He stuck to his word, and she gave him a lot of credit for that. She pointed out all the things that she was pleased with in the report—that it really did make progress—and then she ranted a bit about the things she didn't like. So did the other opposition leaders. They basically gave this a mixed report card.

It was pretty clear that there were certain things that gave the city license to do what they wanted, but the long-time city opponents were able to benefit because the report brought many of their principles to the table for the first time, getting them into water policy in the city in a more legitimate way, without their actually having to sign it. So this was a classic case of their letting the thing go through—without actively opposing it—and, in fact, offering some public praise for it.

So I then felt much better, when I realized the logic of that, from their point of view. That was very exciting. In fact, over the succeeding five or six years, those critics repeatedly referred back to this agreement as almost a covenant that was reached by the city with all the different constituents every time they were afraid the city was varying from that. So, this became a sort of classic text—this was the core agreement. It was very exciting.

There was a commitment in this agreement to an open, public process for future decisions about water. That was important because in the past anybody who disagreed with the chamber of commerce or the city water policy was not only excluded from a committee, they were usually told to leave the room if it was at all a public meeting. They were used to being hounded out and totally excluded. So, the commitment to that open public process was really a key thing.

Now, the reality is that this is the sort of agreement that could sit on a shelf and not amount to anything. But what was important was that such a broad and diverse group supported it and made sure that the city stayed with that commitment as well. That is what set it apart.

Reflections on Power, Process, and Politics

This was a very interesting case because here the powerless or the relatively powerless had built their power, and they had fought and won against the city establishment against all the odds—all the money was on one side. But this strange coalition of people—many of whom were in very poor communities, and many from wealthy communities too—this strange coalition beat the powers that be. So they weren't powerless anymore—in terms of politics and counting votes, they had made their point. They could not be denied.

As for participation by the hardliners, it seemed, going in, that the basic principle was that the people who the city had tried to ignore needed to be at the table. This case had high press visibility. We simply agreed that no one was going to speak on behalf of the committee until the committee authorized somebody to do that. We couldn't keep individual members from talking to the press, but they always had to specify that they were only giving their own opinions, talking as individuals.

The point was that we were trying to create an atmosphere for collaboration. It's very easy to destroy that and to destroy any potential for trust if you're yelling at people in front of a TV camera and then sitting down next to them trying to get them to agree on something. Nevertheless, a few of them violated that because they couldn't resist a sound bite here or a sound bite there.

Race and ethnicity was very interesting here. I've worked on water policy issues for 25 years, and often I've seen cases where people of color were not involved in the discussion at all. Sometimes that was because you were talking about water planning over a 50-year period. You're not talking about some immediate issue in this community, which people can relate to. It gets very abstract, very quickly. But these communities had been engaged on this issue—they were in the fight, and they were well represented at the table.

So, this was an exception—there were issues of discrimination implicit in the basic problem about equity and the fact that the developer community had been leading the city for 20 years to focus investment and development dollars north instead of in the old part of the city. So, that was there, and the rate structure and all those things, and they were all connected.

San Antonio has learned to make plenty of room in the public sphere and in the political sphere for people of color—but not in the economic sphere. But I think they were well represented here.

I love the politics in this work and figuring out what people are trying to gain and what they want, how to define their "threshold" for declaring victory, or loss. Often you have to work with them on that a little bit because they may not be clear, in a strategic sense, when they have won enough, when they need to back off, and when they need to moderate.

The hard-line leaders against city policy had the most trouble with that because they couldn't accept any other point of view as legitimate. After a while, a few of them did isolate themselves because everybody else came to see, "Hey, there are some reasonable things here. We want to move ahead. We don't want to be just held up in this constant struggle," and so those four were alone in the end. It was quite dramatic. They had angered, even alienated, many of their allies.

So I'm really intrigued by all of that. What I learned most from the process involved this question, "What is consensus?" What does it mean to say, "Well, can you live with this, even if you can't sign the document?"

Now, I don't usually imagine that you're going to get 100 percent consensus from a big committee like that. But here were four major spokespersons for a particular point of view, and at the outset it would have been inconceivable to me that if we didn't have their willing acceptance, we would still have an agreement. I had to learn. "Well, they're letting it go ahead, and they're taking advantage of it to this extent—that they wanted to keep an out for themselves for the things they don't agree on, and their way of doing that was even going so far as to offer 50 percent praise in public to their enemies for what was achieved, and then holding back their signatures as a symbolic repudiation of the rest."

In terms of people's interests, I think some people did come out with a changed perspective. I think there were some people who had long opposed city water policy and would never have imagined that they would wind up accepting an agreement that also had the blessing of the chamber—and many people in the chamber wouldn't have imagined that they would get that close to a general agreement.

Did people think about their interests any differently because of this process? I observed a bit of change thinking about interests on the part of the new generation of business people because I couldn't have had a more graphic or dramatic example than having the old guard telling me, "Now, this is the only community you have to worry about. We're the employers. We run the place. That's it." And then having the younger people saying, "That's crazy—they're shooting themselves in the foot the way the hardliners on the other side are shooting themselves in the foot. They say these outrageous things and make these outrageous claims, and they alienate everybody, and you can't get away with that."

There are really interesting internal differences within the parties. There can be many ways of interpreting how basic interests are best served, but those differences are sometimes hidden by loud voices of the more vociferous members. It's hard for outsiders to notice that changes are going on within a group as younger members adapt their thinking and strategies to changing circumstances.

Afterword

The San Antonio water policy case represented one brief chapter in a decades-long controversy about how to manage groundwater of the Edwards Aquifer system in south central Texas. While trying to learn from the record of this one process, it's also important to look at longer-term process scales. Only in that way can you get a realistic idea of the contribution that collaborative methods can make.

Participants, planners, and mediators alike are judged, of course, in terms of immediate outcomes. In the midst of the action, the pressure is intense to get results—in this case a new policy that could draw the city together as never before. After years of conflict that had led to stalemate, everyone wanted something they could rally around as a win, and this process gave them an agreement to point to. The press lavished praise on the new policy, and the politicians used it as best they could to further their careers. The agreement, however, needed a lot of follow-up if it was to be anything more than a brief headline.

This was fundamentally an agreement about a future process for evaluating the specific water strategies that could balance conflicting interests in a substantive way. The necessary follow-up was the institutionalization of that even-handed process. This was done through a second collaborative effort involving the same parties in the form of a citizens committee. It attracted far less public or political attention since it had to do with defining criteria for decision making rather than getting at specific water projects. It achieved the purpose of creating a more transparent process for evaluating future projects according to detailed criteria with regular input through citizen participation open to all interested groups.

This is the sort of follow-up process that should be planned for and put in place following an agreement in principle, as happened with the San Antonio water policy document. Over time, it's all too easy for the business of water politics to resume its usual course, which tends to result in the public being asked to support decisions and projects without ongoing involvement. That sets up the dynamic of decision making in which a project is accepted or rejected as a whole, a process that not only invites public conflict, but also is also wasteful of everyone's resources. The follow-up process offered a step-by-step way to screen projects in a public review. It was not a perfect system, but it was a step in the direction of institutionalizing the principle of collaboration.

In addition to considering a longer-term implementation scale relating to a particular agreement, there is also the need to look at how an expanding group of participants become organized to deal with a regional resource problem. When I first became involved in the Edwards conflict, some years prior to working on the specifics of San Antonio water policy, I worked on a regional process involving six major players, representing a range of groundwater users, including San Antonio. Each of them tightly controlled access to internal decision making about water, and, as a group, they wanted to exclude all public participation. This strikes me now as a good example of a system with tightly closed boundaries. Even though the regional conditions and politics were changing dramatically, this group was artificially constraining the information it was willing to consider as important by refusing to allow participation by newer groups that were beginning to make their influence felt.

One thing we've learned from the study of complex self-organizing adaptive systems is that keeping boundaries open is essential. New participants bring new information and early signs of change that will require adaptation to ensure survival. I think a collaborative approach to major policy decisions permits an approach analogous to that of most complex systems in keeping human use of a regional resource as responsive and adaptive as possible. One way of looking over several decades of history of the Edwards conflict is that the system for managing human sharing of the resource has been forced open in response to numerous pressures, including national protection of endangered species, urban growth beyond the boundaries of individual cities, state-level decisions about water management, and more widespread access to information and decision making by groups that had long been excluded.

I can look back on the San Antonio water policy process as one step in this longer-term change. In that light, I like to think that the trend toward more collaborative efforts has a certain inevitability to it. The reality of our politics, however, is that we continue to have institutions that try to sustain control for as long as possible, exclude diverse perspectives, and impose solutions based on narrow interests and ideology. It falls to planners, mediators, and a few supportive political leaders to work in this setting of fiercely adversarial conflict and to use their influence to add as much of a more open and collaborative approach as possible. While the parties may be searching for an immediate political result, the organizers of a process need also to plan as much as possible to extend the influence of collaboration into the future through some form of institutionalization.

Chapter 10
Facilitating the Land-Use Planning Process for Vancouver Island

Gordon Sloan

Gordon Sloan introduces us to both the complexity of regional land-use planning and the opportunities of managing and enabling multiparty problem-solving processes. Taking on the project of devising a plan for all of Vancouver Island, Sloan convened representatives of 14 "sectors" so that industry and economic development interests clustered, indigenous groups clustered, environmental interests clustered, and so on. These sectors then had their own internal negotiations to consider, along with the strategic and substantive questions regarding how they would present their interests, goals, and uncertainties to the other representatives at the table.

Sloan shows us strikingly that before parties can learn and work together, they may well need to undo, to unlearn, their own strong presumptions of what they're getting into together. But that's easier said than done. So, he argues, intermediaries might often help deeply committed parties early on to presume less and to probe more, so that they can craft options that serve their interests well. When a new and uncertain process itself raises questions for participants about what they might expect, and what they might really get done, Sloan shows us, time spent together on training might help everyone do better, individually and collectively.

In part, too, Sloan suggests in a telling passage, parties can much more easily be skeptical about each other's willingness to work together than they can initially be trusting. So we see a process here involving regional complexity and interdependence, technical, legal, and social complexities, challenges of process design, and parties learning about each other too. Sloan shows how initially plausible, even seductive, presumptions, of "either-or" or "whether or not" might give way to a creative search for "how" options might take shape. Sloan keeps us focused practically on the ways, in complex multiparty land-use and environmental cases, parties might do the realistic and creative work that will enable them, as he puts it pointedly, to "build solutions together that accommodate, not compromise, the interests of everybody." —JF

They're each saying exactly the same thing about the other. That's a piece of information that they should know. It's handy to be able to tell them that when they say to you, "You'll be able to trust what we say, but there's no way you can trust anything they say." It's great to be able to say to them in response that, "You won't believe this, but they used exactly the same words to describe their view of you." They're amazed. "They did! They don't think we're accountable?" They discover that there are all kinds of assumptions that one value system makes about the other that have to be debunked.

I mediated the Vancouver Island regional process of CORE, the Commission on Resources and the Environment. That was a land-use negotiation and resource allocation process that involved setting the strategic land uses for that whole area. Vancouver Island is a huge area of land. It's bigger than many American states. It's probably about 350 miles long. It contains some of the really contentious areas that have been in the papers, Clayoquot Sound, Carmanah Valley, an area known as Robson Bite, which is where the killer whales do their rock rubbing. It has a number of places of international and even global significance with respect to environmental issues, specifically forest issues. It has probably the biggest and most productive temperate rain forest in the world. That's been very heavily logged, although not in all cases heavily modified.

So the battle is typically between development and resource extraction on the one hand, and protection and conservation on the other. It's a very classic pro-con battle. The mediation project involved in that, from a mediator's point of view, was to try to break out of the "either-or," "distributive" approaches to those kinds of problems and to encourage integrated approaches that would involve the parties in actually working together to set a land-use plan rather than to try to defeat one another. There have been lots of other successful arenas for battling with one another. We didn't want to transport that battle into the negotiation.

Beyond Either-Or Negotiation

I felt that the transformation from an "either-or" to a more collaborative approach was an important way to go. In the way I mediate and in the way I teach mediation, that's one of the three or four most important transformations. People have to approach the problem as one that is a common problem for all. If they don't do that, they're going to have to succeed against one another. So they've really got the choice: Are we going to distribute victory over a fixed pie — in this case a plan for an island — or are we going to work together to actually create the pie in a way that is mutually acceptable?

People come into those discussions making the assumption — and I think it's partly cultural, partly contextual — that the question of preservation or development is an "either-or"; it's a "whether-or-not." It's a classic distributional kind of a problem. I think that's a predisposition that people bring to the problem. One of the three or four major things that the mediator has to do generally is to transform that expectation into a very different expectation, one that would center around what I usually describe as a "how" or "what," rather than an "either-or" or "whether-or not." So that rather than "whether or not such and such an area is going to be preserved and protected," the question should be, "How do we deal with this area in a way that brings about the societal, environmental, and economic expectations of everybody?" Then they've got to engage in dealing with that problem together because they can't do it against each other. They can't do it at one another's expense, or there isn't going to be a solution. They would be standing on the bridges, and litigating and injunctioning, and doing all that sort of stuff. But I see that transformation from distributive to integrative strategies as partly a procedural change. It's not just a change of attitude. Mediators have the opportunity to actually make that happen by framing the issues in such a way that they're only capable of being dealt with together. If the issues are framed as "What we've got to solve here is whether or not this will be a protected area," well, you've just set up a distributional approach to the problem. The mediators have a tremendous amount of influence and I think very productive influence in framing the issues in an integrated way.

The Mechanics of the Mediation

In this mediation, there were 14 sectors. It was such a big mediation that we organized all of the interests on Vancouver Island, and in fact, way beyond those of Vancouver Island — they were global in nature. Each sector was defined as a unique perspective on the problem so that rather than any one organization or one corporation or one government being at the table, we simply had whole perspectives that caused them to have to form constituencies. There was a lot of integration that went on in terms of organizing participation away from the table. We spent months doing that before the table even convened—about four months in a preparation and pre-table assessment phase.

Mechanically, what happened was that the commissioner—who is a provincial official, or in U.S. terms a state agency official—announced that rather than simply recommending to the cabinet what land uses he saw for the area, he would rather people negotiated over the uses on Vancouver Island, and he invited people to negotiate in some way. He suggested, "Why don't you contact me if you have an interest in being involved in this," and he was swamped with more than 1,000 briefs, letters, faxes, and representations. What his office did was to begin to organize those into more or less like-minded perspectives. What distilled out of that were 14 different points of view: distinct enough that it wasn't possible for anyone of them to speak for another. That was really our test: How can you gather people around a table in a totally inclusive way, but still be effective? So we used this sectoral model, and it worked pretty well. That idea evolved, I think, through some of the experiences that a number of other mediators have had in Washington, Idaho, Massachusetts, Colorado, and a number of other places.

But I think it really worked here because we had the pulp workers saying, "We're different from other unions. We're different from the guys who work in the forest." We had the forest people saying, "Well, our guys aren't pulp workers. We cut down the trees. We have a different perspective." But no, they all have the broad perspective of forest employment. So we just framed those issues and those identities broadly enough to be able to create a broad base of representation. We had local government, provincial government, forest employment, the forest manufacturers and managers, the big companies, an aboriginal presence, conservation, outdoor recreation, general nonforest employment, tourism, mining, agriculture. Youth, I think, was there as a separate sector. All of those people were at the table.

There's really an infinite number of ways that we could have divided them up. What was going through my mind at that point, not as a mediator but as a convener, was, "We've got to keep this thing small enough that people can still communicate." If you get much more than 12 or 15 people, you don't have a group any more. You have something else. You don't have a group that communicates among its members; you have a group that has to orate, you've got a gym full of people.

Working for Inclusion

It's got to be effective, but it must be inclusive. We can't create this in a contrived way that excludes people. There's got to be a funneling effect, and my worry through all this was that people would feel left out and that they would ultimately say, "I didn't have a voice."

So we just kept structuring the process and structuring the mechanics of the thing to meet that concern. We invited people to meetings all over Vancouver Island, at about a dozen different places. And various people from CORE, or me, or another mediator who was working with me, would go to these public meetings and say, "Look, here's what the commissioner's envisaging. Here's how it appears to be shaping up, here are some perspectives that we see being at the table. We're interested in your perspective. We want you to be involved in an effective but inclusive way. How do you think it ought to be done?"

We just got views, and then we wrote back to everybody who had contacted the commissioner and said, "We think that your perspective is very like the following groups. We are hosting a meeting of all those groups on such and such a day. Do you want to come?"

Each sector then had the opportunity to meet privately and to identify itself. Without people who they viewed as the enemy present, all of the people involved in, say, fishery, got together. There were unions, on-shore workers, independent fishermen, shellfish people, everybody—people who typically wouldn't get together in the same room. They have quite distinct interests, but as a global interest, fishery, vis-à-vis everything else, is distinct. We said, "We think you're what we're calling a sector. We think you're a perspective at the table. We want you to organize in some way that can focus your presence at the table." Then we gave them a suggestion. That was to choose a spokesperson who could change from time to time, instructed by a steering group, which could be three people, 12 people, whatever they wanted, but that steering group would then be responsible to the membership, who might be thousands of people, or 10 organizations, or whatever. It varied from sector to sector. That was the central model that we proposed and the people generally adopted.

Accountability to Constituencies

Each sector was very differently organized. But it was important, once the mediation got underway, that each sector was able to convince each other sector of its accountability. Each had to be able to show that. Each had to be able to show its accountability for decisions that it might make and its accountability up and down the chain. In the case of large corporations or unions, it's very easy to obtain that accountability because they already have the existing organization.

They're politically accountable. In the case of the conservation sector—which was composed of about 80 different environmental groups, from massive international groups to church basement recycling outfits, just a tremendous hodge-podge of people—there wasn't the same degree of accountability. Those who spoke at the table couldn't say with certainty that they spoke for everybody and that they could keep people off the bridges. But as long as everyone at the table understood that and had an opportunity to examine one another's accountability (which they did), it worked.

A lot of this arose before we got to the table. You'd have one group saying about another, "Well, we're accountable. We intend to be there until the end, but those buggers aren't going to be there." Or, "There's no way you can get them to mean what they're going to say, or to perform what they promise to do, once they come to the table." There were issues of trust too in this accountability strategy; it was not just a question of do you really speak for everybody? There was also anxiety about whether the thing could work, whether we trust the other, whether there'll be enough money to do this, how long is this all going to take anyhow, what about this, what about that? All kinds of preconditions came up prior to convening the table. They all arose then, which is ideal, because you have a chance as a mediator to work with those problems. Those are sets of interests that the parties have got to meet somehow. They see them as preconditions: "There's no damn way we're getting to this table until we have funding promised to us." Well, that has to be reframed. That description of a problem is not a pre-condition, it's a criterion for the speaker that needs to be solved.

So, as each of these 14 sectors were beginning to meet amongst themselves, we were actually facilitating those conversations as well. We made that optional. We simply said, "If you want mediation, the commission will pay for it. If you don't and you want to meet among yourselves, it's a deal. You just organize yourselves."

Preparatory Training

So they did organize themselves some with much more sophistication than others. But it didn't really matter. That was a stylistic thing. They could do it any way they wanted. What emerged from that was almost everybody saying, "Look, our problem here is we don't know how to do this thing we're about to do at the table. You've got to give us a hand."

It was apparent that we needed to provide training. So we did something that I don't think has ever been done before: we provided training to each sector separately about basic negotiation and process. Before the table even sat down for its convening meeting, for its first meeting, every sector had privately had 1.5

days of training for their whole steering group and any other interested people. There were as few as four or five in the smallest training session and as many as 80 in the biggest one. It was fascinating. So they came to the table already having a common concept of what it means, at least theoretically, to sit down together and begin to define issues, begin to identify interests, begin to solve problems. I'd never done that before. I'd never had the budget to do it before.

Since about half my work is training, I had trained a lot of people at multi-party tables—usually at a whole table when they were well into their work. You know, they'll decide, "We need a workshop. This thing's not going well."

"Workshop" is code for "We're in trouble." What you do in those cases is that you go in and work through some of the trouble while you're delivering training, but it's not ideal. The neat thing about what I've just described was that by the time they were up and running, they were all of one mind about what it meant to ask open questions, to listen to what people say, to seek interest-based information, to abandon positions. All of that at least wasn't foreign jargon to them, and it made a big difference, a very big difference.

I think that two things led us to do it that way, instead of our usual way of doing it once they're together as a group. One was that they kept saying, "We don't know if we're up to this. We don't know if we've got the skills. What about the big boys? They have the money. They must have taken some training." So there was fear there. Although the big boys were all saying, "We don't know whether we're up to this either. We're used to labor management negotiations. We don't know what this negotiation is going to be like."

So everyone had an appetite for training. That was the first thing.

The second thing was that as we got into the pre-convening phase, it was apparent to us that there was a difference of appreciation out there, both in government and among the sectors, about whether this was primarily a planning exercise or primarily a dispute resolution exercise—that is, a negotiation. What kind of animal was this? I wanted to make it clear that, to the extent that their outputs would be planning outputs, they weren't going to really get to those until they had resolved some of the conflicts. I thought that the best way to make that clear was to teach.

In other words, I couldn't simply say, "You're going to have to negotiate, period," because that wouldn't mean anything to them. We had to demonstrate, teach, and do some skills-based training for them to actually practice and role-play before they had a sense of what it meant to attempt to solve problems with people whose values were so radically different from theirs.

And when I say theirs, I mean every group; each group shared that impression, that it's us against them. It's this dichotomy that you run into all the time in mediation, but it's much more serious in multiparty public policy negotiations: "There's no way that the enemy will ever understand me," because "the enemy" is inherently evil, weak, out of touch, all those things. That being the case, "There's no way we'll ever come to terms." So the way to solve that, it seems to me, is to give people a chance privately and safely within their own sector to air their own anxiety, to practice some of this stuff, and to have an experiential bite at seeing that they can do this. They can communicate effectively; they can deal with stupid behavior across the table effectively. Or at least they have a sense of what that would be like. That was very effective.

How do we have them vent their anxieties in a way that's at all productive when it might also fuel the fires? What's productive is for me to do an orientation on a Sunday-Monday with the green side of this problem and then on a Wednesday-Thursday with the brown side of this problem.

They're each saying exactly the same thing about the other. That's a piece of information that they should know. It's handy to be able to tell them that, when they say to you, "You'll be able to trust what we say, but there's no way you can trust anything they say." It's great to be able to say to them in response that, "You won't believe this, but they used exactly the same words to describe their view of you."

They're amazed. "They did! They don't think we're accountable?" They discover that there are all kinds of assumptions that one value system makes about the other that have to be debunked.

There's a lot more going on here than just teaching them communication skills. Macro-wise, they're just getting a bunch of information. They're finding out about what the process might be like, getting a sense of the great big circus they're getting into because this thing lasted a year and a half, and any long multiparty public policy process is like that. There are survival skills one needs to be able to get through such a process. So, there's the information component, and that was a big deal.

Second, there's a communication skills and negotiation component that they just scratch the surface of in a day and a half, but that's important.

Third, I think they begin to crystallize their own interests. They don't know that yet because they don't know what interests are, but they begin to retreat from positions that they take about the land base, and they begin to identify specific areas of need, desire, concern, fear, aspiration, expectation—what I would call interests—that they've got to be very clear on by the time the negotiation gets rolling.

They do that by way of the exercises in the training session and through the discussions that are going on. They're beginning for the first time to think in terms of what do we really want to get out of this?, rather than what is our opening gambit going to be?

You want to dissuade them off all that. You want to persuade them to disclose to everyone at the table—and persuade everyone else to disclose to everyone at the table—what they're really there for, because you want to build solutions together that accommodate, not compromise, the interests of everybody. That's the objective. So they begin to get a sense of that. I say "begin" because it's a long process, but it happens, and it happens early.

Gaining Power in Negotiations

Were groups empowered? Did this level the playing field in some ways? We certainly heard a lot about that issue, although not specifically from aboriginal people. Aboriginal people were always on the sideline of this negotiation because they have a parallel land claim process in British Columbia right now, so they weren't involved in the same way. They came periodically to observe. But this did help to level the playing field for less organized groups.

There was empowerment both within the groups and between any group and another. That empowerment was played out functionally and structurally too because each group had only one vote. Each group had only one presence. There was no voting, although everyone, of course, assumed that there were going to be votes, but they understood that the input to consensus by any group is as powerful as any other group. So that although one group is cutting $1.2 billion worth of product from the study area per year and another group has no budget at all, they still are equal at the table. It's still as important for the big guys to convince the little guys and the little guys to convince the big guys as it ever was. They're also getting a sense of being able to trust the process. But that really takes time. I don't think they fully trust that process until about half way into it. They come to trust it as they see increased opportunity—that's my experience—and they trust it as they see their confidence build over time. It's really those two dimensions.

When they see, "Holy shit! We can actually accomplish more here than we can by engaging in litigation or lobbying or any of the other BATNAs (Best Alternatives To a Negotiated Agreement)," they really engage in the process. That's trust making; it's very practical.

Until that happens, there isn't a whole lot of trust. But these training sessions did begin to allay some of their apprehensions about the process and increase their level of recognition of others and others' levels of recognition of them. So there were both of those coefficients that Baruch Bush and Joseph Folger are talking about: empowerment and recognition. We saw them beginning to build in the participation process, in identification and participation. It was really interesting. Looking back on it, it's quite surprising to me that that was happening because we'd never done that before. But since then, in several large things that I've done or am now working on, I've insisted upon some element of what I like to call "orientation." Nobody wants to be "trained," but "orientation" they can live with. And so we call them "orientations," orienting each sector to the process. That was a major hallmark of the success of how this negotiation went.

Perspectives within Groups

Another thing that it helps to have, when some of these different sectors are themselves rather large groups, is to have better representation of all the perspectives from within those large groups. So they take it back to the hive, and it infects the way they operate within that group. It makes a big difference. One of the outcomes that's now been researched about this particular process is that there seems to have been tremendous spin-offs after the table finished its work in the communities. I don't know how much of this is orientation, how much is just what went on at the table. There's much, much more empowerment and recognition and just plain communication and coordination among classic enemies than there was before the process.

That makes sense. When this table began to meet, the physical setup was a couple of mediators, some staff from the commission, and then 14 seats around this table. So you had about 17 or 18 people, and then beyond them were their steering groups, typically in the next row in clusters of chairs. There might be three or four behind this chair, 10 behind that chair, one behind this chair. There were a lot of other people. And beyond them were the general public: Joe Forest-worker; a vice president of a corporation who had come over to monitor for that day; three or four people from government who were just curious about what was going on; and townspeople. We even had elementary school classes coming in to sit for a half an hour to see what a big negotiation was like. It was a traveling show that went around the Island from place to place so people did get a chance to see this going on. But the result is about 100 to 150 people at any time in the room. It's a very big, public process, and yet there is great intimacy in the inner sanctum among those who are actually speaking and negotiating with each other. So it was very interesting.

Where we were in the island didn't matter. It tended to be the same faces, but the way we structured this and the way the table crafted its process, procedure arrangements, and agreement, was that a steering group could designate its spokesperson any way it wanted. The spokespeople could change, so as the subject moved from forestry guidelines for setbacks for salmon-bearing creeks to high-altitude logging, or to visual quality objectives in logging areas for tourist purposes, people would change seats. The engineer who was an expert in that would take this person's place, or the person in the environmental sector who knew about rock and ice and protected areas would take a seat. It was quite acceptable to the table for anyone to be sitting there as long as that one person was the spokesperson for that period. That went fine. There was no contest over any of that.

Ceremonies of Beginning

We moved from there into what I describe as joint assessment. They've assessed privately, sector by sector: What do you want to negotiate?, Under what circumstances?, and What are the criteria to make the damn thing work? Now they have to assess jointly. We got them together in a convening session, which is a very polite and somewhat ceremonial event. It went for a night and then the entire next day.

Right away we got them into assessing as a table jointly, "What does this table now need for this thing to be successful?"

One sector had said, "We require another sector to pre-commit to be there the whole time. "

Well, they can't do that. Now that the sectors are all together, what can we say as a group about commitment to attend? There's a shift then from blaming the other to trying to identify as a group what the criteria are for a successful negotiation.

That was really good. That was a commitment: going around the table, each sector saying in very different ways their level of seriousness and accountability and asking, "How do you communicate back and forth? You guys, are you going to be publishing a newsletter?"

A lot of information is exchanged at that point, just prior to ground rules. This is still, as I put it, their sniffing around the hydrant. They're still checking one another out and trying to establish, jointly now rather than individually, "Yes, we want to proceed with this, and here's what we want to do. Here are the criteria that we think need to be in place for us to be effective as a table."

Again, that's fairly ceremonial. It usually involves them making all kinds of demands of government for pre-commitments that the government won't make, but at least it flexes their ego a wee bit.

In this case when we started out, we had the deputy premier, a couple of cabinet ministers, and various people at the convening session just to throw some weight at it, to demonstrate that this was a serious effort by government. The government was pumping a million bucks, or whatever it was going to be, into this process, and that ought to be some message that it's serious. The other thing was that there were so many assumptions and expectations over the preceding months and weeks that when everyone did sit down together, it was very polite initially.

Once they get into negotiating, days and days in the future, you can imagine how the gloves came off, but that was only to be expected. Initially, it was quite ceremonial, everybody expressing himself or herself politely and with great deference to everybody else. It was very nice. I think convening is actually a ceremony, not a ritual, but a ceremony. It's an actual kicking off of something.

It's very like the phony kickoff that the dignitary does at a football game. Sometimes at a football game, they haul out the president or the vice president or the mayor or somebody who does the ceremonial kickoff. Then they put the ball back at the center, and the teams play. It's really simply a signal and a ceremony, a metaphor, an extended figure of speech, saying, "OK, this thing's about to begin. We're serious. We're prepared. And we're all here, and we're glad we're here."

That's a real accomplishment when you take people who have been suing one another for decades and tying themselves to trees and doing all kinds of things for them to actually say that they've committed to spending some time trying to solve the whole problem rather than valley by valley. So that was a big deal.

Ground Rules

But they soon get down to work, and the next phase they go into is what we call process design. That's where ground rules come up. They crafted their own 10-page process and procedure agreement during that phase, which took about three or four days. It was a terrific agreement, it covered everything: what consensus is, how they shall participate, what the organization of groups will be, what spokespeople are, who has the right to talk, behavior at the table, philosophic cornerstones of the negotiation, how to deal with the press, how to deal with media—just everything under the sun.

I was mediating that discussion. That's a negotiation in its own right, and it needs assistance. Mechanically, what I did was, I gave them a template. I gave them a pro-forma that was about four pages long. "Here are some things that other groups have done. Here are some subject areas that you might want to tackle." Then we simply got into negotiating it.

At the next meeting, a number of them brought some wording, and I simply recognized people, reframed what they were saying, periodically summarized that, and gathered things up. Meanwhile a secretary at the edge of the table was typing the changes into an emerging document. Those were projected through the computer to an overhead onto the wall. So you've got 28 eyes, 14 sets of eyes, all staring at the same wording, and you're working as a single organ. That's the objective. You want to integrate this negotiation. You've got somebody across the table saying, "Just a second, move the phrase, 'as best as the table can do,' to before the verb," and everybody's pointing and staring at the same stuff. They're working on one common document at that point.

So you're already building the expectation that this is not going to be a negotiation in which four or five powerful groups each have an alternate scenario that they use to try to out-persuade the other. This is going to be one in which the table as a whole generates its own scenario together because that's what's happening with the process and procedure early on. That's very important. I was quite worried about that.

I was worried about whether that would work because you could get the manufacturers and managers, the big corporations, bringing in their finished document and presenting it to the table and saying, "We think this bears a lot of looking at," meaning "Accept this or else," and the green side simply reacting out of spite to that and coming up with a document that for its own reasons would be unacceptable to the others. Then you could have this early squaring off of extremes, this polarized distributional approach. So I was really concerned about that, but it worked very well. That was a very successful part of this thing.

I did nothing to help that, other than preparing them in the orientation. We did some theoretical work in the orientation about integrated negotiation. I can't think of anything I did other than constantly restating and summarizing what people were saying so that it's said a second time and set out there by some independent person, just in the air where people can look at it and think about it. That's vitally important.

Rephrasing and Focusing Discussions

This whole business of reflective skills, restating, reframing, paraphrasing, what in the U.S. is usually called rephrasing, which are so important in bilateral mediation, family mediation, commercial mediation, is even more important in multiparty negotiations because people get tired and you have a dozen people at the table, three of them waiting to speak. They're not going to listen to the person who's speaking, particularly if it's that same idiot who constantly says the same thing. That's their view of him or her.

So it's much more powerful if the mediator can periodically just punctuate or animate the conversation with a short summary of what he or she has heard. My colleague or I would simply say, "So basically what you're saying, Deborah, and what you've been saying, Robert, together, is a, b, c, d," just that. They nod and then you look around the table to the other dozen people and you say, "Has everybody got that?," and generally people nod. There'll be one or two people who will say, "What was that?" That demonstrates the need to have done what we just did, and then we repeat it again. Deborah and Robert have both said it, and you've tried to bring it together, actualizing the integration of what they've said. You've published it from a neutral point of view with neutral language, everybody acknowledges it, the ones who are asleep wake up, they hear it again, and that communication is complete. If that doesn't happen, I don't know how anyone can be assured that anything actually was understood at those meetings. So I think one of the mediator's prime skills is the constant use of reflection. When I started this kind of work a few years ago, I assumed that there'd be much less of that in multiparty work. But my experience is that that's not the case.

We ran into a lot of instances where, for example, the industrial folks were putting forth some position and the environmentalists just sat with their arms folded or looking away, just tuning out. What I do then depends on the context, but my practice is to try to access some specific skills that are just sitting there on the shelf ready to go, and in the moment that it happens, try to properly analyze exactly what's happening. It's very like what you do in a bilateral situation, but it's just much, much, much more complex because there's so much more going on all at once. For instance, using this example, there might be two or three people—and they're not always on the environmental side, by any means—leaning back, folding their arms, rolling their eyes, or losing it. I think I would probably select "immediacy" as a technique in those cases; that is, being prepared to observe out loud, as the neutral, what I see happening and question why it's happening in the moment that it occurs. "I notice, Dan and Bev, you seem to have lost interest in some of what's being said across the table here. There may be perfectly good reasons for that, but I just noted that it's happening at this point, and I'm wondering if what Darryl has just said, or if what he's just described, is causing you to lose interest."

Rescuing Discussions

Now, that's quite an intervention skill. It puts them on the spot, but it causes them to have to then disclose clearly what it was that was going on in that complex negotiation that put them to sleep or that caused them to react. It's very akin to what you do in bilateral mediation, usually in a more minute way, in more emotional circumstances. "I notice when so and so said such and such that you began tapping your pen. What is going on?"

I would never do that in a multiparty situation, but if it seems to be part of a whole system of ignoring something or a whole system of reaction, then I think that ought to be public, and we ought to talk openly about what's going on. When that kind of thing happens, the party who you've asked, who you've been immediate with, will typically respond by describing their aversion to what was just said by the other. That gives you as the mediator an opportunity to respond by moving from the positions that are disclosed in that aversion to the interest behind it, reframing with open questions to probe where the interest is. It gives you an opportunity to transform positions and interests. But it can be lost if you don't use immediacy in that situation.

There are a lot of other things we would do. We would call a break. We would call a caucus occasionally, although not often. We didn't use a lot of caucusing in these multiparty situations. We would ask for clarification. We would intervene in what had sometimes become an emotional situation.

Mediated Negotiations as a Forgiving Process

I wish I could say that it's just experience here, but it's not. My sense is that it may partly be experience, but partly it's almost an impulse, almost a hunch of what you sense is needed here. But that's no help at all, particularly when I say that to mediators. It's no help at all to say that because how do I put objective criteria around making those decisions? But sometimes that's what it was. I was working with another very experienced mediator, and she and I would debrief frequently over particular things that we had elected to do. We would find ourselves shrugging our shoulders and saying, "Oh, it seemed to be the right thing." Or, "Well, that really bombed." But it's a very forgiving process because you're not representing anybody, so you can make blunders.

Let me give one example of where it bombed. The guy representing the unions was a big, blustery, very, very verbally competent guy. At one point, he slammed his books, shouted, and said, "I just get so pissed off when you guys don't seem to recognize that preserving 12 percent of this land base is nothing. By the time you've netted down all the losses we've got on salmon-spawning habitat and geotechnical problems and slippage and all the rest of it, there's 40 percent of the land base we're not going to be able to touch. I'm just fed up with this whole damn thing." He slammed his book shut, and he turned his chair sideways as much as to say, "I'm not really part of this table, but I'm still sitting here." Sally, my colleague, turned to him and said, "Look, John, I can tell that you feel really frustrated when you hear those kinds of things." But she couldn't even get halfway through that sentence before at least half a dozen people at the table groaned. It was her genuine reaction, right from the cuff, an intuitive selection of active listening as a method for dealing with his comment that bombed.

We talked about it afterwards, and we both agreed that's probably exactly what you would do in four- or five- or a two-party mediation in that kind of a situation. You want to acknowledge his frustration in some way. We decided that it was either the selection of that particular skill at that time that didn't work, or it was just that this was not a touchy-feely guy. He isn't somebody to whom you're going to say, "Gee, you feel frustrated." He's going to tell you to bugger off and don't tell him how he feels, and this isn't a matter of feeling, and then slam his book and go for a smoke. So this isn't the time to acknowledge his feelings; this is the time to do it in some other way. I think what was really called for, and we eventually did it anyhow, was to say, "Look, it's 10:30 in the morning. Why don't we take our mid-morning break, and we'll have some discussions about this and come back together in about 20 minutes." And then we'd go out and chase him and stand out in the parking lot with him and find out exactly what's going on, and talk his talk.

There weren't many, but that was an example of selecting something that we thought would work that didn't. You know why it doesn't after you look at it. But the criteria for making that choice are much more immediate than say, "It's time to use this skill now, and I can tell because of these objective indicators." It doesn't work that way.

I think most mediators know that. The danger is in doing nothing. I think it's far, far better to have an almost innate sense, to try to develop that innate sense of what's going on in the context that it's occurring, and then take a stab at some skill. It's far better to do that than to let the thing broil on, because if you blow it, no problem. It's always possible to turn that into the situation and say, "Well, that was obviously the wrong thing to say." Everyone will laugh. Or, "Well, that was obviously the wrong way to acknowledge your frustration, John." And everyone will laugh.

And John will say, "Fucking right," or something like that, and it will cut through the anxiety.

Now, you can't do that in court as a lawyer. You can't do that in the heat of a negotiation as a negotiator, but as a mediator you really can get away with that: "No, that's the wrong thing to say."

You really can try those things because the process is forgiving. It gives an opportunity for people to explain where they screwed up or explain where they tried something that didn't work, shrug their shoulders, and move on. I've been doing this for about 10 years, and in the last few years, I've become more and more aware of that. Early on in my mediation career, I thought that absolutely every move was strategic, was tactically vital, and boy, you better be right in your judgments or something terrible will befall you, and the whole house of cards will come slamming down. That's just not the case. So I think it's important, and I say this a fair bit in my trainings now: people who are getting into mediation should know that they can experiment with this. They can experiment with skills and process. There's plenty of room for diversity. I really encourage that.

Interest-Based Negotiations

There are other ways we've improvised that have been lasting. Everyone's familiar with interest-based negotiation. Our whole objective here—and it was a stated, published one—was to have an interest-based negotiation rather than a position-based negotiation. And the way we actualized that, about halfway through the process, was to do a short teaching segment on interests to remind people what they were and then to get each sector to develop its own interest statement in writing. So that's a little regime of developing written interest statements around the theme of needs, desires, concerns, fears, hopes: five headings, a template, if you will, of those things.

Then each sector presented its interest statement. It took about a half-day to two-thirds of a day each to present to the rest of the table. Everyone at the table was then invited to question the presenting sector on its interest statement, not to cross-examine them, not to doubt them. They agreed ahead of time that they would be using clarifying, probing, consequential, open questions with a view to trying to be clear about what it was that sector sought to get out of this negotiation. The objective of doing that, of course, was to ultimately show, when it was all over, where the commonness was. We then took the results of those presentations of interest statements, conditioned by a lot of discussion through the questions, and the results of all of that were boiled down into what we called an interest round up. It was about a three- or four-page piece of work that demonstrated about a dozen common interests held by everyone at the table.

The hope is that this is where we've accomplished a turning from "preservation versus development" to a more constructive, collaborative view. The first place that you do that is in setting the task. How do you frame the issues? The things we have to decide. The things we have to solve. The second place you do it is in interest statements. Now that we know what we have to decide, what's important to us about what we have to decide? What are the needs, desires, concerns, fears, hopes, and how are they similar among these vastly different presences at the table, these vastly different perspectives? And how are they similar in the way that, looking to the future, we might now craft an agreement over them or about them? That's another actualization of the integrated issue frame.

Let me quickly comment on how we framed the problem so that it wouldn't be one of either preservation or development. The first thing was that the government dictated it to an extent. It gave the table a task. The task was four or five points long, identifying areas for protection, identifying the working forests.

The second prong was then for the table to again describe that task in a way that it could actually get its talons into it. So rather than, "How much of the island will be available for logging?," which sounds pretty distributional to me, it would be described as, "What zoning can we apply to the island that will provide continuation of its economic viability and adequate preservation of representative species in an integrated frame?" At an early stage, just after process and procedure agreement, after process design, we got into defining the task, certainly well ahead of interests.

Having said that, it was a bit iterative. We jumped around somewhat and found ourselves returning to earlier phases or stages of this all the time, but that was basically the regime. The idea is that it makes some kind of linear sense, or some kind of spiral sense, to have the ground rules and process and procedure in place before you define what it is you have to decide. It makes sense to define what you have to decide before you define what's important about it. It's hard to talk about that until you know what you're talking about. And it makes perfect sense to do all of that before making decisions, which would be the final thing, coming to solutions, coming to agreement, developing consensus, which, again, is certainly the opposite of the way lawyers operate. It's generally opposite from the way business operates, too, where you typically make a proposal and then you whittle away at it. You're proposing a solution before even meeting the other side. That's craziness, just all upside down. So you have nothing, you haven't developed any interests by which to judge whether the proposal's any damn good even though it's your own.

Consensus Recommendations and Turning Points
So, we kept holding back, kept causing the table to not come to terms, kept putting the brakes on it until the very end. I'm not sure that was the best thing to do. It's certainly the way I deal with most mediation because I find people want to make decisions, and those decisions are uninformed by their interests. They've got to flesh out their interests and be clear on what's important to them and why before they can craft a solution. They've got to do that. But in this complex case, I think it wouldn't have hurt for them to be developing a solution on a parallel track at the same time.

I'm saying that from hindsight now. Maybe we shouldn't have forestalled it quite as much as we did because we got down to a time crunch at the end. But they were ultimately unable to make a decision about what specific areas would be protected and what specific areas would be the working forest. They did generate about 60 pages of consensus recommendations on everything else, but that one big jewel in the crown, defining protected areas, they didn't get to. That's always the big contentious thing, and they couldn't get to that. Now I think we could have had a subcommittee or a reproduction of the table, away from the table, churning through that on an ongoing basis, looking at percentages, looking at particular areas, comparing them with computer renderings of the implications of choosing this area or enlarging that area, or shrinking this area. We could have been doing that. But that's hindsight. It's easy to say.

There were a few rough spots, or turning points, that we had in this process. The turning points had a number of different manifestations. There would be those specific moments in the mediation that every mediator longs for, that when they happen, you just can't believe how wonderful it is. Somebody, some sector or group of sectors, changes their mind about something. They decide to give up some position, and they say so clearly. There was a point in this process when there was a big deal at this table about whether there would be 12 percent protection or more or less. Then a set of groups that were demanding 29 percent protection finally said, "We're not as concerned about the numbers as we are about making sure that there is connectivity between protected areas so that there can be the transference of biology over a period of decades or centuries. "

Now, that is a bald and clear retraction, one moving from a position to elucidating the interests and articulating the interests that underlie that position: "That 29 percent is not important to us because that could all well be rock and ice and junk. What we want is contiguous space. We want to make sure that our needs, desires, concerns, hopes, fears, and so on are met somehow in a solution here."

There was a palpable delight around the room with that, among those on the green side and on the brown side. It was good to hear. Those moments happen.

What led to that, I think, was that there had been some good sector work away from the table. I don't think that was anything a mediator did. But what we did do when we heard that, I remember, was to acknowledge—and acknowledgment is such a big part of this—acknowledge the movement that had occurred and the work that had been done, always in terms of the interests that were revealed, rather than saying, "Boy, good for you," stroke, stroke, stroke, "for giving up something," which we preach against. I don't believe in giving in or giving up.

We stroked them by emphasizing how important it was to articulate the interest that had to be accomplished here. So we were into describing the accommodation of interest, the accomplishment of interest, rather than a compromising of position. That was our whole expressed plan, and the parties understood that. So there were those moments, but there were few of them. There might have been half a dozen in the 47 days of meetings we had. They're rare but they're watershed moments—just a treat.

Recognizing Adversaries

Acknowledgment is important for the mediators, but it's also important for other parties to acknowledge something that someone else has done—in this case to articulate their interests rather than hammering away at their position. It's then possible for the person who's just made the movement to see, "OK, I haven't compromised. I'm not seen to have given something up." Without that acknowledgment they're just making that change, and shifting from positions to interests, against a brick wall. It's a tree falling in the forest, and there's no one there to hear it. So they have to have acknowledgment. Typically, in a multiparty table, they get it from those at the table. The mediators don't have a whole lot of work to do in acknowledging because there are so many others there who have done their courses that they know that it's worth doing that. They're inclined to anyhow because they're relieved. But the mediators also have an important role to play, and we thought we did, in giving strokes for those accomplishments. So it was worth doing.

Do we do anything to elicit those acknowledgments from the group if they're not forthcoming? I don't think I do. It seems the conservation sector has gone some distance in articulating what it is they really want to get out of this. "Anybody got any comment on that?"

I think that's as much as I would say, "Anybody got any comment on that?" I don't think it's appropriate for the mediator to say, "Let's have a hand for whoever."

You really are blowing your neutrality at that point. But there were other things. There were things like the social gatherings after hours, where people would get together in the most unlikely groups, career adversaries, people who had been on television during news hours speaking against one another, in a reporter's microphone many times, and these people were getting along. They even went belly dancing one night, a whole bunch of them. It was great. All of that was a real improvement over the norm.

You see people's adversarial inclinations being stored or breaking down, so much so that they lose sight of what the public expectation is. The negotiators do become quite enchanted with their own accomplishments and with their own level of civility and friendliness. But the public, of course, continues to expect them to be at one another's throats and quite demands it. So it's very hard, I think, to take away from the table that new attitude and approach with one another.

For instance, when we would reach various levels of accomplishment and publish those, or the commissioner published those in a press release, we'd get all kinds of editorial commentary in various papers, pooh-poohing the whole thing, simply saying, "There's nothing to it. There's a group that's not going anywhere. These are people who engage in belly dancing and group hugs and this kind of craziness." That was a problem. You can't just develop outputs in response to some guess about the crowd wanting more or less blood. You have to be honest. Ultimately in the public policy arena, although there are dips and valleys (and the dips in public policy formulation are very public), those are things that the public is very interested in. There's an awful lot of material that they never see or care about that ultimately, over the long haul, goes to creating good law and good policy.

Cycles of Community Building, Resignation, and Hope

The public interest is in some ways a flash in the pan. Once they know that the areas have been protected or that logging has been preserved and will go on, that's all they want to know. They don't want to know what the long-term and much more important effects are going to be.

The parties started out in a polite phase, and they didn't permanently change. They remained civil with one another, but as with any group, they go through different phases of recognition of one another and of building community. That's what happens when you have this group of people who meet together over and over and over again for 47 days. My experience is that a table like this is a community. It's not like two people, it's this whole group, and with its arms extended, with these sectors, it gets to be a very, very big thing with 40 or 50 people at every meeting, the same 40 or 50 people getting together every two or three weeks for two days. That's really intensive. So you go through some well-recognized phases—although they're not talked about much—of community building. There is this initial pseudo-community relationship that goes on which is associated with politeness and civility and pouring coffee for one another and talking about fishing, joking about this and that. That seems to give way to some sparring, finally, after everybody gets used to one another. That can be much more realistic. I wish it would happen earlier. That sparring—and it's chaotic—then typically gives way to a little more emptiness.

What they will tend to do at that point is lose hope. About two-thirds of the way through the process, various parties begin to lose hope. "This thing is going nowhere. We're spinning our wheels. We're not getting support from government. There's no way we're going to complete our work in the time we've got." In response to which the mediators would pull people aside or say publicly at the table, "Are you saying you don't want to continue to do this?" "No, no, no, we're not saying that." So there needs to be a level of commitment, but there was this kind of emptiness, this kind of hopelessness and frustration with the fact that it's much harder to get along with a bunch of people than it is to get along with yourself, you know. It's much more efficient to make decisions alone than to have to make them with 15 other people. People slowly learned that and were beginning to talk about it. Eventually that gives way to some genuine community, or some genuine decision making, once people get back in there and take the tools and work with them.

Some people have described a similar thing, but for them there is this one moment where something blows, whether it's the union guy who just says, "This is a crock of shit, I've had it with this," or whatever it is. They almost wait for that moment because that's where it turns. But that's not my experience. I think that's more typical of an arbitrator's style. They wait for that moment of impatience because that demonstrates the people are now pissed off enough that they'll make decisions. I don't think that's a good measure of quality decisions. In other words, to see that people are fed up enough that they're ready to talk turkey is not a good basis for getting a wise and durable output from them. Some think that engaging the union representative at that point is really to find out, "Well, what are your interests? What are your needs here? What's going on for you?" There's an attempt to somehow get down to a level of talking that hadn't happened before. But if that's able to happen because he's pissed off and has gone through a bit of a catharsis and is adrenally shot for 20 minutes, that's the wrong time for him to be talking about his interests.

I'm a little critical of that approach because I think in those circumstances people will regard multiparty mediation more as you do a good therapy session, after about the third or fourth session, where the husband or wife or the individual in therapy finally breaks down. Well, maybe that's appropriate for that kind of a context. I suspect it is. I'm not a therapist. But where people are genuinely trying to understand one another, and they've got you in there to assist them in that and make it easy, to facilitate it, I think it's cheap medicine to be waiting for the magic, almost mystical, moment that no one can really quite put their finger on to be the great tonic that will make everybody perform. I think there ought to be very clear reasons why people perform, and they ought to be connected to their articulating their interests and beginning to work with those interests, not just either getting exhausted or frustrated or impatient enough to begin to give up. As you can see, I'm critical of that other approach, but there are varying views.

One of the interesting things in dealing with the government is that government wants output. They want deliverables. That's what they're up to. And as a result of that desire on the part of government, which is a legitimate interest, they may use any process that will deliver those things. So if soft mediation works, fine. If arbitration works, fine. If exhausting people and keeping them up all night works, "Well, let's try that." I think the ends always justify the means for some parties. But for me as a process person, I think the means are absolutely bloody everything because the means themselves will deliver greater levels of empowerment and recognition as well as greater levels of genuine self-acknowledgment of what the sector needs and wants. That's usually much more valuable than the deliverables. So I think one has to be careful about that.

Afterword

I'm a lawyer, and I have been for 20 years, but really in the last seven or eight years I haven't practiced conventional law at all. All of my work has been entirely in mediation and some training. At the moment I'm doing about 50-50, half training of negotiators and mediators in all sectors, all across Canada and some in the U.S. The other half of my work is mediation. I am really a generalist, although there's been a temptation—a number of times people have tried to persuade me to work in a particular area only. I can't do it. I'm too interested in the whole field. So I continue to mediate everything from the huge multiparty negotiations to bilateral problems involving shareholders in a company, or wrongful dismissal problems, or wills and estate problems, or personal injuries, anything. Sometimes they involve many parties, sometimes a few. I'm doing one at the moment that involves 2,300 homeowners who are complaining about some electrical problems, and they're commencing a class action.

My law practice was located for five years in a big city, Vancouver, and then I moved out to the country, and I practiced there for six or seven years. Then I took a mediation course, really out of curiosity, about 10 years ago, and decided that really had potential. That was something I wanted to do more of. So I did a fair bit of family mediation and moved from family mediation to more general mediation. Then I realized, if I really want to do this stuff as much as I do—and it was beginning to dwarf the interest in my general practice—I've got to get out of general practice altogether and specialize more in this. So that's exactly what I did, about eight years ago.

What I liked most about mediation was being able to deal with the parties, either with or without their lawyers—typically it's with their lawyers—in a more direct and efficient way that encouraged their communication, encouraged them to be more forthright and open and straightforward about their differences. It didn't encourage them to minimize their differences at all—quite the opposite—but it gave them a much more immediate forum for getting things done. The level of client satisfaction and of lawyer satisfaction on the part of their counsel would be enormous, and I just hadn't experienced that before. I'd had lots and lots of cases where I'd acted for plaintiffs and gone to trial and won, but had my client pissed off because although they would have a 100 percent victory and costs awarded to them and all the rest of it, it seemed to be a zero-minus battle. That's very professionally dissatisfying. You can imagine what it's like to do a good job and have clients shrug their shoulders and say, "No, no, I'm very pleased with the way you performed. I'm just pissed off and want to go home." They pay your bill and all the rest of it, but it's not really a satisfactory service. Mediation seemed to offer and does offer tremendous advantages. But it really became obvious to me about four or five years ago that, if this works bilaterally, what about the great big civil problems that the courts are bugged by? And what about problems outside the courts that are really more a question of planning and governance? Couldn't we use an assisted negotiation methodology somehow to really tackle those issues? It was about that time Larry Susskind was beginning to write about this, and others were beginning to toy with this, and British Columbia jumped on the bandwagon and said, "We really want to use this stuff. How can we do that?" So I was one of the people who began to discuss how that might happen. And I've become really interested in that.

I teach a lot of lawyers. Lawyers are generally not very knowledgeable about what on earth this animal, mediation, is. They think it involves arbitration to some extent. They just don't understand what mediation is. So it needs to be clarified and defined in each case so that everybody knows what they're dealing with. I see my profession as being increasingly anxious about losing an edge that they have in the area of dispute resolution and not knowing the nature of the enemy that is out there whittling away at their monopoly on litigation. It's not an enemy, of course. It's something that they can be powerfully involved in and should be as a profession that is at the cutting edge of dispute resolution, but the law is also, as we all know, something of a dinosaur profession, and they've got to make some changes.

We're seeing those changes begin to be made now in Canada. Lawyers are accessing mediation more with a little less trepidation than they did last year. And, bit by bit, I think we're going to see lawyers taking more and more files out of their cabinets and saying, "Maybe we'll mediate this one." I see that happening exponentially just over the last year or two, and I think that increase is continuing. So that's the good news. The bad news is that there are all kinds of movements afoot, both in government and outside of government, to try and regulate this area now as a quasi-profession, to impose standards of one kind or another. I'm not saying that that's always bad news. I think it's probably a good thing at the end of the day, but it's something that has to be fairly organic because the practice of mediation is broad now. You can't simply impose those things from on high.

Since this profile was penned a lot has changed in Environmental and Public Policy dispute resolution in Canada. Experiments such as the process described have in some cases given way to government programs on a much larger scale. The CORE land-use negotiation process was one of a kind, carried on in a dispute resolution vacuum. However, almost 20 years later, mediation and other multiparty, multi-interest exercises are routine in environmental assessment, municipal growth strategies, First Nations government, government negotiations, and land and resource management plans (to name a few).

At the same time, these processes feed public expectation of enhanced engagement in decision making. These processes are part of a growing culture of collaboration in developing local plans and tailoring the application of government policy to meet regional needs. Interest groups have become used to such consultative and participatory processes. This has led to the development of negotiation table expertise on a local level. Government is also developing policy guidelines about what sorts of decisions they will make without enhanced consultation of this sort. The future will tell that story.

Part 6

Deep Value Differences and
Reinventing Community
Problem Solving

Chapter 11
Facilitating Statewide HIV/ AIDS Policies and Priorities in Colorado

Michael Hughes

When deep values conflict, planners risk quitting too early. We have all seen impassioned pleas for deeply held values—Save Open Space! Get Government Off the Backs of Small Business!—and we know too that some of the passionate public cares more about saying what they have to say than about listening to anyone with differing opinions or commitments. When some stakeholders just want to sound off and "decide, announce, and defend" what they have to say rather than listen and respond to others, participatory planning processes may be in danger of grinding to a loud halt.

Nevertheless, planners often face the challenging job of convening task forces, working groups, or staffing committees, whose members might represent deeply divergent worldviews, social attitudes, and even religious backgrounds. What happens, then, when a public authority, for example, asks a planner—asks you—to convene a bottom-up process in the face of such deep differences to address a vital, even life-and-death, issue of health and safety in your community?

That's just what the Colorado State Health Department, working with the National Civic League, asked Mike Hughes to do: to bring together in an inclusive process—in order to devise funding priorities for targeting federal HIV-AIDS prevention dollars in Colorado—gay community activists, religious fundamentalists, sex workers, representatives of communities of color, public health officials and experts, school representatives, and still others.

As a result, then, in a series of meetings that ranged from as many as 110 people to 50 for the most part, a process developed that Hughes describes through ups and downs, through venting and storytelling, through pain and cooperation, to create a practical working agreement about funding priorities despite the stakeholders' obvious deep value differences.

We see in this striking case that even when such "deep value differences" loom large, practical agreements can still be possible even as doctrinal divisions remain. We have seen this same lesson emerge from Frank Blechman's story above. Stakeholders with deep value disagreements may "fundamentally" disagree about doctrinal issues (in that case, about abortion) or about allegiances or priorities, yet they may still be able to fashion practical and creative working agreements on other issues that they also care about.

So it's the job of planners to listen and learn enough when parties articulate deep disagreements to explore practically when and whether these "apparently irreconcilable" differences between stakeholders really do, or really don't, matter in any given case.

Hughes's story suggests what can be practically possible, even when others might think that the cast of characters involved surely has irreconcilable differences. What might mediated negotiations or consensus building or facilitative leadership accomplish in the face of deep value differences? No case experience might answer that question better than the one Mike Hughes recounts in this chapter. —JF

> We had gay people, straight people, bi people. We had people who were HIV positive but didn't have full-blown AIDS. We had people who did have AIDS. We tried to cover all the bases; one guy stood up and said, "I think I'm supposed to represent white straight people," and he got a huge laugh. He was from the Denver Department of Health. From the beginning, his message was. . .that acknowledging these differences—in life experiences, political perspectives, and socioeconomic backgrounds—would be crucial to the success of this project.

This case describes a consensus-building process for HIV prevention strategies in the State of Colorado. The case came my way in 1994 and was a significant professional accomplishment: A very large (110 participants), diverse, and impassioned group reached consensus. Over an eight-month period, my involvement in this life-or-death topic profoundly influenced my approach to subsequent work.

This case will be presented both chronologically and thematically. Woven throughout the descriptions of meetings I mediated are many of the tenets and challenges inherent to consensus building. The following pages will describe how relationship building, common language, celebration, and rigorous consensus checks enriched our process. They also include details of several disputes within the meetings, as well as their resolution.

A CDC Directive Means Change

In the early 1990s, the state health department received a directive from the U.S. Centers for Disease Control (CDC). From that point forward, health department funding for HIV prevention would be linked to how successfully the agency was able to gain community-based input in the area of HIV prevention strategies. The CDC funds the health department directly and provides funds that pass through the health department to community organizations doing AIDS prevention work.

The CDC set goals for a new project, Coloradans Working Together (CWT). This project was supposed to develop a plan for statewide prevention; it was also supposed to comment on and, if possible, to concur on the state health department's application for funding. In light of the CDC directive, the health department sought to engage the multitude of groups affected by the epidemic: gay men, African-American and Hispanic populations, relatives of those infected, and professional service providers, such as health care professionals and social workers.

This project took place in the atmosphere of Amendment Two, and people were painfully aware of the deep political divisions in Colorado. This amendment proclaimed that it would be illegal for any local government, city or county, to adopt an ordinance explicitly protecting the civil rights of people who are gay or lesbian. Amendment Two was a ballot initiative. Its passage led to boycotts and a legal battle that went to the U.S. Supreme Court, where the amendment was finally overturned.

The Ad Hoc Process

In 1993, at the request of the state health department, the National Civic League became involved in the planning stage of CWT. This preliminary work jointly conducted by the Civic League and the health department was called the ad hoc process. Its aim was to design community planning for HIV prevention in Colorado, statewide, and to set the stage for CWT.

Members of the ad hoc process hoped to lay the groundwork for a public participation process that could bring potentially antagonistic groups to the table. They envisioned a process that would create enduring strategies for HIV prevention. First, they focused on stakeholder identification: Who cares about HIV prevention?; Which groups are out there doing it?; Where do they get their money?; and What do they need to be effective?

The ad hoc process also focused on participation. Ad hoc process participants were aware that any plan unfavorable to the people who put Amendment Two on the ballot could be stopped in its tracks. Participants said, up front, "We have to get different religious points of view. We have to get different political points of view. We have to open the doors and mean it when we open the doors." More than anything else, participants didn't want to spend a lot of time and effort and then end up with something that couldn't be implemented. The political debate did not need to be inflamed one step further.

They recruited religious evangelicals and politically conservative, religious fundamentalists—not too many, but some. They tried to cover the political spectrum staying aware of who could stop this plan from being implemented. To achieve this kind of balance in Colorado, invitations must be sent to Colorado Springs, to Colorado for Family Values; in short, the people who put Amendment Two on the ballot. Despite the efforts of ad hoc process participants, the religious right and Amendment Two advocates were underrepresented. Many of them viewed the health department as partisan, dominated by the political left. The health department director is appointed in Colorado by the governor—a Democrat at that time. The governor had not dramatically advocated for gay rights, but he was well known to be anti-Amendment Two. I think the religious right believed that the deck was stacked from the beginning. There was a lot of skepticism on their part.

CWT had to represent a number of interests and points of view. The health department in Colorado was politically on the left in terms of AIDS prevention. It emphasized school-based education and condom distribution, and was beginning to move toward anonymous testing—all of which were controversial. In the context of a broad political spectrum, HIV prevention activists and the health department were aligned pretty closely. However, activists in Colorado saw the health department as conservative. These community-based groups wanted more and faster action in the fight against AIDS. Finally, various minority groups felt that funds had been unfairly diverted from their communities. They hoped to gain more autonomy and decision-making power regarding service delivery. At times, these groups were critical of the health department for tightly maintaining fiscal control and for going slowly in changing prevention programs.

Ad hoc process participants did a great deal of talking about what a good process would be. They talked about openness and confidentiality and how to balance those two things. They discussed ground rules, the number of meet-ings to be held, and "What is collaboration? How do you do it? What makes it go?" All their discussions underscored just how much conflict there was in the area of HIV prevention. The National Civic League hired us (CDR Associates) as a subcontractor to mediate what they expected to be a very charged policy dialogue.

Before they completed their work and disbanded, the ad hoc process par-ticipants drafted a request for proposals for facilitation and mediation services. Then they turned over the process and the facilitation team to the CWT Coordi-nating Committee. The committee's role was to serve as the "memory" from the ad hoc process, providing guidance and direction as well as monitoring progress. This committee consisted of veterans of the ad hoc process as well as some new players. All told, the group included about a dozen of the most prominent AIDS activists in Colorado, including those doing HIV prevention in the state health department, gay rights activists, and AIDS prevention and care specialists. The membership reflected the diversity of the larger group, CWT; there was some balance of ethnicity, a pretty good balance of men to women, and a pretty good balance of gay to straight.

The Process Takes Off

The policy dialogue began with an organizational meeting. It was a huge kick-off with a great deal of publicity. We had 110 people in the room; the energy was incredible. Internally at CDR, and again with the coordinating committee, we discussed the feasibility of mediating with so many active participants. Had the process design been ours, we would have chosen some kind of stakeholder representative group. The coordinating committee could have done the negoti-ating, with the 110 others watching and providing input in a different way. But the ad hoc process had guaranteed the most open process I've ever seen. When I said that we would find a way to get consensus from 110 people, a part of me didn't believe it. I knew we would have to develop mechanisms for the process unlike any I'd used before.

Meeting number one established the foundation of our work together. My co-facilitator—Derek Okubo from the National Civic League—and I intro-duced ourselves. I also briefly reviewed my preferred style of facilitation: You're in charge and I'm here to safeguard your process. I always try to let groups know what I'm doing as the facilitator, and why I do what I do. Finally, I described my idea of consensus: an agreement reached after struggling with all interests to find the best solution ("best" meaning the solution that satisfies the most impor-tant and the widest range of interests). We knew we couldn't have 110 people introduce themselves efficiently. So we split participants into groups of five or six. After they spent some time talking, the plan was for one person to stand up and say, "These are the names of the people who are sitting here. This is Pete and Bill and John and Joe and Sam and Dolores. And among the six of us, the thing that we have in common about being here is...."

I told them that in their small-group introductions, people should state explicitly if they did not want to share particular information with the larger assembly. That way they could maintain confidentiality. The coordinating committee and I were hoping that they would go to the heart of their life circumstances: "I'm here because I'm sick," or "I'm here because somebody I love is sick." But we didn't want to put people on the spot in front of 100 strangers.

Their reaction gave me great confidence. They looked at me like I'd lost my mind and said, "No, that's not a big deal. We'll talk about what we want to talk about." And for the most part, people were willing to disclose personal information. One person stood up and said, "This is so-and-so, and she's a prostitute. She has AIDS." I think the truth is that people who are used to working in this arena—talking about sex, talking about death, talking about disease—have learned not to hide. It's part of the activism to speak out rather than remaining silent.

We did some team building. We convened a diversity panel in which every shape, size, color, and preference that we could imagine was represented. Someone from the African-American community began the discussion. She stood up and spoke to these questions: Who is my community? What has been the effect of this virus on my community? What don't you know about my community that I want you to know? We had a member of the Latino community and a Native American. We had gay people, straight people, bi people. We had people who were HIV positive but didn't have full-blown AIDS. We had people who did have AIDS. We tried to cover all the bases; one guy stood up and said, "I think I'm supposed to represent white straight people," and he got a huge laugh. He was from the Denver Department of Health. From the beginning, his message was about people's differences. He stated that acknowledging these differences—in life experiences, political perspectives, and socioeconomic backgrounds—would be crucial to the success of this project.

Although there was an open atmosphere and we were off to a good start, there was a lot of resistance when we started to talk about the process. A flood of questions arose: What does it mean to participate, and how many meetings are there likely to be? Where will meetings be, and how long they will take? What are the ground rules, and where are the data going to come from, and what's the purpose of this anyway? What's the CDC after, and what agenda is the health department going to push? There was lots of skepticism and discussion about whether this process was authentic: Who was missing from it? What would its outcome be? While a few questioned the process, most were quietly taking it in and at times meeting number one was ominously quiet. The suspicion, fear, and anger around HIV prevention would not instantly dissolve. People were absorbing what folks from the ad hoc process were telling them. I observed moments of one-way communication and passivity, and speculated that most participants were not ready to take ownership of the process.

Relationship Building and the Use of Language

People were sure of one thing: If this group was going to be able to work together, its members were going to have to embrace the group's larger mission. In developing a plan, they would have to go beyond their own personal agendas. They couldn't think in the back of their minds, "Look, my agency wants this money. That's why I'm here." People expected a lot of turf battles and struggles over money. To help build the sense of shared purpose, we created a statement of shared purpose called What We Believe. Among the values were parity, a commitment to give everyone an equal place in the process, inclusion, a promise to value everyone, and representation, a guarantee to draw all points of view into each decision.

We hoped to help people see that what they needed to accomplish for the State of Colorado was bigger than their own goals and, it was hoped, inclusive of their unique priorities. We certainly didn't accomplish this goal at the first meeting. But something equally important occurred: People began to feel as though they knew each other. We used a number of techniques to help people learn each other's names and establish rapport.

I also introduced the idea that much of what we would do together centered around the development of mutually acceptable vocabulary and grammar. We would focus on creating language for the plan that, we hoped, the whole group could live with. That way, we would move away from "I have to change your mind about this" and move toward "Well, what words can we find together?" We had to shift from confrontation to the collaborative development of language.

Warning Signs and Stumbling Blocks

The biggest challenge to teamwork was the probability of a high level of conflict, so we set about building systems to cope. A whole set of ground rules related specifically to dispute resolution.

When disputes arise, what do we do? When we can't deal with it as a whole group, where does it go? I did a one-hour training segment on how to raise conflict productively. When you're angry about something, or when you see your interests are not being attended to in some way, what do you do about it?

I gave participants 10 key ideas in this area:
- Take care of yourself. Relax, breathe, and make yourself comfortable before tackling controversial issues.
- Carefully consider timing. When is the best time to raise an issue?
- Be clear with yourself about your real concerns.
- Use "I" messages. Avoid blaming, finger pointing, and so on.
- Focus on the future. Communicate the way you want things to be, rather than dwelling on what you don't like about the present.
- Frame concerns in terms of your interests, rather than making demands: "Here's the interest I'm trying to meet…".
- Assume that other viewpoints are possible.
- Don't propose your favorite answer too soon.
- Don't escalate conflict by insisting you are right.
- Everyone has a right to the way he or she feels: Work to accept other people's strong feelings as well as your own.

It took time for participants to internalize these principles and begin to put them to use. In the beginning, participants didn't raise difficult issues in the meetings; instead, negative feelings carried over after the meetings. Participants called us to say, "You know, I don't trust the health department to do this" or "You know, the health department's too much in control of this" or "There were too many speakers from the health department." These misgivings eventually worked their way through the grapevine to the coordinating committee. People were grumpy about the presenters and the data. There had been some attrition, and we talked about that as a group. People said, "You know, that's the truth of it. That's how this is going to work—people will drop out."

In general, we stressed that people were going to have to talk openly and raise sensitive issues. We also made an effort to anticipate what wasn't going to work and to make adjustments. There was one obvious thing that the ad hoc committee, the coordinating committee, and the facilitators missed: We scheduled meetings from 8:00 a.m. to 5 :00 p.m. Now, I'm notorious for getting caught up in the subject and resisting taking a break. But we learned right away that eight hours was way too much for somebody who has AIDS, or for somebody who is trying to fight the infection and stay well. Participants needed to spend less time each day, so we multiplied the number of days.

We cut the schedule back to 10:00 a.m. to 4:00 p.m., with, at a minimum, a mandatory 15-minute break in the morning, an uninterrupted hour for lunch, and a mandatory 15-minute break in the afternoon. We kept saying to the group, "Does this work for you? Is this the right purpose for this group? Are these data to your liking? You know, it's yours: You have to take ownership of this. This is your process." We did everything that we could think of to encourage feedback. At the end of every meeting, we asked, "What went wrong? What didn't work? What do we need to change?" I talked to people informally individually during breaks and at lunch.

We started off meeting once a month, then moved to every other week. Meeting number two introduced the epidemiological profile: these are the people who have been sick; these are the people who are getting sick; and these are the rates of infection for different communities. A needs assessment, based on interviews with AIDS prevention organizations, was also explained. The presenters were from the health department or members of the ad hoc process. The discussion that followed uncovered resistance to both the process and the data.

In session number three, there was discussion about whether the health department was just paying lip service to new strategies for HIV prevention. Would this process really make a difference, and would that difference result in money flowing in new directions than in the past? Was the health department prepared to lay-off staff to get money out into the community? Health department staff was in the room, and they fielded hard questions about whether the prevention plan would be implemented according to recommendations.

The third meeting was rough, both in terms of the process and the substance. We tossed problems back at the group: "So, if you don't like the data, can we go get more? What would the data cost? Who would go get them? Who would you trust to have them?" We worked through some of those issues so that we could move forward in the next meeting.

At this point, our group was down to 60 or 70 people at each meeting. Some of the original 110 had come only to confirm that their own interests were represented. For example, people said, "Well, you know, if ACT UP (a gay rights activist group) is here, I don't have to come." Or "If there are enough members of the Latino community here, then I don't have to come." After the kickoff, some people had gone their merry way. But we still felt that we had reached pretty far into the community and had attracted a wide spectrum of people.

In the third meeting, the power in the meeting shifted, and I felt a huge transfer of ownership happening. We stopped talking in Meeting 3 about anything that had come before. The ad hoc process stopped, didn't exist any more. From here on out, anything that happened with this process was in the participants' hands. One way I recognized this shift was that in Meeting 3, they came after me. Big surprise! I have learned from these large-group efforts that the facilitator is often a lightning rod. If you don't want that role, don't pick up the marker! Don't be a mediator if you can't accept the idea of being a target.

In the opening meetings, we set up the room in such a way that all 110 participants faced in the same direction. That way, the presenters could reach the whole group, and communication would go through the facilitator. The room was small, and we were elbow to elbow. The seats were theater style, with several big arcs of chairs. I was calling on people from my spot in the front of the room. When 40 or so hands went up, I would say, "I'm going to start over here on the right side of the room and I'm going to keep coming around, and I'll catch up so those of you that are way over on the left side of the room, you'll go first on the next question."

As I'm sweeping across the room, of course, new hands come up. By the time I got over to the other side, somebody went berserk and said, "I'm going to talk now, let me in!" I then acknowledged that the facilitation wasn't going very well. They said, "Yeah, you're too slow. You're not calling on us fast enough. You're not letting us talk." Suddenly, it was all my fault. I said, "Yeah, we've got to fix this process, and you've got to fix me and make sure that I'm doing this well." I knew we had to respond to their reaction to the facilitation. It became clear that we needed to structure our work so that all participants were thinking at once and working together. We would need to mix and match open discussion, small group, and individual work. We also decided to assign tasks both during and between sessions. Some objectives would have to be accomplished off-line, with subsequent opportunities for group discussion. And in the larger meetings, we needed a new structure. For the next meeting, we moved the chairs into concentric circles with a small table and four chairs at the center. And we made aisles that led to the center of the room so everyone could easily move from the back to the front.

With this set up, I could get out of the way and let people come to the table and talk rather than waiting for me to call on them. We explained the procedure to the participants: "When we are ready to open discussion on a topic, we will clearly mark the transition: Now it's time for discussion. Then we will get out of the way. If you've got something to say, come sit in a chair. There are four chairs, and four of you can talk with one another loudly, so we can all hear it. When you're done, get out of the chair. If you see somebody waiting, make room for him or her. When we think that the discussion has wound itself to some sort of conclusion, or we want to ask if you have come to consensus, we'll interject to move the process on. But when it's time to talk, it's time to talk. You don't have to be called on. You don't have to raise your hand."

They loved it. They took to it both because the structure made sense and because they sensed our responsiveness. Through the remainder of the work, we used this system.

This method worked beautifully much of the time, but it was not without its downsides. At least twice, I was much too far away. I was down the aisle in the back of the room, and I should have been at the table with them. After some tough going, I suggested a modification. We had a room with mostly teal green chairs, but there were a few that were ugly pink. I suggested that we use green chairs for the four discussion seats, and add a fifth one — ugly pink for the facilitator. That chair belonged to me or to the co-facilitator. When necessary, we could sit down in it and mediate the conversation.

Visual Tools and the Use of Celebration

Throughout the process, we used a visual consensus check: you hold your thumb up if you're in agreement, even if you are willing to go along but you're not ecstatic; you hold your thumb sideways if you're not quite sure, or you want to ask a question, or you want more data; and thumbs down means, I'm not in consensus, and you can't go forward without me. We'd gotten used to doing this kind of consensus check on wording and on process. We'd work through the thumbs down, and then we'd work through the thumbs sideways. When everybody could hold their thumbs up, we'd move on. We used this method a thousand times if we used it once.

We all rode an emotional roller coaster in the months we spent together. Celebration and exuberance came not from me, but from the participants and the coordinating committee. We played music at a lunch break. With some instruction and encouragement from one participant, people took each other arm in arm and danced around the room. One of the members of the coordinating committee was in an improvisational acting group, and she got the whole group involved in acting exercises at a break. She picked people out of the group and said they had to pretend, with gestures only, to demonstrate that they were angry or afraid or even constipated. It was hysterical. The dancing and other planned and impromptu team-building events had an important common element touch.

In one of our first meetings, we asked the participants to get in pairs. We gave each pair a piece of paper and a pen. We asked the two to put their hands together on the pen and, without speaking to each other, to draw a picture. Each pair quickly discovered the need to cooperate and to give one another power over the pen and over the picture itself. Each person found ways to signal his or her partner through the simple release of pressure on the pen or a slight touch. The pictures were funny and hopeful, giving all of us one more opportunity to laugh and to look ahead. The act of drawing together, hand in hand, while trying to find answers to a disease passed from one person to the next through intimate contact was a powerful one. Contact could be part of healing as well.

As our work went on, it became clear to me that this group needed an opportunity to celebrate something, anything, because they were dealing with very depressing things: life and death, disease and destruction. In late fall, we actually lost one of the members of the group to AIDS. We grieved together over that. If we were going to grieve together over Joe's death, we certainly ought to celebrate together as well.

A Plan Emerges, Things Heat Up

The substantive core of the plan began to take shape at the fourth meeting. The CDC had strict guidelines about the content of this plan. For example, it mandated that we articulate the most important needs in HIV prevention in Colorado. Our group was challenged to identify populations affected by the epidemic and to prioritize those populations. What an awful thing to ask people to do, to choose one group over another, but that's what they demanded: a ranking of jeopardized people. The group also had to identify preferred strategies for preventing the disease in those populations.

We started with needs. We asked each individual to generate a list, and we ended up with something like 150 different needs. At lunch, we scrambled to organize the list as a point of departure for discussion. We told the group that before the next meeting, volunteers would further pare down these needs: remove the redundancies, categorize them, and make this list more manageable.

The small group was able to compress the 150 needs statements into 13 by lifting them to a level of generality that captured what was underneath. Of course, we hoped not to lose the nuance, but we needed these 13 as broader categories. As the discussion continued, a participant who would eventually contribute the 14th need spoke up. This wonderful participant—he was brilliant—came into the circle, and he said, "Here's a need that is missing. There is a need to shift the discussion of AIDS in Colorado from a moral issue to a public health issue, and I refuse to participate in moving this plan forward until we wrestle with that."

He made an eloquent speech about how moral barriers to effective AIDS education were killing people. His statements weren't accusatory. They weren't blaming. He didn't denigrate Amendment Two supporters or folks who opposed certain prevention methods on moral grounds. He was angry, but his emotion didn't take the form of a personal accusation. The whole room was captivated. Other people ran to the table and started talking with him. The folks from Focus on the Family and from Colorado for Family Values talked about why, for them, this was a moral issue and the meaning their values had for them. People engaged in the discussion with renewed intensity. They started working on different levels, dropping down in those chairs and talking to each other person to person. The guy who started the discussion kept one of the four chairs for quite a long time. Then he got out, other people came in; later he was invited back.

Amazingly, no one broke the ground rules. People were speaking to one another respectfully. They were doing their best to listen to one another. The person who began the discussion simply said, "Amendment Two and the moral barriers are in place, and because they're in place, this is the effect." It was depersonalized, meaning "not accusatory." But it was clearly personal from his point of view. It was very much an "I" message. "This is how I see it." It set the right tone.

We came upon another issue later on, where people stood up and said, "All of you people…." It was a racial issue. "You white people all are…." The stereotypes flew out, and the room exploded. But that didn't happen on this one. He didn't say, "All you religious bigots…. All you Bible thumpers…." Instead, he said, "These barriers are in place."

He didn't say who put them there. He didn't point any fingers or make any inflammatory statements. He just spoke from his own beliefs and his own anger and his own pain at seeing people that he cares about die. It was emotionally very powerful.

In the ensuing discussion, others said, "Well, those aren't the facts. In fact, why people are dying is because we can't, in our culture, frame these things in moral terms, because we're losing the moral ground underneath us." These people were taking the opposite point of view. They said, "No, you don't understand, this must become a moral issue. If it isn't a moral issue, people will continue to behave in ways that put them in danger. Once you have moral underpinnings to keep people from behaving in those ways, that's when people won't die."

When the discussion had reached the point where people were beginning to repeat themselves, we would step in. We might say, "Look, this discussion hasn't led us to some kind of consensus point of view, that's clear. So what do you want to do with that conflict? You have to account for this in the plan. You have one person who is not with you unless the plan says something about this. We're going to have to do something. We're going to have to write a 14th need statement. Or we're going to have to find some other way to resolve it. So, what mechanism?"

Small Group Mediation: Morality and 14 Need Statements

We had ground rules about conflict resolution. When an issue couldn't be resolved within the group, we would resort to small group mediation. For this conflict—the one about morality—the four people present included the person who had presented the issue, a person from Colorado for Family Values, and one person each for support of their point of view. Luckily, the person from Colorado for Family Values selected someone with a moderate stance from an organization called His Heart (a Christian organization that cares for people with AIDS). The person who presented the issue, from the Colorado AIDS Project, selected a colleague who was a collaborative, calm presence in the group. From my point of view, these were wise choices.

The five of us sat down between meetings with the large group and did a mediation, and we developed language that the four of them could live with. It was clear that what we were doing was writing a plan. Instead of getting mired in "I have to change your mind about this" kind of talk, we focused on "What words can we find together?" And they did it. We walked out of that mediation after two hours with a message that all four of them agreed to.

The way I did it was to take the process that we were using for CWT and compress it into two hours. First I said, "We're going to begin at the beginning. Let's make sure we all know one another." We did introductions. I continued, "OK, let's get the ground rules clear. This two-hour session will work if you talk one at a time, you respect one another, you use language that's appropriate, and you avoid personal attacks."

I laid out the familiar ground rules to make clear how careful we would need to be when we spoke to one another. I laid out a process. Each person would talk about the importance of a particular wording, so they could educate one another about their respective views. Then each would suggest options that would take into account the needs expressed. Finally, we went into a problem-solving mode. Attending carefully to language was a task they were willing to accept. After all, we had already wordsmithed 13 needs. We had taken out commas and worked on the grammar and substituted one word for another. So they knew how to approach the 14th need, and they went at it.

I proposed this approach because I knew that underneath the wording there was a common concern: to stop this disease from spreading. I knew that unless they really saw that they ultimately were aiming at the same thing, just aiming at it in absolutely opposite ways, they were just going to keep aiming in opposite ways and would not find language that the other one would find acceptable. Recognizing their mutual interest in creating a plan acceptable to each of their constituencies was key. Once all four of them heard this message from the others—that they too wanted to stop the disease—it became a joint task. They suspended confrontation for long enough to discover that they could in fact find words that would be satisfactory to both sides, and they didn't have to give up their points of view. They also found that they could agree to disagree. That was part of it, acknowledging that they weren't going to change. Regardless, they had to write a document that both sides could live with. That was simpler, so I focused them on that.

The language they all agreed on was this: "There is a need to remove moral objections to HIV prevention and education that is appropriate to the behaviors of the target community." Now that's somewhat vague. But then they followed with "For communities that include members with a range of moral perspectives, HIV prevention methods need to be appropriate to that range of moral perspectives by presenting multiple prevention messages." The subtext of this statement is that not everybody in any community is going to share every moral perspective. Therefore, if you give people prevention messages, the messages should encompass a range of moral points of view. In other words, prevention messages should present multiple options that correspond with those different moral perspectives.

The only way that we could get the gay rights activists to accept sentences two and three was to include sentence number one: "There is a need to remove moral objections to messages that are appropriate to the target community." In concrete terms, this means that for settings such as gay bars, you can use sexually explicit material. Why? Because, in a gay bar, sexually explicit material is within that audience's moral parameters. But if you go into the schools, and you've got students who come from a fundamentalist Christian point of view, both those students and their parents would likely be uncomfortable with sexually explicit material. Thus, the wording encourages a range of messages that are tailored to a spectrum of moral perspectives.

In two hours they hammered out three sentences.

It became difficult only at the very end. I said, "Look, you're all done, the mediation's over, hurray for you. You get to go back to the group and say, 'We have a draft for you.' Now let's all go home."

But, instead of leaving, everyone stood around and started talking about whether being gay is a lifestyle or not. They hit on the word "lifestyle" and suddenly started to have an argument. I interrupted and said, "I think it's a mistake for you to continue this conversation. I think you should get in your cars and go home."

They laughed and shook hands, and said, "You're right. We did well today. Let's go home."

But I can tell you they were not going out for a beer together afterwards.

They went back to the big group with their draft, and I stood on my head to praise the four of them. I wanted to send the message that they shouldn't take this kind of breakthrough lightly. If we hadn't been able to resolve this one, the extreme factions on each side might have dropped out, and the credibility of the plan would have been damaged. As it turned out, the exact wording didn't stick. The larger group changed it. But we celebrated the four of them. We all knew that this issue could have blown the whole group apart.

Things fell into place after the group decided on the 14 needs statements. But there was more hard work after that because we had to prioritize those needs. We also had to identify populations within each category and prioritize those. We had groups that developed strategies to meet the needs for each population and, again, to prioritize the strategies.

The Racial Divide

The task of prioritizing populations triggered a discussion about race, oppression, and homophobia, and what it meant to be hated or ignored. At that moment, having the table and those four chairs was almost not enough. Prioritizing populations raised questions about whether the well-being of African-Americans or gay men or Latinos was a higher priority than for some other group. This highly charged confrontation made the "Is this a moral issue?" discussion look manageable by comparison. There were a lot of tears shed. It was sad, both because the group was pulling itself apart and because the issues themselves were painful to begin with.

Early in this part of the agenda, a man stood up and said, "All of you white people…." The stereotypes flew out, and the room exploded. Participants aired their beliefs about how funds had been allocated. They believed that prevention money had been allocated disproportionately and that communities of color had not gotten funding commensurate with their rate of infection. I couldn't bring myself to stop this frank discussion about how hard it was to choose one group's needs over another's. Opinion is still divided about whether that meeting was a good or a bad thing. I have to take the mediator's role and say it was both.

I later learned that the discussion was very uncomfortable for a lot of people. They saw it as divisive and destructive, rather than ultimately healing. People came up to me and said, "Stop this thing!" A couple of people got out of their chairs and came over to me and said, "You're the facilitator, make this stop." (They were white.) I said, "I can't. If I stop this I will add insult to this injury." Then I added, "But if you think this should stop, there are chairs up there in the middle of the room. You stop it. You're part of this. Take a role in the discussion and see if it's best that we stop it." I let the interchange go, and the group kept going, until people were emotionally and physically exhausted.

For some, the discussion about race was too much. They believed that the acrimony drove a wedge in the group. I think it simply named the wedge that was already there and gave them a chance to talk it out. At the next meeting, people stood up and said, "I hated that. I thought that was painful and awful." Then other people stood up and said, "Yes, it was painful. Yes, it was awful, but I needed to do what I did in that meeting and I needed to have that conversation, and it was time well spent."

Picking Up the Pieces

I had thought long and hard about how to open the next meeting. By happenstance, I had been reading a book called *The Soul of Politics* by Jim Wallis. A quote from that book hit me over the head, and I wrote it down. I showed it to one of the people on the coordinating committee and I said, "I think this is what happened in the last meeting." He said, "That's it, absolutely, and I'll read it at the next meeting." What Vic read was from pages 162-163 in *The Soul of Politics*:

> Compassion. The word compassion literally means to suffer with, to put yourself in someone else's position, to walk for a little while in his or her shoes. Compassion always begins with listening. The listening that leads to compassion is the beginning of understanding. In America we build walls we desperately hope will keep people away from us. But these same walls are ultimately unable to prevent us from experiencing the consequences of abandoning our neighbor. The walls divide us, but they don't protect us. Those illusory but oppressive walls must be broken down and nothing does that better than the experience of listening directly to the people on the other side of the wall. Getting close enough to see, hear, touch, smell, and taste the reality of others is what always makes the difference. In listening to the stories of those so seemingly different from us, we find similar but unexpressed voices inside ourselves. Hearing one another's stories is the beginning of new understanding and the foundation of compassionate action.

In reading this quote, Vic made room for everybody to express different points of view about what happened. That was a very wise 30 minutes we took out of the agenda. People had a chance to decompress and let go of anxieties over what had happened in that difficult meeting.

Then we tried to pick up the pieces. We still had to get these populations prioritized. And participants rose to the occasion. They were able to say, "Look, let's step back from this, and let's get this right. Let's make sure that we are understanding why you would put a group in the highest priority, and why you would put a group in a second-level or higher priority, and why you would put the group in simply a high-priority population."

We talked about the criteria. We talked about their concerns. They made those difficult decisions and reached consensus on every priority.

Before the last meeting, we gave people a draft of the plan and asked people to identify any reservations they might have. On sticky Post-it notes, people had to write down the specific page number and the specific wording they wanted to change to make the plan acceptable to them. We stuck all these Post-it notes up on the wall. Everybody went and read them, and we worked through them at the last meeting. One by one, barriers to consensus came down from the wall.

People were nervous. There was a lot of anxiety about whether we'd get consensus. The coordinating committee members responded this way: They made worry beads for everyone. (These beads were the kind you hang on Christmas trees—segments of eight or 10 plastic beads.) If we started to get stuck a little bit, people would run up and grab worry beads. If we were making progress, they would throw their beads back in the bowl. People started hooking worry beads together, putting them around their head, and weaving them into their clothing. Every now and then we'd hit a tough barrier to consensus. We'd get through it, changing the wording. People would hold their thumbs up and start tossing the beads away.

At the end, I said to the group, "Thumbs?"—and they started to hold up their thumbs.

Then, one person said, "No," in a very loud voice from the back of the room.

I thought, "Oh, we don't have consensus. There's something else—what haven't we done?"

But this person said, "No, don't hold your thumbs up, stand up."

I looked around and said, "Is that OK?"

And everybody said, "Yeah, let's stand up."

People started getting out of their chairs, and the next thing you know, not one person is sitting down. I said to the group, "Well, I think you've done it. You have consensus." And a cheer went up in the room, and people started to hug one another and shake hands and celebrate. And all of a sudden the beads started flying through the air. There was a huge shower of beads in the middle of the room, and I'm standing and I'm watching these beads float through the air and land in the middle of the room.

They were able to come to consensus on the plan, something that many people had thought impossible. Even I had doubted they could throw the doors open, let anybody come in, and still get real consensus. People were ultimately able to agree to a ranking of populations, lined up under the needs statements. Groups were prioritized as highest, higher, and high. They did it! At the project's conclusion, they had jointly worked out a document that described needs, populations, and strategies.

Time to Heal Wounds

One stroke of genius that had come from the ad hoc process, from the health department, and from the CDC was this: The plan wouldn't be a one-time effort. People dedicated to HIV and AIDS work saw the need to do long-term, sustainable work in the planning arena. For this reason, CWT created one more CDC goal: We are going to take time to heal wounds. That was their exact phrasing, "time to heal wounds." Participants promised each other that when we hit a painful subject, we would take the time to work through it, and heal as a community. They spoke about the depth of people's pain, and how best to offer relief. It was a promise they made to each other.

This was important, too, for me personally. I have a friend who has AIDS, a close friend. I'm executor in the will and will be a primary caretaker when it comes to that time. We're not there yet, thank goodness. More than 10 years we've known each other. And I've lost other friends to AIDS as well. This made it hard for me to keep my nose where it belonged, to be a good mediator and not a participant. There were a couple of times when I could feel myself slipping, feel myself being pulled in.

I can say without reservation that this work is the most important I've done in my professional life. With this group, we reached each other's deepest wounds and were able to regroup and move on. I came to care deeply for the participants and for the Coordinating Committee members. I came to care deeply about the work they accomplished. While facilitators ostensibly adopt neutral stances, I believe my emotional engagement with participants was critical.

Any good I was able to do as a mediator came directly from being involved with them emotionally every step of the way. As the work progressed, the participants were able to raise difficult, emotional issues in large part because we were able to create a safe environment. To the best of my ability, anger and pain were attended to with compassion. As a human being, to remain detached from participants' sadness would have been unthinkable. As a mediator, to remain at a distance from the CWT members would have made me inaccessible at critical moments of the deliberation. This realization has colored my subsequent work in this field. I cross freely into that more vulnerable place, trusting that empathy and personal connection enrich—rather than compromise—mediation of consensus-building processes.

Postscript

It is October 26, 1998. Today, I had the chance to talk to Bob, the current CWT coordinator. He is now preparing for CWT's sixth year of community planning. A CDC study of prevention programs before and after CWT confirms that funding has changed significantly in response to the plan. CDC staff have invited Bob to share the success story and help those in other states who struggle for the elusive consensus we built. He acknowledges that each year requires hard work to keep the spirit of cooperation alive and to solve the next problem. But most important, in Bob's opinion the delivery of HIV services is much improved in Colorado.

Afterword

It was extraordinary to reread the profile from so many years ago and it is fascinating to think back over the years. After doing this work for 20 years, I realize how much one project can influence the way I work. Profoundly moving experiences have changed me, and this was one of those watershed experiences that I know changed the flow of my professional life.

I know—and have known since this project—that there is no level of emotional reaction that I can't accept, incorporate, and embrace in my work. I know so many in our field who are afraid that they won't be able to build a process for dialogue and decision making strong enough to contain the expression of deeply felt emotions. I have no such fear. After this project, I think my work became more imaginative and more spontaneous, and I think I became more nimble as a mediator. I attribute that to the confidence that comes from fearlessness.

I think I always trusted my own gut reaction to the situations I find myself in; after the work described in this profile, I trust those reactions more and follow where they lead more willingly.

Looking back, I see the elements of the conflict that were about the identities of the participants. Many were fighting for more than HIV funding; they were fighting for recognition and respect for an essential part of their identity. Identity-based conflicts, I think, can transform or reinforce the mediator's sense of her or his own identity. I think I knew myself better at the end of that work, and I see myself more clearly today as a result. When I have helped others find a voice and speak about the truth of who they are, I find afterward that it is easier to speak truthfully about who I am.

Chapter 12
Activist Mediation and Public Disputes

Lawrence Susskind

No one has done more than Larry Susskind to demonstrate the promise of mediation, facilitative leadership, and consensus building for governance and planning in the face of conflict. For more than 40 years Susskind has worked not only with local organizations to resolve housing, land-use, and transportation disputes, but with international organizations to address global environmental issues—more recently, for example, challenges of water diplomacy.

Susskind fits no stereotype of a typical university professor. Teaching in the Massachusetts Institute of Technology's Department of Urban Studies and Planning, he has complemented his steady stream of publications with an even more active professional life as a mediator, trainer, and policy advisor, in the U.S. and abroad. In any given year, Susskind has been in the middle of a half-dozen multiparty, multi-issue disputes involving, for example, the siting of hazardous waste facilities, the design of controversial regional public housing plans, the creation of city-suburb costsharing schemes to ensure regional water quality, or the crafting of toxic waste cleanup strategies involving industry, government, and community members.

Susskind's vision of public dispute mediation and his successful practice make him a widely respected, if at times controversial figure in the dispute resolution community. Both his vision and practice challenged the popular wisdom of the field that regards "neutrality" as sacred. Many mediators might have concerned themselves with process alone, leaving the substance of agreements to the parties themselves. The demands of neutrality, according to many public dispute mediators, prevent them from focusing on power imbalances among negotiating parties. Other mediators working in the public eye wonder if mediation can be a viable strategy when participants number 30 or more, the process is highly political, and parties vary enormously in their expertise, resources, and political experience.

Susskind rejects mediator claims to pure neutrality. He suggests, instead, a stricter notion of nonpartisanship and the provocative idea of activist mediation. He has argued that mediators must address power imbalances among the parties to public disputes by, for example, providing premediation negotiation training to all parties.

Susskind's early statements to the planning profession remain accessible, clearly argued, and practically relevant, even as they gave way to his more monumental *Consensus Building Handbook* and smaller guides to practice (for example, *Breaking Roberts Rules*), with other volumes documenting emerging ideas and practices published in between and since. Susskind's influence has been extensive, and it has contributed as well to the broader Program on Negotiation at Harvard that he has shaped since its earliest days.

The profile that follows presents Susskind's responses to a series of questions I raised to learn more about his views and practice of mediation. I guided our lengthy interview sessions with three primary goals in mind. First, I wanted to learn how his work had developed. Somehow, Susskind's dispute resolution practice had grown from his earlier work on public participation in urban planning and policymaking processes. How did this happen?

Second, I wanted to explore the controversial positions Susskind has taken regarding the ethical responsibilities of mediators working on public issues. If being neutral, for example, was an inadequate, if not altogether deceptive, characterization of the responsibilities of public dispute mediators, just what alternative did Susskind have in mind?

Third, I wanted to press him about actual cases and how he handled them. In the heat of practice, faced with angry, skeptical, politically contentious parties, what did Susskind find most challenging, most perplexing? What did he find most satisfying, most difficult? To introduce each of these three sections, I make several brief observations.

This profile, in Susskind's own words from early in his career, presents a classic, arguably unsurpassed, statement of the promise and practice of public dispute resolution. —JF

❦

People start this process with needs, desires, wants, concerns, ideology, uncertainty, and interests. All of them. And I expect people to

change—to inform their sense of what they would or wouldn't like to have happen by listening to what other people say. Mediation is not a question of plugging into the computer answers to questionnaires from each person and printing out the maximized joint gain resolution. Learning and inventing goes on, and reconsideration goes on, and argument matters.

Public Dispute Resolution, Not Environmental Mediation

I knew that Susskind had long been interested in the promises of active citizen participation in government, and I knew he had taught, written, consulted, and practiced widely. But I didn't know much about how these pieces of his professional life had developed, complementing or tugging at one another. So I began by asking Susskind about his own training and the subsequent development of his practice.—JF

Let me describe what I [Susskind] do as public dispute mediation, and not environmental mediation. What I did in the late 1970s was environmental mediation, but I've tried to broaden it since then to be the mediation—the resolution or the management—of disputes in the public sector. I work on three types of public disputes: first, disputes over the allocation of scarce resources—like a piece of land or a body of water; second, disputes over policy priorities—Should we emphasize environmental protection in this context or economic development? Should we emphasize meeting the needs of this group or that group?; and third, disputes over quality-of-life standards, environmental standards, human service standards—disagreements over the standards that ought to be set within a policy that has been made or is being made. I don't view the last grouping as primarily environmental any longer, though I did at one time.

When I was an undergraduate at Columbia, I majored in sociology and English literature. I was interested in studying drama and poetry. But I didn't act; I wrote and produced plays. If you look at my work on role-play exercises and simulations now, it traces directly back to my work in drama, particularly in stagecraft. I think this probably has a lot to do with the way I manage events within the context of dispute resolution. It has something to do with writing and producing plays too, as a matter of fact.

The work in sociology led me into urban planning. I went to the School of Design at Harvard, and I thought I was going to become a city planner. I thought that had to do with design, which I had to learn, so I went to what was called the Design School. Little did I know that I was hitting the place at a moment in time when nobody knew what the hell they were doing, or what city planning was. At least that's the way it looked to me.

That first year in planning school I got involved in advocacy planning with Chester Hartman, who was my first instructor. We worked on a grassroots project to try to get a rent control bill passed in Cambridge. I thought, "This makes sense to me." But the Harvard hierarchy was telling Chester, "You're not getting tenure; you can't stay here. What you're teaching is not going to count for credit." And I'm thinking: "Oh no, this is not right. What you guys are doing doesn't make any sense at all." It was an unhappy situation for me at Harvard that year.

I transferred in the middle of the Harvard program and finished my master's degree at MIT the next year. My sense of planning, when I transferred, was confused. Having studied with Charlie Abrams at Columbia, I thought planning was going to be about how you develop cities—particularly in developing countries, and particularly neighborhoods within cities—in ways that respect both the politics and technical expertise that planners ought to be able to bring to things. I got to Harvard, and they weren't talking about that at all. They had a notion that it had something to do with land use, and they had rules about land use.

I applied to the Master's and Ph.D. programs at MIT at the same time. I said very clearly on my Ph.D. application that I wanted to teach urban studies. I wanted to work some in the university, and I wanted to get involved in how change happens in cities. But I also wanted to move back and forth between a scholarly role, a consulting role, and an activist role. I think I've done that, in my own way.

Lloyd Rodwin became chair at the MIT Urban Studies and Planning program and said, "Why don't you help me run the program?" I said, "Sure." They admitted me into the Ph.D. program, and Lloyd said that we had to build an undergraduate program, and I thought, "Good, that's what I like, teaching undergraduates." So, my job was to create a proposal for a bachelor's degree in urban studies in MIT and get it through the MIT bureaucracy. That worked, and I taught there and headed the program for its first three or four years. We had a hundred majors! It was a major new program at MIT at the time.

I wrote my master's thesis about the problems of planning new towns. I'd looked at the programs to build new cities, both in the U.S. and elsewhere. The problem was you couldn't talk to the people who were going to live in the place to find out what they wanted. You couldn't talk to them because you didn't know who they were. So you turned it over to some "experts," and the planning process just didn't work.

By the time I was doing my doctoral work, the Nixon administration had passed the revenue-sharing legislation of the early 1970s. I was interested in a couple of questions, primarily what level of authority should reside with whom?, and what level of authority should match what spatial level?

These questions actually emerged from the "new towns" work that was going on then at MIT. In the planning of new towns, one reason that the damn thing didn't work was that you had too much of a centralized plan, and you didn't have neighborhoods having control over how they evolve and grow. "Oh, but if you give them complete control, then the advantage of planning the new town, the economy of scale, would be lost," the argument went. My question was, when you switch the level of authority of the allocation of the block grant, do you increase or decrease the responsiveness, in the use of money, to the needs of different groups? That's a participation question. In other words, people knew how to lobby city hall under the old program because they could sort of play-off the city and the feds. With this new program of revenue sharing, it wasn't clear whether low-income and poor people were going to be better off or worse off. I studied the LEAA and Partnership of Health programs in great detail, and the gains and losses the block grant programs meant for the poor. That was what my dissertation was about.

Because of that work, I was hired by groups on all sides of the question—the League of Women Voters, the Brookings Institute, Arthur D. Little, the Center for Community Change—who wanted to monitor what actually happened with these general revenue-sharing and block grant funds. Everybody thought it was either going to be good or bad to make this change, and here I had written about it, and people said: "What would you look at, what would you watch?" Dick Nathan had put together these monitoring studies at the Brookings Institute, and then the citizen activist groups said: "We want to have our own citizen-monitoring study." So I got hired by a lot of the grassroots groups to design citizen-monitoring studies. For a while it seemed like I was working on every monitoring study everywhere.

I tried to design these monitoring studies in a way that would leave people empowered to continue tracking and monitoring this stuff on their own. It wouldn't just be data gathering; it would be education in a way that would leave people with an ability to follow what was going on in their own communities on an ongoing basis. This was a very different approach to the issues from that of many economists. I wasn't interested in equity/efficiency trade-offs. I was interested in power. Do you get better allocation decisions—more accountable to the people that really know what they need—when you switch the locus of power from the federal level to the local level? All of this got me tagged as a citizen participation type.

Then I got invited into a small town on the north shore of Boston—where I knew the town and I knew a lot of the people—to help the citizens there do a plan for the town because the town government wouldn't do one. This was in Rockport, and we did something called "Planning for the Future of Rockport," which was a completely citizen-based process for growth management and planning for the town. For me, that project was motivated entirely by the desire to find a new model of how to teach planning. I liked what I'd done as a student with Chet Hartman. So I brought students from MIT in as the staff from beginning to end. We had a community-based laboratory, with a real client. We had real political restraints; we had time pressures. And the students were the staff; I had undergraduates and doctoral students all working together.

That led to the town of Arlington, a Boston suburb that borders Cambridge. The town government invited us in, saying, "Look, you did this thing up in Rockport. We're interested in having citizens involved here too." What I learned from Rockport was that we hadn't left behind any institutionalized organization because we were, in a sense, fighting city hall the whole time. We weren't really working for the town government in Rockport; we were working for an ad hoc citizen's group. The group of folks who had been on the planning board, citizen members, had invited us. They said "Look, the city government isn't going to do this. We want to get citizens from the whole town doing it."

In Arlington, we worked to create the citizen involvement committee, and that's a group that still existed many years later.

About that time, something called the Citizen Involvement Network was created by the Rockefeller Foundation. They wanted to pick the 25 best examples of citizen involvement in the country, support them for several years, and document how citizen participation really works. The Arlington Citizen Involvement Committee was chosen as one of the 25, and I got hooked-up with the national Citizen Involvement Network. I started advising them, based on the work of the monitoring studies, about how they could have citizens monitoring this rather than having some evaluator come in and write it up. I felt the citizens could learn themselves by looking not just at their own community, but also at the other 24, and they could pass ideas around. That was the key to the Citizen's Involvement Network.

In Arlington at that time we didn't have an "outside professor" problem. There wasn't a racial issue. There wasn't a problem in moderate-size towns like Arlington with outsiders coming in. They had no model cities history; nothing like that at all. There was this feeling of, "The university is agreeing to help us. Isn't that wonderful!" And there was tremendous respect for the university resources coming in. And we brought the money. We didn't ask them for a penny. I raised the money for all those projects and said that we would pay for them. And we actually provided money to the citizen's group.

The problem came in the next project, which is really where my mediation work begins. The Red Line, the subway, was about to be extended out from Boston's inner city to Route 128, with a major stop in Arlington—the Alewife station. The citizen's involvement committee said, "You just can't do this. There has to be citizen involvement in this decision." And they went and lobbied the governor, and they had very strong state legislative representation from Arlington at the time. And out of that came a request that we create a regional citizen-involvement process for the detailed planning of the Red Line extension.

It helped that I had been a gubernatorial appointee for the six years before that. The regional agency was put in charge of the planning process. Since I had good contacts in Arlington and with the state, when they said, "Let's do this," I turned it into another student involvement project.

The governor appointed me to chair the regional citizen advisory committee for this process, with the concurrence of the four communities that were involved in the subway extension: Arlington, Cambridge, Somerville, and Watertown.

"Well, we need staff," I said.

"We have professional staff," various officials responded.

"I know," I said, "those are engineers. We need people to really work to help the citizen's group gather the information it needs to have some real input into this."

Fifty—maybe 60—people were appointed by the four towns, the governor, the regional park authority, all the ad hoc environmental groups, the watershed association, the business community. It seemed like everyone had a chance to appoint someone to be on this committee. We had this huge crowd turn out. The meetings went on for 12 or 13 months, every Wednesday night. I will remember it for the rest of my life. From six to midnight, with preparatory stuff between meetings, it was an incredibly elaborate process.

What I kept trying to do in the meetings was to say, "Let's pick some topics, let's gather the information we need, let's understand the assumptions, and then let's try to reach some type of agreement on what we want to recommend here." But then, halfway through the process, it dawned on me that the real problem wasn't getting everybody heard. The real problem was how to avoid having the whole citizen advice-giving process undercut by the fact that the citizen types couldn't agree on anything. So I tried to say then, "What the real issue here for all of us is, is to get consensus." And I announced that to the group. Otherwise, the whole process was going to end up having no effect on what the engineers were telling the state to do. So I had to try to get an agreement among the people with different views.

I thought, "Geez, I've worked on all of this participation stuff starting back with getting rent control in an advocacy mode, and then I watched rent control erode in Cambridge a piece at a time. It's there on paper, sure, but it's not what it was intended to be in the beginning. There was really no way to hold it in place given the constant battle that was taking place politically." So the goal here was really to get some agreement on what the smartest thing to do was.

The citizen involvement committee's main job was the environmental impact assessment, which had to be done under federal and state law for that project. The assessment rested on the choice of alternatives that the various people involved would consider. So we spent a lot of time trying to tell the engineers about new alternatives—"Don't extend the subway at all. That should be an option." Or "Have buses down the same right-of-way instead of a fixed rail." And the engineers were saying "No, no, no. That's not a realistic option." The initial battle was over what alternatives to consider. And that's where I discovered the power of the impact assessment process as a way of structuring citizen participation.

The assessment process requires citizen participation. It requires that you scope out options. It requires that people have a chance to be heard, to write their comments down, and to get reactions to their comments. So I then decided to try something that was an absolute shot in the dark. I remember the issue got very hot and heavy about the size of the parking garage that was going to go with the subway station. The engineers projected that we needed to house 10,000 cars. The citizens group wanted no parking because that wasn't their idea of promoting mass transit. And the engineers wanted to pave over a sensitive environmental area too.

So I said, "Let's have a slide show showing us images of parking garages of everything from 10,000 down to nothing." The engineers who were working for us at the time and paid by the state said, "Where are we going to get slides like that?" I said, "I don't know. Call around the country, the world, and get pictures other engineering firms have worked on."

And so we had a slide show. "Well, here's a picture of a parking garage of 10,000 spaces: Logan Airport." People said, "There's no way you're going to put that many cars here." And the engineers said, "You know, that's probably right."

We had these images of different garages, and I then started using straw polls at the end of each meeting, and said, "This is not binding on anybody, but let's just see. Here are some ranges now. Could we get an agreement that the garage should not be more than 2,500 cars?" Ninety percent of the people agreed after the slide show. So when we really had a sense of what this was about and it wasn't just a symbolic debate, it was a lot easier to get agreement. That became the key turning point in the process.

The same thing happened with the discussion of the forecasting models. When you get behind the statement of what is and what isn't acceptable from the technical people to the assumptions they're making, you open the black box. You bring everybody with you. You test the assumptions. You jointly generate the data. You jointly make the forecasts. You jointly imagine the image.

The slide show on possible garages was the joint imaging of what the thing was that we were really talking about. People saying, "10,000," had no idea what it was when they said it, because they thought, "The engineers say we've got to have it. I believe the engineers. People who are environmentalists don't want cars; they're just saying they don't want it. So I'll vote for 10,000." Until they saw it, and suddenly they were more able to really participate in the conversation. Then everybody backed off. The engineers backed off. Everybody backed off. It was fascinating. I hadn't expected anything in particular. I was trying to promote good discussion, an informed discussion.

But the project ended on a very sour note. By the end, we'd reached an accord on a new option for what should go where. And the option included a set of trade-offs that no one had envisioned in the first place, which was: Could you improve the environment in exchange for allowing this development to go ahead—all the watershed improvements that you've always wanted, the bikeways you've always wanted?

And we reached an accord in which we had a new option to study in the impact statement. Everyone said that's the option, that's what we should do. Everyone, the whole committee, agreed. Everyone said, after this process of hammering out, bit by bit, all the pieces that we were done. Everyone. So we took our recommendation to the state. And they picked an option without all of the promised compensation in the form of bikeways and the waterway improvements. The state included some of the ideas, but not all. So we said, "What's going on here? We put all this time and energy in." We called in the Massachusetts Secretary of Transportation. He said, "It's beyond the scope of this group to tell us to do this."

And then, acting on behalf of the group, I said, "We're going to file legislation to formalize this group as the ongoing manager of this process." The group wanted to do it, but the Cambridge City Manager, who had worked out this deal with the state for the option he wanted, wrote a letter asking that I no longer be chair of the group and saying he didn't want some new ad hoc authority that would take away the power of the cities. He didn't mind an advisory group, but he did not want to deal with an organization with power.

I thought the only way the group was going to get what it wanted was to get some institutionalized standing. So we drafted legislation that challenged the authority of those in power. And those in power un-appointed me, declared the task force's work over, and thanked us for our work. But we had the agreement.

The Alewife project went ahead pretty close to our option, but without a lot of things that had been promised—embittering a lot of people who'd worked very hard to generate this new option and who'd thought they had given away a huge amount to agree to not litigate against the whole thing. That's the only reason the Alewife station on the Cambridge-Arlington town line got built; otherwise it would still be in court today.

There was a lesson here: you needed to have a clear mandate. I'd started with Chet Hartman, with the advocacy work, completely on the outside of the establishment. Then I moved to the monitoring studies, and then to institutionalized citizen participation; so the next step was to move completely within the circle. I started completely out of the circle, got closer and closer, and now I'm in it, but I want to change what goes on in terms of the understandings in the circle. I want to be in a relationship that clearly establishes who has what authority to make what decision, and in which we are going to get those in power, in the beginning, to say, "Rather than have gridlock, rather than be in conflict forever, we are going to try to work this out."

Now, I didn't know you called that mediation. Nobody did. It wasn't called that; it didn't exist as mediation. When I wrote about this experience, I called it consensus building in the land-use planning process. But, having done that, having seen that you could convert citizen participation, I then said, "Look, I want to look at some other models of citizen participation."

That led to the European study, reported in my book *Paternalism, Conflict and Co-production* (that I edited with Michael Elliot). The model of co-production was, I realized, what I had created in the Alewife station case, but there were all these European antecedents of it. So we did all these case studies—we discovered these antecedents—and I said, "Coproduction—that's what I'm going to call it." But nobody knew what coproduction was; it was too awkward a term. But the European study did convince me that this idea wasn't crazy. What I learned from Rockport, Arlington, Alewife, and the monitoring work was that you can stand on the outside being an advocate throwing bombs—you can do what I did when I worked with Chet—and you can win some victories. But those victories will probably be short-lived, and they won't really redistribute power.

Then I got a call from the Kettering Foundation, saying they had this experiment they want to try called a "Negotiated Investment Strategy" (NIS). They were going to have a federal team, state team, and a local team in three different cities trying to come up with a long-term development plan. Kettering had had me out several times to talk about my work on citizen participation. They had come up with this idea of the "Negotiated Investment Strategy," and they had gone to the Carter administration and asked for support—it was the last year of the Carter administration. Marshall Kaplan in HUD suggested maybe they should get one urban planner in one of the three cities. Bill Usery, the former Secretary of Labor, was the mediator for St. Paul. Jim Laue was the mediator for Gary, Indiana, and I was the mediator for Columbus, Ohio. They called us facilitators. Frank Keefe (former Massachusetts Secretary of Administration and Finance) and I did that together, and it worked. There was front-page *New York Times* coverage of those three experiments.

What we did was help the federal, state, and local teams, each with 20 to 25 people, to agree on long-term public and private actions to promote development in the cities, including ways to coordinate all the federal programs.

These three groups met in a big room, with three big tables and a little table up here for the facilitator. Our job was to get an agreement on a five- to ten-year public and private investment package for the city. I wanted Frank there because I felt I didn't know the inside operation of government well enough. Because this was really involving the details: the nitty-gritty of federal contracts, with letters going to the state, "Could the state do this?" The policy debate was incredibly elaborate. It was unbelievable, just unbelievable.

We negotiated the agenda. We negotiated the ground rules. That's where it occurred to me that these people were not going to let someone decide what the agenda was going to be. We're talking about having the most senior people in that situation that you could have.

We said, "Frank and I will meet privately with each group and ask them what the issues are that they're concerned about." We'd write a summary of that and hand it out at the next meeting to see if we could get an agreement on it with everybody. The next meeting would come, and everybody would have rearranged it, and so we negotiated the agenda.

Then we asked each group to prepare a position paper on each issue on the agenda. We divided the next several meetings into periods for discussing the collection of those papers.

We met and people presented their papers. Frank and I then tried to look for the points of agreement and disagreement, sharpened the agreements and disagreements another time, and then said, "Look, here is what we agree and disagree on, but don't close on this issue until we look at the next issue."

We went through all of that and began to develop a single text. Then we looked for trades across issues, and then we developed one overall document. Then those groups all took it back for ratification. Basically, we went through the set of steps we now go through—pre-negotiation preparations, then negotiation, then postnegotiation followup.

Nobody "walked" because huge amounts of federal money were contingent on the consensus. HUD's Kaplan had good connections to Eisenstat (in Carter's office) who said, "You guys reach an accord, and you're going to be first in line. You're going to free up a lot of discretionary funds. We want to demonstrate that this can work." So there was a very clear incentive.

I wrote a report that summarized the agreement that went into effect. I then wrote a report about the process, which was the first thing ever written about the negotiated investment strategy process. I was reflecting on this, thinking, "This is different from Alewife—all these groups accepted the fact that the product was going to be the thing that got implemented."

It was the natural next step. I thought, "The agreement is going to hold, the agreement is going to be, because we have all 'the powers that be' here, and we also have representatives of citizen groups and others. What we come up with is going to be the agreement, and my job is to help them get an agreement."

Four Debates in Public Dispute Resolution

I next wanted to explore how and why Susskind had come to be a controversial figure in the world of public dispute mediation. I knew he had challenged the virtue of "neutrality" as the essence of mediators' practice. I knew he'd also touched off a flurry of debates when he'd argued that public dispute mediators should be held accountable for their work. If "neutrality" was an unworkable or even misleading ideal for mediators to aspire to, what alternative did Susskind have in mind? He had written about "activist" mediation. Wasn't that a contradiction in terms? What could activist mediation mean? Susskind began with central controversies in the field. —JF

Four debates permeate the practice of environmental, or more broadly, public dispute resolution. The first has to do with the timing and mode of entry. The second has to do with the activism of the neutral. The third concerns the expertise of the neutral about the subject matter and the institutional terrain, not just the subject matter. And a fourth involves the ongoing responsibilities and accountability of the mediator for the quality of the outcome. These are the dimensions along which there are substantial ideological and practical differences in the field.

I can describe my own practice to illustrate the issues. With regard to entry, my interest has been in creating some sort of first-order neutral auspices to market the notion of dispute resolution—the state offices of mediation, legislation creating legitimacy around the use of mediation in the siting process, or the U.S. Administrative Conference legislatively having the authority to say, "Now it's time for negotiated rulemaking." In other words, creating an institutional legitimacy for the use of mediation and auspices that will not do the mediation, but that will alert people to the possibility and the advantages of it and get it started. I think that's absolutely crucial.

Someone calls you and says, "I've got a dispute. Can you help be the mediator?" That's how most private dispute resolution has worked. Most dispute resolvers wait to be called by one of the parties. But it's too hard to create legitimacy when you're invited in by only one side. I wanted to solve that problem, and that is why I invented the concept of state offices of mediation. That is why I think we need rosters of mediators, preapproved. That's why I worked with the EPA and the U.S. Administrative Conference on the federal legislation creating negotiated rulemaking.

I had this idea of the state offices on the plane out to a meeting in Colorado, and so in my talk there I said: "Look, I'll give you an illustration of what I mean by institutionalizing a demand." And I proposed something called the "Governors' Offices of Mediation." I wrote about that talk, and I started talking it up to various groups, including the National Institute for Dispute Resolution (NIDR). NIDR, which was just getting started at the time, decided to take the idea and run with it, and so they offered grants to the first four or five states that would put in proposals. I worked with the states of Hawaii, Massachusetts, and Minnesota. The only early ones I didn't work with were Wisconsin and Alaska. Gerald Cormick worked with Alaska, and Howard Bellman worked with Wisconsin, and most of these states put in proposals and got the money from NIDR to create the state offices. Those were the seeds.

Back then, I was also working with Massachusetts and other states to get siting legislation, and I was working with the EPA to get negotiated rulemaking, and now I'm trying to work with public utility commissions to get negotiated rate setting around the country. It's institutionalizing the demand to solve the entry problem.

Of course, there are clearly cases that shouldn't be mediated, and that is where these state offices also help; they save the time. Len and Suzie Buckle (professors at Northeastern University) wrote a wonderful report on the New England Environmental Mediation Center before it went out of business, showing that it had to go sniff out 12 to 20 cases before it found one that you could actually get. And it used up all of its resources looking into cases, meeting with the parties, trying to get this side to accept mediation even though they had been called by the other side. That's what is killing these offices: no one is paying for that overhead. That really struck home.

So the first issue is, "What is your theory about entry?" It's not that I wouldn't come in if one side called me. But that's not my view about how we ought to organize the field, and it is not my view of what's going to make it possible to be successful more often.

But institutionalizing demand doesn't mean that mediation is a panacea or the cure-all for everything. What a state office can do is look at 15 cases to find the one you ought to mediate. It has the institutionalized support to pay for that.

My metaphor—my image, my slogan—for the state offices is that they match up dispute "havers" with dispute "resolvers" when it is appropriate. They have a roster of the resolvers; they get a call from the "havers," or they go find them, because it's legitimate. It's in the state's interest to go snoop around. When they see a situation where it might work, they tell the parties all about it. The mediator isn't there selling a service, so it's a lot more legitimate; you're not a consultant selling your wares.

I need to say, categorically, that at the local, state, and federal level there are disputes over scarce resources, over policy, and over standards that are not handled fairly, efficiently, wisely, nor do they produce stable results when you use the conventional approaches to handling them legislatively, administratively, or judicially. I can document it; I can demonstrate it. There is no question that is true.

We just don't do as well as we could on those four standards of effectiveness. I know it. *Fairer, wiser, more efficient, more stable outcomes: That's the logic of it.*

I do try to be sensitive to the issues of power, precedent, and the vulnerability of the powerless, and I tried in the last chapter of my 1987 book, *Breaking the Impasse*, to address the issue. I'm still in the same groove on this one, though maybe it's a rut. It's the "as-compared-to-what?" point of view.

I am not prepared to abandon dispute resolution because it doesn't achieve the ideal. Especially when I can demonstrate that it does better for those that the critics say that they're most concerned for than all of the other options currently available to those groups, including direct action and the law. If we care about relatively powerless groups, we have to recognize when they're going to do better compared to what they're likely to get from court or from direct action.

I'm not making any argument in principle against courts or against direct action. Not at all. I'm not prepared to say that in every situation dispute resolution will do better. I'm prepared to describe the attributes of situations when we shouldn't use it. But many times, it is better.

It's true that some practitioners have made statements that have damaged the credibility of the dispute resolution profession. Some have made understated claims about mediator activism, for example—that mediators have no business being concerned with power imbalances or unrepresented parties.

But in my view, mediator activism is appropriate. First, it is appropriate for a potential neutral, a neutral who may potentially be acceptable to all parties, to go out and recruit parties. To go out and recruit representatives of interests who the parties already at the table feel should be present but aren't. I think it's appropriate for a neutral to go out and round up representatives, or even help groups coalesce to become enough of a group to name a representative to know that their interest is at stake. That's activism on recruitment.

There's a second step in activism. The parties are there. They've framed the agenda narrowly. They don't see a potential linkage. It is, I think, appropriate for a neutral to ask in the form of a question whether they might want to expand the scope of the agenda because this, and this, and this other case or other experience might suggest it. That's activism.

It is appropriate, third, for the neutral to provide skill-building training to parties who need it, as long as the offer is made to all parties, to enhance the prospect of maximizing joint gains. That's activism.

It is appropriate in my view, too, for the neutral, when meeting with the parties privately, to push them to consider their best alternatives to a negotiated agreement (BATNAs) and the ways of improving their BATNAs and thus their attitude toward what the option of no agreement really means to them.

It is appropriate to question people, to cross-examine them in private. "Do you really know what you're going to get if you don't accept this? Have you thought about that? Is there anything you can do to improve your fallback if you get no agreement?" To push them hard, to cross-examine them, to understand whether and when they should agree or not agree to certain packages—that's activism. It's appropriate to suggest items to put on the table, that the parties themselves haven't suggested—things to trade.

It's appropriate to do this either in caucus or together, in the form of a question, an added possibility, as an option: not to advocate it, but to raise possibilities, to broaden what's available to work with—and to be the initiator of that and not to pretend that you're not. That's activism.

You ask questions: "Have you thought of this? Have you considered this? What about that? Have you taken this three steps down the line and thought about what this means to you? Did you know about this thing over here? Might that be relevant?" I'm not pretending that by asking it as a question, you're not being an activist. Quite the contrary—I'm saying that's the form of activism that I would personally prescribe, and I would say that I would be an advocate for the agreement back with the constituents of the parties. So, we work together at the table, and one guy says, "Well, I see why this is reasonable. Will you come and help me sell it back to my people?"

You bet I'll go, and I'll represent the interests of the whole group if told by the whole group it's O.K. — back with the constituents of one group or with the press. That's activism. So there's activism about recruiting parties, about raising other issues, asking about the issues, providing skills, cross-examining the parties about their alternatives, even suggesting items to explore that maybe no one has brought up yet. The rest of the environmental mediation or public dispute resolution community are scattered along the continuum of views on activism, starting from, "Don't do any of those things at all because the parties won't own the agreement.... It will fall apart, they'll disavow it, they won't own it, they'll think it's yours," or "Who the hell are you to interfere? It's their dispute, not yours."

This kind of criticism can come from some scholars with a labor orientation. But the most experienced labor mediators I know say, "That's a crock. I do all of those things in here." It's a myth about the labor realm that you don't meddle because the parties won't own it, that they won't feel it's theirs, that you'll be injecting your values inappropriately, that it's unethical.

I'm not neutral with regard to the outcome. I'm nonpartisan. That's a big difference. I refuse to adopt the interest of one side as being more important than the interest of any others. I will not side with any party, including the least powerful; I'm not siding with anybody. For only pragmatic reasons, I won't maintain my role in the dispute if I'm viewed as partisan.

But I'm not neutral with regard to the quality of the outcome. I want an outcome that maximizes joint gains, that doesn't leave joint gains unclaimed. I want an outcome that takes the least amount of time and that saves the most money for the parties that I can. Maximizing joint gains means that you haven't left something on the table that would have been better for both sides because the parties didn't propose it.

In any event, the rest of the dispute resolution community arrays itself across this continuum of activism, and there are little markers that move up and down on bringing parties in. Some people are with me on that. On generating options, no way. On generating data, on bringing your experience to them from other cases, no way. On offering to be an advocate for the thing out there in the public and the press, no way: "Hey, you don't want to get identified with any one thing. Then you won't be viewed as neutral by other people who might not like it later, and you might hurt your reputation. You're just a process person. No substantive involvement." That's the view.

But the patronizing tone of some of the critics gets to me: "These dispute resolvers are coming up with stuff that's just cooling off these people who would get more if only they would go to court."

Wait a minute: Who decides this? The people can't decide for themselves whether this is OK? Only you, the great paternal observer knows? I have a lot more confidence in people's ability to know their own interest and to make comparisons and to make risk assessments for themselves than the critics do. So when anyone objects to my activism, I want to remind him or her about the voluntary nature of the agreements here. Also, because some people have relatively few resources and may be there because they don't have a better alternative, I want to remind the critics that activism can also mean training.

That's why I want another piece of activism—bringing resources to the table to ensure that nobody is disadvantaged. We create the resource kitty in negotiated rulemaking cases, in which any group that can't pay the fare to come to Washington can dip into that fund. It's a kitty. We do it with the concurrence of all the parties already in. Everybody has to agree to every move. You have to have a resource kitty; you've got to have an equal playing field.

The people who bring up the issue of co-optation seem to say that a resource kitty and training may look attractive in the short run and so co-opt weaker parties. But what they're really saying is, "These dumb people." You have to follow the logic here; "these dumb people" are being conned into accepting something that they don't realize isn't as good for them as something else.

You can't believe in co-optation without being patronizing. That's it in a nutshell. Because then you're saying that you see it, and they don't—that they're giving something away, that they're being fooled, tricked, or sold a bill of goods. That's what co-optation means. But people know their own interests. Even if they begin with insufficient information, expertise, organizational capacity, they're likely to do better in a public dispute resolution process than if they go through the normal process.

Bringing people into a process, giving people a feeling of participation, and then not empowering them to have any say was the problem with citizen participation; it didn't really promise you anything. But in dispute resolution, you have a veto. You can always step back out. You can always take whatever position you want. You can always go back and use your other options. I don't think the critics are paying enough attention to that, as compared to every other option available.

Another dimension of activism involves expertise. There are people who believe that you sell process. You go in, and you don't need to have ever worked in the past in that institutional context. You don't need to know the system of rules, laws, and informal understandings. You don't need to know even the technical language; you can learn it. The parties know; it's their agreement. It's O.K., you don't need to know it. You're not supposed to know it well enough to contribute substantively anyway. You're only a process person.

But first, you're a drag on the inventing process if you don't even know what they're talking about. They can't stop to educate you. You've got to know at least what they're talking about. Second, you're less than a helpful advocate of a good outcome if you can't bring to them the experience of others that they don't know, with regard to the range of solutions you could invent. I got involved in a land-use case, for example, where the people never understood that you could have property value insurance as part of a siting process. I said, "Well, here's a case, here's a case, and here's a case of property value insurance." And they said, "You mean we can do that? Wow, that solves a big problem for us."

It's perfectly appropriate—even necessary—for a mediator to do this kind of thing. It is, certainly, if we care about the efficiency of the outcome, meaning joint gains maximized, stability of the outcome, and wisdom of the outcome, as the measures of whether we did a good job. Wisdom of the outcome here simply means that, in retrospect, you did not forgo the available technical knowledge with regard to options that you had. You consulted what was there by way of options. And in retrospect you won't say, "Oh God, are we dumb. We didn't even know that possibility existed."

So the notion that the mediator or facilitator shouldn't have any expertise because you'll screw it up doesn't make any sense. It's only if you say, "My job is to help the parties reach an agreement amongst themselves. I don't care about the agreement; I have no responsibility for the agreement. I'm neutral! I'm neutral with regard to the quality to the outcome. I don't care about the outcome; I'm a process person"— only if you say that, do you then argue, "I don't need any expertise except process expertise." But it really doesn't make much sense.

This leads to the issues of responsibility and accountability, which are terribly confusing ones to talk about. I got myself in a lot of trouble with a *Vermont Law Review* piece on the accountability of mediators because I didn't qualify stuff enough to get across the point I wanted, and so people said, "Oh, you mean you're so concerned about the quality of the outcome that you would advocate the interests of those least able to advocate their own interest? Well, then you're clearly not neutral, and you're not a mediator."

I said, "Now look. When I say I'm committed to the best possible outcome, it means several things. It means the outcome is viewed as fair by all parties. It means I ask questions. It means I help put more options on the table. It means I help train people to advocate their own interest, but I offer the same training to everybody. It doesn't mean I take a side."

It's very hard to find a way of saying that the interventions that you make, while offered equally to everyone, help some disproportionately, particularly those least able. So you are having a disproportionate effect on those people's abilities to pursue their interests, but what you're doing, you're doing equally for all, except that it has a more beneficial effect for some. Now that is a very hard point to get across.

So when I say I'm accountable for the quality of the outcome, people say, "Well, then you're not neutral because then you're trying to steer the outcome toward a particular thing you think is good." And I say, "No."

Accountability for the quality of the outcome—providing training for everybody and helping them maximize joint gains—is the element of activism here. It's all in the phrase, "maximize joint gains."

Efficiency is a function of not leaving potential joint gains on the table. That means you have an absolute concern about the quality of the outcome, the substance of the outcome. You can look and say, "Oh my God, they're not maximizing joint gains. I have to say something here to squeeze out all possible joint gains." I'm accountable for helping to manage a process that will produce those gains for the parties.

I'm partly to blame if it doesn't come out. If the thing doesn't get implemented later because we didn't anticipate a boulder in the road, I'm partly to blame. I had a responsibility to help them think clearly about the steps for implementation. But many of my colleagues will take no blame—"I'm not responsible for implementation. That's the whole point," they'll say. "It's the parties' agreement. It's not mine."

This is a very hard point to get across, particularly within the community of mediators because it's such a sensitive issue. You say a word like "accountable" or "responsible," and they explode before they hear the rest of the sentence.

Frustrations and Rewards in Public Dispute Resolution

My conversation with Susskind next turned to the issues I most wanted to explore: his "feel" for his own practice—the difficulties and challenges, the satisfaction or worry, his own emotional and reflective response to the complexity and movement of mediation practice. How, I wondered, would Susskind feel about dealing with angry and doubting parties, with the irrationalities of politically charged public conflicts? How would Susskind make sense of the real messiness of practice?—JF

The work itself is enormously satisfying—to work out a resolution in some contentious public dispute—because it basically achieves what I organize my life around trying to do. I set out to stay involved with issues on the ground in everyday life, people's struggles in their everyday life, to find a way, by working at the intersections between theory and practice, of doing that while still keeping my eye on the bigger picture and still remaining primarily an educator. No small chore. I want it all. I want to stay in the university. I want the satisfaction of being an educator. I want to be a theory builder, but I want my theory to come from practice. And I want my practical intervention to solve problems in the world. Then I'll be happy. And I think I'm getting that. That's what's satisfying.

So, for example, I get a call in the Hartford case: "We've never tried this before, but we're trying to get all these communities in the Hartford region to agree on an allocation of affordable housing responsibilities. What do we do? Are you interested?"

The first exciting part for me is trying to construct an image of what the process would be like, costing it out, putting a team together, and selling it to the people involved. In this case, they had a review committee that had eight, 10, maybe 12 practitioners and companies invited to come and make presentations. So I knew I was one among many, and I thought, "Look, I'm going to tell them," as I always do, realistically, "This is what it is going to take. This is one model of the process. These are the choices you'll have to make. This is why the team I can put together can do the job. These are the issues that are going to come up. This is what I've worked on that's like this that is helpful. These are the problems that I don't think you've addressed yet. Are you sure you want to do this?" I don't pull any punches when I come and do those interviews. In a way, we're back to stagecraft.

So I went and was interviewed by a team of all the people, state and local, who were going to be involved in these negotiations—if they were going to go ahead. I knew all the competition that was being interviewed, and I liked getting the contract. I like explaining to people what they're getting into and how to think about it.

It's a challenge to convince people that there's a right way, based on experience so far, to think about the questions they need to ask themselves, and I try to turn those occasions into a situation in which—even if I don't get the job—they'll know a lot better what they need to get, and why and how they need to do what they need to do.

I really relish those occasions; I'm never the least bit nervous about them. I look forward to them; I enjoy them. I've never walked into a situation where I've had any stage fright at all having to do with dispute resolution. I'm nervous about lots of other things, but not about this. In just about any situation now, I really believe I'm going to have a sense of what I ought to do—based on a lot of experience at this point.

The frustrations and satisfactions emerge in different kinds of ways. In this Connecticut case, for instance, we get the contract, we agree to do it, I put the team together, I go down, and we meet with all the parties, and it's a high. I'm doing what I want to be doing. I see the possibilities; I know this can work. I'm excited to meet a brand new set of people, all of whom have strong views. All of whom are very able, who have never heard of dispute resolution before, for the most part, who don't see what's coming and I do—what the process is going to lead to, the problems that are going to come. But I can't tell them about it all at the beginning because it won't mean anything.

We start, and then there's six, eight, 10, 12, 24 months of exhaustion, and many letdowns because I see very clearly the steps we have to go through, the problems we're going to have to resolve, the confrontations we're going to have to have, the learning that has to go on, and they don't.

I may not know anything about the particulars; I just know there's a set of dynamics that are going to have to work themselves out. Some people are going to emerge as strong speakers and others aren't. Someone is going to throw a bomb somewhere along the way. Someone is going to have a bright light turned on and decide that dispute resolution is the greatest thing that ever happened. There are going to be moments of real anger. There are going to be moments when someone is going to leave, and we're going to have to fight to get him or her to come back because they think leaving is the only choice they have. I know that all that is going to happen.

It's like having this ability to predict the future and trying to figure out what to tell another person. You come down from another planet. You know their whole history, and you know where it's going to go, and you come from the future, you come back. You can't tell them what's going to happen! It isn't going to have any meaning. It's very much like being a time traveler if you do enough of this stuff after a while.

I can see what we have to resolve. It's grueling. It's absolutely grueling, sitting in a room with 20, 50, 100, 200 people. They're all just paying attention to what they're concerned about; I'm trying to pay attention to what all of them are concerned about.

I'm watching all the nonverbal stuff. I'm trying to keep a script in my head. I'm trying to be responsive. I'm trying to watch every face. I'm trying to watch the relationships between the people. I'm trying to keep tabs on the clock. I'm trying to worry about how I'm being perceived. And in the end, I'm exhausted. I'm sweaty. I'm tired. I come home and I go into a deep sleep. It's an incredible outlay of energy—every one of these events.

And doing it, week after week after week, when you know that you could consolidate it if you could just "fast forward." But then you know that you can't. You want to, but you can't. They have to live it; it's theirs. It's their dispute; they have to live it. But it's frustrating a lot of the time. And you can't let on any of the frustration. You can't share it with any of the people in the group, which makes it even more frustrating.

Even when you think something is going to a dead-end, you have to let it go. Unless they know it's a dead-end, it isn't a dead-end. So, there's great frustration because of the commitment of the time and energy, yours and theirs, that in one respect you know might be shortened but in another you know can't be.

You're constantly trying to keep it moving, but you have to be very deft at those interventions. I'm constantly editing what I'm saying; I'm on a delay loop. I have to think about how it will be perceived, if it will help or hurt.

I make mistakes all the time; I still do. I guess my thinking outdistances my ability to talk, and my ability to talk outpaces my ability to listen. So I'm constantly thinking ahead; I'm half listening, and I'm then trying to speak. Sometimes I'm talking too fast for them to get it, or I'm trying to run the whole thing on slow motion for them, when I want to speed it fast forward for me. It's very crazy.

When I screw up, I try to make a joke. I try to use humor more than anything else to deal with mistakes. Say I said something, someone's getting angry, and I realize that it's because they thought I said something that I didn't mean. But they think I said it, and they're just going to get angrier. So I stop and I say, "Maybe this is a good time for us to run this back and start over again. Could I be allowed to edit out what I just said because obviously I just screwed up?" Or I'll say, "Maybe I ought to ask this person to come here, and I'll go over there and sit down and listen because obviously I'm not hearing how I sound very well."

A lot of the time I use sarcasm as a form of humor because it's the easiest form of humor for me. I'm not much good at punch lines, so it's sarcasm — but with myself as the butt of the joke. Or I'll make my eyes big and say, "Whoa! He's angry at me now!" And I'll say, "What did I do to get you that angry at me? I haven't been yelled at like that since my son did yesterday when I took his toys away!" I'll try to make light of what is going on to ease the tension in the room.

If there's going to be anger, I want it aimed at me if it's going to be aimed at anybody, rather than at the process. I want to be able to soak it up, absorb it like a pillow; I don't ever hit back.

If someone is angry at what is going on, I want them to get angry in a way that doesn't hurt their relationship with another person in the room. Getting angry is OK, but getting angry and out of control isn't. People often get out of control in these circumstances, and so I have to try to find a way to wrap some humor around it and let the person save face and not have them walk or ruin the relationship.

They might stand up and make a speech, and everybody will start their eyes rolling, and they're saying, "Get this jerk out of here," and I know that that person is going to have a hard time gaining any respect from the rest of the group. And yet I work for that person as well as the rest of the group, and I want this person to be able to recoup their respect from the rest of the folks there.

So when they're done, I'll say, "Gee, I really agree there's a concern that you have about this, this, this, and this," and I will try, as best I can, in a pithy way to take the most legitimate part of what they said and say it again to the rest of the group on their behalf so the rest of the group will see, "Gee, there was really some important meaning in that."

I'm trying to keep everybody working on the problem, rather than going at each other. It's not easy—it's hard. A lot of these situations involve incredible stakes for a lot of people, and they're very highly charged.

But it's not the meetings part that's hard; it's the part that's between the meetings, after the meetings, writing it up, organizing the staff. The drag for me is managing the administration of it. A lot of stuff happens between meetings. All the phone calls, all the follow-up review of the material, writing the press releases, making sure that arrangements are all set for the next time. I used to do all of that, but I don't anymore. I now have staff to do all that. But fatigue is a big issue.

In the meeting—getting it to work, dealing with the flow of things—I'm not worried; I assume it's all going to work out fine, and I'm going to know the right thing to do. I'm prepared; I've thought about this stuff.

But I do get very frustrated when somebody can't express their own views well to the rest of the group and the rest of the group is pouncing on them. I know that if I intervene, the person would take it as an insult, and yet I know I could express that person's view in a succinct way that would help them. Then I have to call a caucus or call a break, and during the coffee go over and talk with the person, and try to say, "God, I know if I were where you are, I would have been really upset with this group. Maybe you could try it this way, or that way." You can't do it publicly, and then it takes more time, and so you're constantly fighting the clock.

The clock is the worst enemy because you know people want more time to talk about things, but you also know that they don't know that the last item on the agenda needs a half an hour, and there's only 20 minutes left. If you cut it off, they're going to be angry, but if you don't take the last item up, you're going to screw up the whole process.

So you say, "Hey look, guys, I really think we've got to go on to the next issue," and you start to talk like you've gone on to it, and wait to see if you can get away with it. There is always an immense amount of adrenalin flowing because I'm fighting the clock.

I'm operating on some other plane when the mediation starts. It's like I'm having a conversation with each person simultaneously. Partly I'm teaching. But how do you teach without being pedantic? How do you teach without being explicitly Socratic? How do you teach without giving lectures? How do you teach without appearing to teach?

I do it by saying, "If I were in that situation..." or "Might you...?" or "Imagine if..." or "What if...?" or "Could that be construed as...?" Everything is questions. It's all questions. It's not questions in the Socratic sense, where I'm manipulating what comes next—because the parties often tell me to shut up, and that's it, and they're going to go ahead and do this.

I'm not fishing for anything. I'm just saying, "God, have you thought about this?" I'm just talking about it as I'm thinking about it, and I'm trying to reveal a thought process that I'm going through. That's the teaching. I'm trying to let my thought process come out loud with them. Some people will say that a lot of this is the force of personality—that I'm underestimating the extent to which the individual mediator's personality has a lot to do with how this process works. But I'm not underestimating it—I know it's important. But I can't do anything about it. I may as well just be who I am.

There are a lot of issues here about general trust building. Take the Maine low-level waste-siting process, a case I worked on through Endispute. After the first meeting of the stakeholders, there were bunches of letters to the editor saying, "This group of professional manipulators from Endispute Inc. has been hired by the Authority to co-opt the members.... People should refuse to join the advisory group, they should boycott the process." And the press showed up to the next meeting with television cameras and everything else, and I had to figure out a way to start off the meeting in a way that would build trust.

So I said, "Before we begin today, I want to make a statement. I want to respond to some of the letters that have been published this week in the newspapers and to some of the concerns that have been raised. If anybody in this group at any point in this process thinks that I am trying to steer this toward a particular outcome, call me on it. Point it out. Interrupt. Say that you think it's the case. If I don't make an adjustment in response that satisfies you that I'm not partisan, I'm out of here. I don't need this. You don't need me."

And the headline the next day was: "Mediator Promises To Withdraw If Bias Detected." All the rest of the discussion—all the substantive stuff that we thought was going to be the debate—they picked up, and after that I didn't have any problems. I said, "I work for you. Hold me accountable."

I did have a private go to with the most obnoxious, difficult person up there last time, and I said, "You know, I'd like to help you."

And he says, "Sure you would."

"I'd like to help you get your interest in this process," I said. "I know you don't believe that. You think I'm working for the power authority or the nuclear plant or something, but try me! Call me during the week. Tell me something that you want on the agenda. Tell me something before the meeting, before you write a broadside to the paper. Give me a chance. Test me on it. If I screw up, then don't believe me any more. Give me one opportunity to demonstrate that I mean what I say. You're not giving me a chance. I work for you."

He toned down the rhetoric dramatically. He's still writing his letters because he uses it as an organizing tool, and I said to him, "I know you need to do this to keep visibility, you have to keep your members abreast of what you're doing, and you want to raise money. I understand that, that's fine. I don't have a problem with that. I don't take it personally. I'd just like to see you get more of what you want. I think I can help you do it." And I said, "And I'm making the same statement to everybody here, and I know that doesn't fit your model of how things get done. Try me."

In the Hartford case, a guy who was very important to the process came but said nothing for the first two meetings. Finally, I tried to move an item off the agenda, and I said I thought we had an agreement on something, and he said, "We don't have any agreement on that. What do you think—this is your agenda? I thought that was going to be the case. I don't need to be here if you think you know what the answer to this whole thing is."

And I said, "Hey look. I thought we had an agreement on that." I took a magic marker and put a big X through the page where I had written the agreement. I took off the page, crumpled it up, and threw it in the garbage can, and I said, "Here, come up and write what you think you agreed to. I missed it. I'm sorry, I missed it."

He came up and said what it should be, and he became one of the key supporters of the process for the rest of the time. It was a very crucial moment. I misconstrued what I thought the group had agreed to. I thought I heard one thing—he heard it right; I heard it wrong. And he took my writing it wrong as an effort to say that that's what they had agreed to when they hadn't. The group said that he had it right, and I had it wrong. After I made the corrections, I didn't have a problem dealing with him the whole rest of time. In fact, he became an activist for the process. He said, "This process is really and effectively accountable to people. We have a chance here to shape this policy. Let's do it."

A lot of people have become almost embarrassingly supportive of a process that they only partly understand. "Oh, we should do everything by consensus. We should always have processes like this. We need neutrals for all of our public meetings." They do this because they feel a sense of efficacy. It's not like going to a hearing where you say your piece, you leave, and you have no idea whether there is any uptake, or you know it's getting done behind closed doors.

Here they see the embodiment of an ideal that they have, which is that people can sit, reason together in the political world, and an intelligent outcome that takes account of everybody's concerns will come out. They'd like to believe that's possible. I think most people in the public sector would like to believe that's possible. They're cynical about the possibilities, given what they see. Here they see it working. That's very uplifting.

People know what's happening. They come in to the public policy mediation process skeptical. They come in realists, not cynics: realists, with skepticism and cynicism floating around, and they wait and see what happens. And if they get an agreement and they feel they've been heard, and they've watched something that works to get everybody heard, and the strongest didn't prevail—logic prevailed, interests were served, politics wasn't ignored, the thing has a chance of being implemented—it's enormously positive for them. Why wouldn't they become advocates for it?

There are two light bulbs that come on. You can see them flashing around the table at key moments. One is, if you don't like what someone just suggested, don't just say you don't like it, try to suggest an alternative that meets their concerns but that's also better for you too. They stop saying, "That's crazy! We're not going to do that. I'm opposed to that...." They realize that the way to get what they want is to offer the other person something that, in fact, responds to their needs but also responds to their own needs, whereas what they heard didn't. You can just see them start.

The first couple of meetings, and for some of the people most of the time, it's, "No, no way! We'll never go for that"—that's all they say. To get past that attitude, I try to say, "Well, what if that person had said this and this and this, would that be better?" They'll respond, "Yeah, that would be better, but it's still not there." Then I say, "What would you add to it to make it better?"

That's this question-asking process. I am modeling the process; I'm hoping they're going to use in dealing with each other. I'm taking this person's side when he says, "No," and I'm saying, "Now you're saying, 'No,' to him. I can see why you're saying, 'No,' but what else could he have said that would have satisfied you?" I'm getting him into the mode of making proposals in response to things that he doesn't like, rather than negative statements, and they're seeing that that's the way to deal with the person that you disagree with in this kind of process.

At some point I see the light bulb go on. The next time something comes up that he doesn't like, he says, "I don't like that as much as this and this. Could you live with that?" And he looks over and smiles at me. You can just see it; it is a very obvious event. He gets it. He gets it, and it's very intriguing.

And then you'll get a lot of people coming along the way saying, "You know we had a thing at home last week, and I tried doing this thing, and it really worked with my kid." I get it all the time in the sidebar conversations—people taking the same model and trying to apply it in their personal lives or at work.

The essence of the process here is acknowledging the other's needs and your own, and making a proposal that tries to meet both. Arguing that you don't like what they want, and you want something else instead, which is the old model of hearings, doesn't get agreement. Remember we're trying to get an agreement here. And we're not going until we get agreement.

When people stay in the mode of No, No, No, I have to act on their behalf with the rest of the group as if they were doing it this way. I say, "Well, John said, 'No.' I think we can all understand why he's not completely enthralled by Jane's idea, but maybe, John, what if Jane had said this and this and this? Would that have been better?"

He'll grudgingly say, "Yeah, it's better."

I'll say, "Could you live with it?"

He says, "No, I can't live with it."

"What would it take for you to live with it?," I ask. "You don't have to commit to anything, but just help us understand what's bothering you about it." Those are the kinds of interventions I do.

John either moves, or he doesn't. If he doesn't, I say, "Well, John, if I were you, my God, I might suggest this and this and this. Would that be moving in the right direction?"

He says, "Yeah."

I say, "We're not committing John to anything but let's work with this for the moment. What about the rest of you, if John had said this?"

It's all "If this, if that, what if...?"; "Could you...?" I don't think I ever make declarative statements about what the group should or shouldn't do, or has or hasn't done.

We take breaks when people can't sit anymore. One of things I'm bad at, I know, is releasing people soon enough for breaks because I could sit for the whole day. I don't need breaks. It's part of being impatient. I don't want to waste the time.

But people need more time, just to get up, walk around, socialize, and stuff like that. So every break I turn into caucuses between me and someone, or I just motion a few people over and say, "That was great, what you did. That was a super proposal; that really broke the logjam. Can the two of you add anything to what she has been saying that will get those guys over there who won't budge on this to...?" I don't call it a caucus—it's a mini-mediation within a mediation.

The time to deal with just one party is between meetings. We don't do it at meetings. We use a lot of written stuff. I will put a draft together and send it to everybody and ask them to send their individual comments back. So I'll know where everybody is on every proposal beforehand.

I get back completely contradictory comments, but at least I know where everybody is. Then I try to formulate something or to lay out two poles and say to the group, "We got all your comments back, and we got a bunch of you here and a bunch of you here. I don't see that it makes sense to just put one of these up. We have to do something about this. Who's got a suggestion?"

The parties are there for lots of reasons. They're in because someone from their organization told them to come. They're in because they don't want the embarrassment of having to explain why they didn't come in. They don't want to get hassled by someone above them or at the same level. They're in just out of curiosity. They're in for thousands of different reasons. And some aren't in at the beginning, and some drop out during. We have to go and get them back, or decide to go ahead without them. It's very intriguing.

In this Hartford case, there was one woman who was a real ringer from the very beginning. She was the only really off-the-wall person there, very vocal, and you never knew what she was going to say—except that it had nothing to do with what anything anyone else said. But she represented one of these towns. She was a citizen type, who talked her way in as the town's representative. And everybody kept trying to accommodate her, but no matter what they said, she would say essentially, "No, No, No, No."

We got all the way through to the very last day, trying to get everyone to sign up. Do we have an agreement? Everyone said, "Yes" (over here). Over there, "Yes." Over there, "Yes." OK, so we hand the written agreement around, and she leaves without signing it. We have every other signature. But there's no agreement unless everybody is on board. Nobody else but us, the mediation team, knew that she hadn't signed when she left.

We called the board she was allegedly appointed by and asked to meet privately with the head of it, and said, "Every week you've gotten the summary of every meeting. Your appointee has been at the following meetings; she missed these meetings. She had these concerns; we think we have responded to all of them. She left without signing; I don't think that was inadvertent. All the other 36 towns want to know why your town hasn't signed. Do you want to sign or not?" They signed.

You can always look ahead and know that at some point somebody is going to threaten to walk. It's a source of power, they think. I can make a list of tactics that someone is going to use with 90 percent certainty in every dispute. I know what they're going to do—I know how people will respond. There are always surprises, but basically I know what to expect.

There's the person who goes to the press and announces that the group did this or did that, and it's not true. And then the next meeting they don't want to come; they don't show. So people are really angry.

So I ask, "What do you think we should do, group, about John and the article in the paper?" Someone will respond, "That wasn't true. We had an understanding, we had a ground rule: No negotiating through the press. He broke the ground rule."

And I say, "What should we do?"

"Oh, screw him, who needs him?" is the response.

"Well, I think we really need him," I'll say. "We need him back."

"Well, you call him," a participant will say. "You get him to come. I'm not calling him." "You want the mediation team to call him? OK, we'll call him," I'll say. "What should we tell him?"

It's the subject of negotiation, with the group, what to do. Everything is negotiated.

Now, anyone can go to the press any time they want. They can say anything they want as long as they don't attribute something to the rest of the group or to someone else. You can't tell political people that they can't talk to the press. But you can have a ground rule: Don't attribute something to someone else. You can say anything you want for yourself.

We do a press release after every meeting. Even if we meet for 10 months, we do a press release after every meeting. We always do a public notice of every meeting. Every meeting is open. You can't have a meeting like this and not have it open to the public or the press. There is no secrecy; there is zero secrecy.

What about between meetings? I don't announce my phone calls to the press. We do a lot between meetings. But I want to know, by what comparison is this process secretive? Compared to what?

I do have a sense of the limits of this model and my own style. I am an inappropriate guy for a bunch of disputes. I'm an inappropriate guy for disputes in which the parties are looking for therapy, personal therapy. I'm just not good at that kind of endless sidebar conversation about how you feel and how I feel. I'm focused on solving the problem. I'm not in the therapeutic mode; I'm in the problem-solving mode, to use Sally Merry and Susan Silbey's distinctions about mediator styles. And I don't have a lot of patience for it.

I'm probably guilty of not listening carefully enough to the possibility that there's no solution. I just work and work and work on the assumption that there is one. I just keep pushing and struggling. The other thing is that some people are truly put off by the pace at which I go. For instance, I'll ask them a question, then another question. I'll say, "OK, I hear you" and before they finish the sentence, I say, "Yeah, yeah, I know you're going to say this—and then they're going to say that. But if you do that, then they'll do this, and then what are you going to do about that?" I can be too fast, and people are just put off by it.

I have to work very hard to keep everything at a better angle. The closer we get to being near the solution, the more propensity I have to say, "You're going to say this, and they're going to say that, and this one will say that, and the only choice you'll have is this because you're concerned about that...." And people don't want to hear all that. They want to live it. They don't want me to live it for them. They want to live it. And I'm probably wrong some of the time, which is even worse.

So the pace has to be in control, but for those that want a much slower pace and a personal touch along the way, I'm the wrong guy. I don't have the time to put in. I'm probably the wrong guy when the parties know each other really well, and they're just rehashing all this old stuff, they're reliving all these old battles. I just don't have a lot of patience for that. When I say that I don't have a lot of patience, basically I opt out. I try not to stay with disputes or get involved with disputes where I don't feel that I'm the right guy, and I try to put other people into those.

I got a call the other day. Would I work on a dispute having to do with the merit pay system in a certain state, on a dispute that's going on between the executive and the legislative branch? I'm not terribly interested in merit job descriptions and merit pay stuff. If I'm not excited about the subject matter, I'm not going to be very enthusiastic. I'm not going to be the right guy for it.

I'm very, very selective, and I can afford to be because I don't have to make my living doing this. But I imagine if I were to try to make my living at this, and I had to take stuff that I thought was boring, I'd be really awful. My mind would be on other things.

There are times in the process when we try to keep people from rehashing history. The point is not to interpret what happened, but to get an agreement on what to do. So I'll say, "Why don't we just sort of give each person a few minutes to give their account of what happened, and there will probably be real differences, they're probably going to disagree. But at least we'll understand more about what people are proposing if we understand where they're coming from, so let's listen to it. But once we know it, let's not try to get agreement about what happened. We want an agreement about what's to be done."

People start this process with needs, desires, wants, concerns, ideology, uncertainty, and interests. All of them. And I expect people to change — to inform their sense of what they would or wouldn't like to have happen by listening to what other people say. Mediation is not a question of plugging into the computer answers to questionnaires from each person and printing out the maximized joint gain resolution. Learning and inventing goes on, and reconsideration goes on, and argument matters.

People discover something about their own interests in the process, and so that's why you talk, as opposed to just pouring the stuff into the microphone and having the computer console be the source of integration, maximizing joint gains. People are not just collections of interests; they have all kinds of tacit wants and needs.

You know that if you're representing a community, there's a diversity of views within the community, not just a single hierarchy of weighted interests. There's what's spoken and unspoken; things you would like to admit, things you wouldn't like to admit; there are things you realize and things you don't yet realize; there are a lot of inchoate concerns.

You listen; you hear what other people say; you identify with that; you're informed by argument and debate, and you could never predict at the beginning where you are going to come out on the issue of your community's responsibilities by the end.

I don't mean that everything is known in the form of interests, that all interests are knowable at the beginning of mediation, or even at the end. I mean: When confronted with a package or choice, when we have come as far as we can, when we don't have any more time or money, when we've explored and plumbed and probed this thing, and when we ask, "Do you want this package or the alternative, which is no agreement?", then you know what is in your best interest, relative to what the options are likely to be, better than anyone else can know at that time.

That's what I mean when I talk about interests. I don't think of interests as completely known quantities from the beginning to the end. If I were to use the economists' multi-attribute decision analytic frame, I'd say that between the beginning and the end, we've added a large number of attributes, we've changed the rank ordering, and we've changed the rationale for the weightings and the rank orderings along the way. But the list of what is known changes because of the conversation. The conversation matters.

There is a danger if a mediator walks in thinking, "You have your interests, you over here have your interests, you over there have your interests, and now we're going to talk." If you don't presume that people are going to learn anything from the conversation, you won't promote the conversation. If you don't presume that people will alter and adjust their calculus as they go, then you won't honor and value the learning that needs to go on: the clarity of communication, the usefulness of bringing new information. That's a big danger.

Arguments about bringing knowledge and expertise and being activists and so on all honor the fact that people don't know everything that they want and need and can't be explicit about it at the beginning. Otherwise we wouldn't go through all this inventing.

I don't assume some perfect rationality from everybody in the room. I assume, first, that emotion will overcome logic lots of times in the course of the process, that it will preempt it. Almost everybody will often do things that, if they thought about it beforehand and were asked, "Would you do that?," they'd say, "No." But they—we—will do it anyway because emotion dominates logic. I think there's lots of recent research on this, suggesting that emotion dominates logic.

I expect it to happen. I expect someone to blow up, even though blowing up at their ally is stupid—but they'll do it anyway. I expect it. Which means we have to give people room in the process, that we have to give people a chance to save face, that the mediator has to absorb a lot of that and deflect it from somebody else. The person will be glad you did it because they'll be the first to tell you that emotion overwhelmed logic at the time. They won't say it that way, but that's what happens. They'll say, "The guy just pissed me off, so what can I do?" So I expect that.

Second, I expect people to say, "Option one is better than option two, option two is better than option three, but I don't believe you that one is better than three."

"Wait a minute!" I'll say. "One is better than two, two is better than three, but you don't think one's better than three?"

I expect that because certain things have symbolic meanings to people that we don't understand. So I try to remember, "There's something in option three that means something to you that I don't understand, which means that it's better for you than number one, even though one is better than two, you agree, and two is better than three, you agree—but if you had a choice between three and one, you would choose three."

I try to understand things like this. I expect people not to be able or willing to communicate to me explicitly lots of overlays of value they attach to things that I don't understand. I expect that what we'll read out is an "illogical" statement—but "illogical" for good reasons.

I try to respond not by convincing people that they're wrong, but by taking what they've said at face value and trying to understand what it is about option three that makes it better than number one. I have to cross-examine people to make sure that that's clear—as much as possible. But it may not even be possible a lot of the times.

Third, people let personal likes and dislikes outweigh their known strategic advantage. I might say, "It'd be great if you had that guy as your ally."

"Screw that!" is the response I might get.

"But if the two of you were arguing this, it would clearly carry the day," I'll say.

"I don't like the guy. Period," they'll say. "I'm not having a private meeting with him; I don't like him." Or they'll say, "You're right, it would probably help. But I'm not doing it." This is more of a personality thing than a symbolic or a value kind of thing.

I also expect people to have a bad day—they've had a fight with their spouse the night before; they didn't get enough sleep, they're cranky; they're worried about something. I expect all that stuff to happen.

Anyone who doesn't expect problems like this hasn't tried to mediate. So much of what is written about mediation is written by people who haven't tried to do it, who haven't looked at it closely. It drives me crazy!

Now, think for a minute about the definition of democracy that most people have. The definition that theorists have has to do with rights and freedoms, and not responsibilities. But if you really look at democratic theory, at least in the way I think it ought to be looked at, it's a balance between rights and obligations, or rights and responsibilities. You have a right to express your own views; you don't have a right to get everything that you want. You have a responsibility to behave in ways that respect the needs of other people and doesn't infringe upon their needs.

And what are the mechanisms of democracy that seek to balance rights and responsibilities? There aren't very many left. Voting? Voting's a big thing. You go, and you vote. Are you balancing rights and responsibilities? Not really. Especially with referenda—you pick one side and take no responsibility for the downside.

Where do we work on this balancing? Participating in processes of government? That doesn't look to me like you're sharing much responsibility. You're going and you're complaining; you're lobbying; you're going to a public meeting; you're saying what's good for you.

The mediation of public disputes is the only mechanism at the moment that I see in which we are trying to find a way to allow, to encourage, and to enable people to balance their rights and responsibilities as citizens.

And why? Because there's no agreement unless you listen, hear, and respond to their concerns. There's no action unless we all accept the responsibility for accommodating the needs and interests of everybody else.

Where's there another forum, another mechanism of democracy that is doing that? I don't see any. Maybe that's too extreme, but I don't see any. You go to court. Are you balancing anything?

The need of parties to respond to each other brings out a sense of responsibility. It recalibrates what I think was the initial notion, the Jeffersonian notion, of democracy. People come in with, "I want this, I want that," and leave with, "We need to do this," in every case I've worked on.

But when you see someone, starting with the mediator, attempting to accommodate your concerns, it behooves you to seek to accommodate other people's concerns if you're going to get what you want. It is too hard, face-to-face, to say, "Well, now that you're doing what I want, that's great; I don't have to do anything for you." It comes down to that. It's too hard. I don't care how toughminded you are. You can't encounter another person face-to-face, have them demonstrate that they want to help you get what you want, and then not accept responsibility for helping them get what they want. It's too hard to do; people can't do it. But you don't have to do that in a public hearing; you don't have to do that when you vote.

As a mediator, I create a context in which that is what happens, a setting which is protected enough, and where there are rules and rewards and encouragement for behaving in that way, and the usual impediments to it are taken away, and the burdens of it are made clear. Is there any other setting in which your responsibilities are balanced with your rights?

The whole process is the epitome of what I think democracy is really supposed to be like. It's not that people are no longer concerned about what they need. It's that they now realize that the only way to meet their needs is to respond to what others need as well, and therefore to come out with something that we can do together that meets each of their needs. And all this doesn't happen for altruistic reasons. The "we" here is special. This "we" can help get what each of us wants and needs. There's no loss of "I," but there is recognition of others, of differences.

Participating politically usually means three things: lobby, vote, and stand for office. What else is there? Those don't promote the kind of balancing of obligation and responsibility that facetoface, joint problem solving or collaborative problem solving creates. I wouldn't argue that my model of direct democracy is to abandon all the conventional mechanisms and have everybody sit around and solve all these problems. I'm in favor of representative democracy. But I do think we can supplement it on occasion in the ways that I've described, and I think that it does produce "we" decisions in an informed way.

What's interesting to me is: What is the option? I don't know what the option is.

Finally, of course, there are public disputes that shouldn't be mediated at all. I don't think disputes concerning rights—constitutional rights; human rights; basic rights—should be mediated, even if you could meet the interests of all sides. We have certain basic constitutional, human rights that are decided and legislated in a different way. I don't think that those ought to be negotiated.

I wouldn't mediate here to try to find a resolution, but I think there are skills and tools in dispute resolution that can help us have much better public, or even private, debate and discussion, so that we can learn to live with our differences. I don't think we are going to resolve differences through mediation when rights—fundamental rights, constitutional rights—are at stake. And there are a lot of them; there are huge numbers of those questions. So if someone came to me and said, "We would like you to mediate the state policy on abortion," I'd say that there's no point in reaching a negotiated policy agreement on abortion. It's a constitutional matter.

Afterword

Over the past several years, I've come to believe that mediation is best understood as informal problem solving. When added as a step to formally mandated policy-making or administrative procedures, informal problem solving can yield agreements that will otherwise elude the parties. Trained intermediaries—including trained planners—have an important role to play in making such problem-solving work.

However, whenever I suggest that informal problem solving (i.e., mediation) can be helpful, public officials still raise the following questions:

- But if nongovernmental neutrals or planners facilitate and manage informal problem solving, doesn't that mean that we must relinquish our power and authority? Or,
- But can informal problem solving really work when the parties disagree in fundamental ways or their exchanges are already quite contentious? Or,
- But won't reliance on informal problem solving undercut formal procedures that we may have to rely upon in the end?

Many governmental bodies still don't realize that by hiring a mediator, they don't relinquish authority. The product of informal problem solving is invariably a proposal, not a decision. Final decisions are still made by those with the statutory authority.

Also, most agencies still don't understand how mediation, or what I've also called "facilitative leadership" in *Breaking Robert's Rules*, can proceed in the absence of trust and in the face of conflicting values. While mediation builds trust, informal problem solving can proceed while that is happening—to identify diverse interests, to bring in expertise, to visit sites, to get new information, and much more. The key is to know how to use a professional intermediary to manage the conflict in the absence of trust. Deeply rooted conflict will have to be dealt with using formal methods. Why not take advantage of an informal setting in which the parties can learn more about each other's views, work through their differences in a less adversarial way, and not be locked in to precedent?

In the same way that public agencies have to carry out their formal administrative responsibilities when parallel legal proceedings are underway, informal problem solving can proceed while formal procedures are held in abeyance. The fact is, adding an early stakeholder assessment and joint development of ground rules—which informal problem solving always requires—can clarify who the real stakeholders are and what the agenda ought to be when formal procedures begin.

Governmental bodies have an easier time accepting mediation or facilitative leadership when it is clear that it serves as an add-on rather than a replacement for what the agencies usually do. So mediation enhances agency decision making; it does not substitute for it. In addition, informality appeals to nongovernmental clients who are put off by the formality and cost of formal administrative or legal hearings.

Someone asked me recently, "If mediation or informal problem solving is such a good idea, why isn't it being used more often?" Well, the answer is, it is being used in diverse ways, many of them "below the radar," informally and not in the limelight. Every effort to work things out informally either before or after formal processes are initiated is a kind of informal problem solving. Whether professional mediators are used or not, informal problem solving (not behind-the-scenes deal making) is expanding. We have lots of evidence to support the idea that professional helpers can make such processes work more effectively. Even if the supply of well-trained public dispute mediators is still limited, it is better for agencies to try informal problem solving without the help of an external neutral than not to use it at all. I would note, though, that even in lean times, legal budgets don't seem to get cut. So, we should be urging agencies to set aside part of their legal budget to support mediation—which might very well save them money in the long run. It's just a matter of time before most public agencies add informal problem solving to what they do. I hope this book will help.

Conclusion
Planning, Learning, and Governing Through Conflict

John Forester

When I began the interviews that led to this book, I was interested, first of all, in what planners could learn from those who had to work "in between" conflicting, distrusting, angry, suspicious, and deeply if differently committed stakeholders all the time. Because I have written *Dealing with Differences: Dramas of Mediating Public Disputes* (Oxford, 2009) with the central question of "lessons for planners" very much in mind, I will try in these closing comments not so much to repeat the highlights of that book, but to build upon them to address the practical challenges that planners face in contentious situations involving passionate differences of priorities, interests, values, and identities.

Good Outcomes, Not Compromises, Not Process Alone
The practitioners in this book—who might have learned the skills and techniques of dispute resolution like mediation, facilitation, and group problem solving early in their careers—have come to see themselves as helping disparate communities learn to bridge differences and to work to solve their own problems. As Frank Blechman beautifully put it, the skills of organizing, mobilizing, and conflict generation could be retooled and refined not only toward the goal of conflict resolution, but also even more powerfully to the goals of practical decision making and implementation—to creative negotiation. But creative negotiation, in turn, implies that parties can craft workable options to solve pressing problems in ways that meet their interests and deep value commitments.

So these practitioners' stories have a surprise in store for readers: the word "compromise" almost never appears. These stories have been about practical planning and processes whose goal has not been compromise but creative problem solving producing workable, interest-satisfying decisions and options instead.

The stories of practice we've considered here have involved even more than multiple actors with multiple priorities and differing interests and values. The cases also have always been complex, some involving legal issues and technical issues and even religious and moral commitments. So these stories have always involved far more than any simple processes of bargaining, trading, or deal making. Rather, these processes have always been about learning, appreciating the complexity and issues of the interests at stake so that proposed solutions could be still more robust, more creatively complex, and more satisfying to the range of stakeholders involved with their multiple and diverse interests. In this way, these stories echo the earlier planning literature on "social learning," but they do so with added value: now, learning becomes not just edifying and insightful, but also tangible and practical. By seeing how astute negotiations link process quality to outcomes, we see the creative invention of workable options. So these stories, throughout this book, have been about agreements and outcomes every bit as much as they have been about procedures and processes. We see in these cases not only gains in knowledge, but also gains in actions to be taken, actions to be legitimated by the stakeholders involved. So, here we have processes of learning that address questions of both epistemology (what and how we know) and ethics (what we ought to do). We see not just gains in relationships built, crucial as those may be, but we see specific decisions and commitments made, outcomes realized.

Learning to Listen, How to Listen, and When Not to Listen

In virtually all of these cases, we see lessons about how to listen (and how not to listen) in situations of disagreement, debate, and differing priorities and claims. These practitioners urge us to respect differing claims and yet to take them as tentative, as depending on the settings in which they have been raised, as depending on the information that has been available up to any given point in time. So, in many of these cases we see the intermediary—or facilitating or convening or mediating—practitioners work to get new information to everyone at the table, to go beyond whatever's just been said, emphatic as it was. We see the intermediaries carefully convening in the same room, often for the first time, players and parties who're confident about what they want but who may never have actually sat and listened to the others' stories—instead of having "heard" those stories earlier as filtered and distorted by the media or by public posturing.

So these practitioners ask planners not to argue with initial positions but to respect them and yet remain open to the possibilities that yesterday's positions can develop into creative new ones as everyone involved in a case learns more about what's going on and about each other, about what's technically possible, and about where parties really do and really don't disagree.

But we learn much more too, here, about the important work that astute listening can do, not so much by collecting new information or leading us to recognize new problems but instead by simply (or not so simply!) showing respect to others, taking others seriously as adults, even or especially when they're upset, impatient, and deeply suspicious of one more well-intentioned process. Listening attentively conveys recognition, regard, and respect; listening inattentively, easily seen as being dismissive and disrespectful, can be as insulting as name-calling can be. Whether in Adler's insistence on making space for personal stories, or Blechman's emphasis on early interviewing, or Beutler's or Richardson's creating times and spaces for learning, we see the ordinary work of listening attentively not only gathering new information, but also doing the extraordinary practical work of building new and trusted relationships that make future learning and future action together possible.

Intermediaries Are Midwives, Not Parents

These cases show us too, but in greater detail, the wisdom of two simple propositions I wrote about much more briefly in *Dealing with Differences*. The first speaks to the curious role of the planner who acts in between distrusting and contentious parties, and it goes like this: intermediaries like mediators don't make agreements any more than midwives make babies. The parties involved produce their agreements step by passionate step: they share their stories, challenge each other's claims, then gather information and expertise, make and refine and craft proposals, then decide what will work for them. They decide what they will do, not the facilitating planners, even as the planners working with them can help at every stage of the process.

So, the planners and intermediaries in our cases have not been parents—but they have been the catalysts and the coaches and the enablers without whom the contentious parties might never have resolved important issues, not perfectly but practically to their satisfaction, together.

Disagreeing About the Creator, and Agreeing Where to Put the Stop Signs

We can put a second striking proposition that these cases illustrate this way: When we find ourselves facing apparently irreconcilable, "deep value differences," we can at times still disagree about what our gods require of us and yet come to agree about where the stop signs should go. In other words, parties can steadfastly continue to disagree about matters of doctrine and deep values, even as they can find practical agreements about specific moves or actions or investments at the very same time. In short, planners or intermediaries who convene passionately and "fundamentally" divided parties must take care not to confuse deep doctrinal disagreements with far more specific possibilities that they might practically explore together. Frank Blechman's example of Adrienne Kaufman's work makes this case powerfully.

The hard-won wisdom of the point here suggests the important differences we need to appreciate and even insist upon between two very distinct forms of "discussion" (a word whose ambiguity thus gets us into trouble). Sometimes as planners we might wish to help parties debate their rival claims of doctrine, but far more often we might want instead, and altogether differently, to help parties engage in a dialogue about who values what. Once we see how "debate" and "dialogue" can take different organizational forms, how they can get in each others' way, how we as planners might act differently to encourage one or the other, then we might design more sensible and more productive planning processes as a result.

But if we think carefully about this book's cases, we will see that they have interwoven not two strands but three. Not only do these practice stories teach us about productive moments of dialogue (think, for example, of Peter Adler's efforts to prompt storytelling or Lisa Beutler's "mind-mapping" exercises) or sharp moments of debate (think, for example, of Ric Richardson's or Beutler's sessions devoted to engaging experts), but also they all culminate in a third practical process that we might simply call "negotiating practical agreements about outcomes." Sometimes, indeed, parties don't need to settle differences of doctrine at all before deciding where the stop signs should go to protect their children as they go to school.

Going Slow to Go Faster

These cases raise crucial questions of timing and efficiency, and an underlying question, largely ignored in the scholarly literature, about what we might call the ongoing costs of unmediated conflict. This suggestion echoes the popular saying, "If you think education's expensive, consider the alternative." Susskind puts this powerfully and simply when he urges us to evaluate the promise and the cost of mediated negotiations by asking pragmatically, "Compared to what?" We might paraphrase this as, "If you don't want to try mediated processes, OK—but just be sure you have a workable, less expensive, more satisfying alternative that will actually work for you!"

Consider Lisa Beutler's success with the California Off Highway Vehicle Roundtable after she inherited the contentious land-use and environmental conflict that had been stewing for 20 years. We find no suggestion in her story to lead us to believe that the State of California could not have asked for, and succeeded with, a similar intervention 10 or even 15 years earlier. Can we, in any reasonable sense, then, worry about Beutler's intervention being slow or time-consuming—after the alternative problem-solving processes had failed for 20 years? In Blechman's case of the county transportation wrangles, or in Adler's case of tensions between the real estate interests, bankers, and Native Hawai'ins, we see interventions in situations where the parties certainly had tried alternatives, but they'd been wrestling with each other for years, with continuing acrimony and without workable agreements they had crafted themselves. So the practice stories we've considered suggest ways that might at first look indirect—certainly less direct than a judge ruling about a winner and a loser on a legal claim—but that might present strategies of community problem solving in which multiple stakeholders might in fact go slow to go much faster than they (or we) otherwise would.

Being Practical Often Means Working Backwards

If we want to go out tonight to eat Italian food, we might wonder about what our options are and what we know about quality, cost, distance, timing, and ambiance. So, we might work back from there to consider the time we need to prepare or to change clothes or to get in the car (or on the bus or bicycle) to get where we'd like to go. Once we have a destination in mind, we work backwards, if only because the further away the restaurant, the earlier we might have to set out to get there at a reasonable time.

The cases in this book tell us a similar story about how practically to reach the destination of well-informed, interest-satisfying, multiparty agreements. One of the real lessons here has been that creative negotiated agreements can hardly be reached before the parties have considered a range of options they might package in complex ways to address their interests: we'll regulate noise in this way; we'll limit access in that way; we'll re-route the buses this way. So before negotiating decisions, parties need to package options creatively.

But parties can't refine workable packages of options like that until they can invent and propose combinations of moves, investments, and actions (e.g., the lawyers say we actually can regulate that, the engineers say we'd need X feet of protection, or the transportation planners say these headways and not those are workable).

But the parties can't know what options they actually have without learning more about the complex cases they're facing; parties know a lot about some things, but no one has full information, especially about future costs, future consequences, perhaps demographic trends and projections, or shifting legal environments. So, in order to invent new options and moves, parties need to involve expertise and to learn, to ask, and to address very practical questions.

But what the parties need and want to learn will depend on their breadth of interests—not only their top two priorities, but also the fuller fabric of what they care about. So, before any experts can address the right problems, the parties at hand need to be able to define together what they'd like to know more about. In Albuquerque, we've seen this meant learning together about urban design options and best zoning practices that could address a variety of needs and interests. In California, in the Environmentalist-OHV negotiations, Lisa Beutler used "mind-mapping" to discover what the stakeholders needed to learn, and only then they brought in experts about sound and land-use law.

Before learning, then, there's convening: parties have to sit and listen and talk, to tell their stories, and to define their shared uncertainties, their need to learn, and their concerns, worries, hopes, and interests, as Peter Adler so cogently showed.

But before a planner or facilitative leader might convene contentious stakeholders with differing priorities and vulnerabilities, that planner or intermediary needs to "assess the conflict," to identify the primary parties or stakeholders who might be practically interconnected here, so practically interdependent that they are wrestling with each other about the problem at hand. Who's affecting whom and who's limiting whose ability to "make things right" (as they see it)? Who has enough of a stake in the problem at hand to come together with skilled facilitators or mediators or planners to try to craft a new way out, a new resolution that might not just be stable but be much better than a resolution handed to the stakeholders by some outside agency or judge? So, then, the early work of convening depends on an earlier assessment to figure out who needs to be at the table!

Working practically and backwards, then, we see a simple and significant lesson emerging from these practitioners' stories: when buy-in and ownership and practical agreement matters, negotiation decisions come last, at the end of a no-nonsense process in which the stakeholders can all say what needs to be said, can learn about technical and legal and social issues that will affect them, and can craft creative solutions and strategies together. In this way, we have seen, practical agreements can emerge from no-agreement beginnings because they can be built interactively and cumulatively with the help of skilled planners and intermediaries.

So, we have considered cases here, remarkably enough, whose successes were driven not by trust, not by expertise alone, not by the intermediaries' rocket science, but by the well-harnessed passions and commitments and interests of the stakeholders themselves. In a certain sense, the planners knew how to get out of the way. Lisa Beutler put it astutely: it's the parties anger that reflects how much they care about the issues at hand, and so the planners' job becomes not avoiding the anger but channeling the passion and commitment it represents to productive ends and outcomes—far less "Calm down!" and perhaps more, "I can see why you're angry, because you care a lot about these issues, and that's why we're here together: to figure out what to do now."

Works Cited in The Profiles

Bennis, Warren, and Patricia Biederman. 1998. *Organizing Genius: The Secrets of Creative Collaboration*. New York: Basic Books.

Boyte, Harry C. 2004. *Everyday Politics: Reconnecting Citizens and Public Life*. Philadelphia: University of Pennsylvania Press.

Forester, John. 2009. *Dealing with Differences: Dramas of Mediating Public Disputes*. New York: Oxford University Press.

Forester, John. 1999. "Dealing With Deep Value Differences," in *The Consensus-Building Handbook: A Comprehensive Guide to Reaching Agreement*, edited by Lawrence Susskind et al. Thousand Oaks, Calif., Sage.

Fung, Archon. 2004. *Empowered Participation: Reinventing Urban Democracy*. Princeton, N.J.: Princeton University Press.

Peters, Scott. 2010. *Democracy and Higher Education: Traditions and Stories of Civic Engagement*. East Lansing, Mich.: Michigan State University Press.

Podziba, Susan. 2013. *Civic Fusion: Mediating Polarized Public Disputes*. Chicago: American Bar Association.

Podziba, Susan. 2006. *The Chelsea Story: How a Corrupt City Regenerated Its Democracy*. Milan: Bruno Mondadori (Italian only).

Surowiecki, James. 2005. *The Wisdom of Crowds*. New York: Anchor.

Susskind, L., and J. Cruickshank. 2006. *Breaking Robert's Rules*. New York: Oxford University Press.

Susskind, Lawrence, S. McKearnan, and J. Thomas-Larmer. 1999. *The Consensus Building Handbook: A Comprehensive Guide to Reaching Agreement*. Thousand Oaks, Calif: Sage.

Wallis, J. 1994. *The Soul of Politics: A Practical And Prophetic Vision For Change*. New York: New Press; Maryknoll, New York: Orbis.

Discussion Questions

These questions explore central themes, insights, and challenges presented by the cases of public dispute and conflict recounted in this book. Students, teachers, planners, public managers, and public policy analysts should all find them useful.

1. The stories in this book talk about conflict and the construction of practical agreements to resolve disputes, but there's very little mention of compromise. Obviously, no single party is getting everything it wants—so why does compromise seem to be an irrelevant concept here, practically speaking?

2. These practice stories show that before negotiation there must be inventing; before inventing there must be learning; before learning there must be convening; and before convening there must be an assessment of who's affected, who might be represented, who's interdependent. How do the practitioners accomplish these prerequisite stages that make any eventual negotiation possible?

3. These practitioners show us diverse strategies to encourage learning on the parts of impatient and sometimes overconfident stakeholders. How do they do that?

4. These practitioners show us how to avoid several traps that threaten participatory processes—personal attacks, poorly informed negotiations, exclusion of affected stakeholders, and lack of buy-in by decision makers, to give several examples. What practical moves and steps can help us avoid these traps?

5. The cases described in this book begin with conflicting stakeholders distrusting each other. How did the facilitative leaders shape processes that enabled these distrusting, skeptical stakeholders to build relationships so that they could work together and create well-informed, interest-satisfying, good outcomes?

6. All of these practice stories are outcome-oriented; none describes process for the sake of process alone. How do they integrate concerns with process with concerns with outcomes?

7. If some agreements can be better (or worse) for all parties than other agreements, how can planners evaluate working agreements produced by affected stakeholders in any given case? Susskind explicitly suggests four criteria that allow us to judge the quality of outcomes or negotiated agreements. What are these criteria and what must planners or facilitative leaders do to try to satisfy them?

8. If facilitative leaders or planners who work in between multiple, interdependent parties don't produce agreements any more than midwives produce babies, how can they nevertheless work to help those parties make their own agreements?

9. These practice stories show us that there's nothing participatory about just calling meetings where bad can go to worse, where fraying relationships can suffer, where experts can baffle or intimidate citizens, where no decisions will be made, and where attendees leave more cynical than when they arrived. What beyond "having meetings" do these facilitative leaders teach us about the requirements of creative, effective, well-informed participatory processes?

10. These practitioners describe cases in which passionate parties with deep value differences managed nevertheless to make practical agreements—for example, about health policy or land-use regulation recommendations. We learn that planners can actually work in between parties with such deep differences. How can they do that? How might public planning processes move beyond doctrinal differences to make less abstract and more specific, pragmatic agreements that are not just good intentions but actual commitments?

11. These practice stories suggest that asking questions can be one of the most effective moves that planners and facilitative leaders can make. How might the questions of intermediaries direct attention selectively, open possibilities, encourage engagement and participation, and even pay respect and give recognition to vulnerable stakeholders? What kinds of questions might be crucial?

12. The drama in many of these cases involves the precarious and surprising cogeneration of new options, senses of "what can we could do now?" emerging against a background of deep mutual suspicion or animosity felt by disputing or agonistic stakeholders. How have facilitative planners been able to encourage and enable new options in the face of such skepticism?

13. None of these stories involves suppressing emotions like fear or anger; on the contrary, several practitioners here stress the importance of harnessing, channeling, or enabling the passions of the parties to fuel the cooperative and agonistic/adversarial search for creative options. How can planners do that?

14. The ambiguous promise of neutrality confuses students of planning and conflict resolution. Several of the practitioners here reject neutrality as a goal even as they claim they do not take sides that would weaken their abilities to work with all parties. What positive commitments, values, or even responsibilities should a public-serving facilitative leader embrace instead of pretending to be strictly neutral or value free?

15. These practitioners have presented no one-size-fits-all recipes, but they have offered us lessons in process design as they crafted steps, procedures, and processes oriented toward producing well-informed, interest-satisfying, stable, fair, and responsive outcomes. What central elements of process design do they ask us to consider?

16. Technical planning expertise matters in all of these cases, but these practitioners suggest that planners must introduce expertise quite carefully. What are the problems lurking in bringing expertise into the planning process?

17. The significance of place plays an important role in many of the cases discussed. Even though parties can have strongly differing views of the places at issue, and their definition of place may embrace social or historical "place" as well as physical places, how does attention to place help bring parties together to solve problems?

18. Larry Sherman began by suggesting that he didn't drop architecture or planning to do mediation but that he learned mediation so that he could do better planning and architecture. Larry Susskind characterizes the mediation-like work involved in all these cases as "informal problem solving" that does not substitute for, but enhances, formally authoritative political institutions of governance. How do these cases inform practical planning and governance work that honors both formal and informal aspects of public policy disputes?

19. Because these cases suggest strategies of solving problems that normal planning processes may not traditionally use, the facilitative leaders have had to establish their own legitimacy. How did they do that? Put another way, who did these intermediaries work for?

20. What role does traditionally established government play in these cases?

21. How do these processes relate to traditional advocacy planning? Why might some argue that advocacy takes one party's side for justice's sake while mediation or facilitative leadership takes all parties' sides for justice's sake? Why would weaker parties take advantage of inclusive, mediated planning processes?

22. What diverse forms of learning do we find in these multi-stakeholder cases?

23. How do these cases answer skeptics who worry that facilitative leadership as exemplified here might erase or ignore conflict, privilege stronger parties, ignore relevant expertise, or just be government by dysfunctional committees?

24. In these cases, what helps facilitative leaders move the parties from mutual blame to listening to one another and crafting proposals for action? How do creative, practical proposals emerge for real consideration by contentious stakeholders who have real interests to satisfy?